GREEK APOLOGISTS
OF THE SECOND CENTURY

Books by Robert M. Grant
published by The Westminster Press

Greek Apologists of the Second Century

Gods and the One God (Library of Early Christianity)

GREEK APOLOGISTS
OF THE
SECOND CENTURY

Robert M. Grant

The Westminster Press
Philadelphia

Book design by Gene Harris

First edition

Published by The Westminster Press®
Philadelphia, Pennsylvania

PRINTED IN THE UNITED STATES OF AMERICA
9 8 7 6 5 4 3 2 1

Library of Congress Cataloging-in-Publication Data

Grant, Robert McQueen, 1917–
   Greek apologists of the second century / Robert M. Grant. — 1st ed.
      p.   cm.
   Bibliography: p.
   Includes index.
   ISBN 0-664-21915-2

   Early church, ca. 30–600. I. Title.
BT1115.G7 1988
239′.3—dc19   88-822
                                                                        CIP

Contents

List of Illustrations

Unless otherwise stated in the caption, photographs are by the author.

1
The Background of Christian Apologetic

Apologetic literature emerges from minority groups that are trying to come to terms with the larger culture within which they live. Apologists do not completely identify themselves with the broader society, but they are not advocates of confrontation or revolution. They address their contemporaries with persuasion, looking for links between the outside world and their own group and thus modifying the development of both. An apologist who finds the link in philosophy or cultural life will lay emphasis on aspects of philosophy or culture that favor his own group's attitudes and ideals and, at the same time, will emphasize a philosophical or cultural analysis or structuring of his group's views. His primary goal is to interpret his own culture—religious, philosophical, or artistic, as the case may be—to the broader group. Some apologists simply try to vindicate their own culture and religion in relation to the surrounding culture and religion and usually try to prove that theirs is more ancient, more authentic, and more expressive of common values. On either approach, success is limited, for the larger group's self-confidence and inertia keep it from changing its attitudes.

The apologist is not completely at home in either his own group or the larger society. He is too much of a generalizer for his own people, and too closely related to minority specifics for society at large. He stands on a borderline, overlapping parts of both areas but not fully identifiable with either the part or the whole. His critics from within sometimes admit his "subjective" loyalty to the group's beliefs but they deny that it is "objective." When Loisy modernized Catholic history nearly a century ago, his opponents accused him of betraying Catholicism. There is something to such a charge, for an apologist's efforts are likely to produce significant changes in the ways the minority looks at itself. As he tries to present its ideas as persuasively as possible, the persuasion is likely to convert the converted and modify their ideas at least in form.

He is also defending the group against accusations spread by the majority about minorities, who are treated as responsible for social divisions or even for various catastrophes that shake up the society as a whole. Tertullian puts this well when he insists that Christians have not participated in recent revolts against the Roman empire but are being blamed for "every public disaster, every misfortune that happens to the people." "If the Tiber rises to the walls, if the Nile does not rise to the fields, if the sky is rainless, if there is an earthquake, a famine, a plague, immediately the cry arises, 'The Christians to the lion!' "[1] Opposition to such groups increases under stress from both social and natural causes.

The thesis of this book is that while there is a certain timeless character to the Christian apologists of the second century, they are deeply involved in the political and social struggles of their time and cannot be understood apart from the precise circumstances in which they are writing.

The Roman Empire in the Second Century

The attitudes and persecution of Trajan's reign (chapter 3) naturally led Christians toward defensive apologetic addressed to the state, though we have no record of apologists earlier than the reign of Hadrian. They began the movement which lasted in its "classical" phase until the reign of Commodus, exactly overlapping the brilliant period of Roman life for which everyone inevitably cites Gibbon.

> If a man were called to fix the period in the history of the world during which the condition of the human race was most happy and prosperous, he would, without hesitation, name that which elapsed from the death of Domitian to the accession of Commodus. The vast extent of the Roman empire was governed by absolute power, under the guidance of virtue and wisdom. The armies were restrained by the firm but gentle hand of four successive emperors whose characters and authority commanded involuntary respect. The forms of the civil administration were carefully preserved by Nerva, Trajan, Hadrian, and the Antonines, who delighted in the image of liberty, and were pleased with considering themselves as the accountable ministers of the laws. Such princes deserved the honour of restoring the republic, had the Romans of their days been capable of enjoying a rational freedom.

This rather effusive statement obviously reflects and presents propaganda for the Roman regime and its supporters. There were certainly Jews and Christians who agreed, but many related to the martyrs would have raised questions. The "virtue and wisdom" of the emperors did not seem evident to all their subjects. It is odd that Gibbon's statement appeared under George III in 1776.

Edward Luttwak presents a similar picture, clearly showing how secure the empire seemed to be.

> The Antonine era, as it became known, was a period of stability and consolidation, of secure frontiers and systematized defenses; it was the climax of impe-

rial success, the result of a sequence of good and long-lived emperors and of favorable circumstances. Having weathered the great crisis of A.D. 69—when it had seemed on the verge of dissolution—the empire of the Flavians, Trajan, Hadrian, and the Antonines had seemingly achieved a system of everlasting security, a pax Roman and eternal.[2]

Whether or not we accept every item in these laudatory comments on the second-century empire, it was the achievement of the second-century apologists that in the face of this overwhelming political reality they believed they could present their petitions to the supreme rulers from Hadrian to Marcus Aurelius. Hadrian chose Antoninus Pius and his two adopted sons, Marcus Aurelius and Lucius Verus, to be his successors. Antoninus reigned from 138 to 161, while of the co-emperors Lucius Verus died in 169 and Marcus Aurelius continued until 180, unfortunately leaving his son Commodus as his successor.

The apologists (Tatian excepted) were of the church and wrote in the church, not just for the church but for the larger world outside. They began by presenting petitions to Hadrian when he visited Athens in 124. After the martyrdom of Polycarp of Smyrna, Justin wrote to Antoninus Pius around 156. After a revolt was suppressed three others addressed Marcus Aurelius in 176. This appeal failed with the bloody martyrdoms in Gaul, and Tatian delivered a violent counterattack addressed not to the emperors but to Greeks in general. A few years later Theophilus, bishop of Antioch, created an apologetic Jewish-Christian theology which was soon modified by better theologians. Petitions to the emperors had ceased and apologists wrote for non-Christian groups or individuals in order to tell outsiders about Christian truth. These writers were contemporaries of the Gnostics but took a very different path. Instead of esoteric spiritualism the apologists confidently used philosophical reason, and though they attacked philosophers they used their language whenever they could. They thus created the basic method of traditional Christian theology.

We should add that apologists do not argue just about religion. Ordinarily they adhere to the religion of their group, but they are trying to integrate the group into the broader culture at all levels and thus are concerned with political, social, and cultural themes as they defend the significance of their own groups in a broader context. Apologists write about the meaning of education and the history of nations. Since they are involved in traditional discussions between and among cultures, they find predecessors among the national apologists of the Hellenistic and Roman periods such as the oriental historians opposed by Josephus—who himself was a leading oriental historian and apologist.

Egyptian, Chaldean, and Jewish Apologetic

In the Hellenistic age there were apologists for various ancient nations now ruled by Greek descendants of Alexander's generals. Apocalyptists and prophets might look for the end of Greco-Roman culture, of Hellenistic kingdoms and of the Roman empire, but other Hellenistic authors—chiefly priestly and therefore preservers of tradition—wrote histories to commend the antiquity and originality of their particular oriental nations.

Writing for the Seleucid king Antiochus I, the Chaldean priest Berossus made such claims for the Babylonians. He was "a Chaldean by birth, but familiar in learned circles through his publication of works on Chaldean astronomy and philosophy for Greek readers." In his apologetic work he "followed the most ancient records."[3]

Among the Egyptians, the priest Manetho wrote about 287 B.C. for Ptolemy II, the Greek king of Egypt. He relied on ancient temple records (now found by archaeologists) for his lists of the kings, setting them forth in Greek for the new era. His *Egyptian History* began with the gods, the demigods, and the spirits of the dead before turning to "the mortal kings who ruled Egypt down to Darius, king of the Persians."[4] He was determined to prove the Egyptians more ancient than other peoples.

These apologists supplied a way for Jews and Christians to argue for their own antiquity. Josephus quoted from them. He was followed by Theophilus, while Tatian and Clement relied on other orientals with similar goals. Under the Ptolemies and the Romans many apologists wrote for Jews and Judaism. The most important of them were the philosopher Philo of Alexandria and the retired general Josephus. They wrote at the beginning and the end of the first century A.D. Philo's long exercises in the allegorical method explain much of the Pentateuch as essentially Middle Platonic philosophy, while Josephus gives historical insights into the recent Jewish rebellion and, in a larger work, the story of humanity from the beginning. Christian apologists took over the methods of both, though without explicit quotations until the end of the second century, and Christians transmitted the texts of both.

Philo

Philo's importance for Christian apologists lies chiefly in his interpretations of the Greek Old Testament and Jewish traditions in the light of Middle Platonism. He often spoke of the "Logos" as an intermediary between God and the world and thus anticipated theological developments in second-century Christianity. He probably died around the time when the Christian mission to the Gentiles began, though the church historian Eusebius later seized upon his description of the Jewish sect of the Therapeutae as proof that he actually knew Christians at Alexandria.[5]

All Philo's works are ultimately apologetic, but the only books specifically apologetic were the fragmentary *Hypothetica* and the less important *Providence* and *Animals,* now extant in Armenian.[6] We should probably identify the *Hypothetica* with the "apology on behalf of the Jews" also mentioned by Eusebius.

In this apology Philo explains that dreams and visions gave novel ideas to the growing Jewish population of Egypt and led them to return to their ancestral home. He evidently knows ethical criticisms of the Hebrews' capture of Canaan and (like the later Origen) defends them on rational not historical grounds. The "probabilities" about their entrance into Canaan must be based not on the "history" but on reason. The biblical story of the conquest of Canaan is not reasonable, for the Hebrews were weary after forty years in the desert. The Canaanites must have "voluntarily surrendered their land."[7]

As for the law ascribed to Moses, "whether what he told them came from his own reasoning or was heard from some divine being, they referred it all to God." Philo claims that Gentile laws were excessively flexible and proceeds to praise the strictness of the Jewish law, for the present treating it more rigidly than in his exegetical treatise *Special Laws.* He ends with praise of the Jews for their observance of the seventh day and the sabbatical year.[8]

Another fragment is entirely concerned with the communal life of the sect of the Essenes, who have no private property but do have common meals and medical care. Philo concludes by emphasizing their rejection of marriage, based on awareness of the innate selfishness of women.[9]

The apology thus defends Jews against the (current) charge of misanthropy, treats the law as not only severe but ethically beneficial, and explains that the Sabbath was not made for idleness. The Essenes represent the highest class of philosophically-minded Jews for Philo, whether or not he accepts all their tenets.

It is not possible to date the *Hypothetica,* but it may have appeared around the time when Philo himself was directly concerned with the persecution of Jews at Alexandria and elsewhere. He describes the pogroms under Caligula in his treatises *Against Flaccus* and *The Embassy to Gaius,* though they are not exactly apologies.

In 38 the Jews at Alexandria tried to get their citizenship recognized, and the Palestinian king Agrippa interceded in their favor. Riots ensued in which synagogues were burned or torn down, and Flaccus, the prefect of Egypt, ruled against their citizenship. Riots and lynchings continued until Agrippa persuaded the youthful emperor Caligula to recall the prefect, confiscate his property, banish him to an island, and finally put him to death.[10] In 39–40, however, Caligula demanded sacrifice not for himself but to himself and planned to erect a statute of himself in the temple at Jerusalem. The Jewish community at Alexandria sent Philo and others to Rome to ask for exemption from such demands. He described their encounters in the *Embassy to Gaius.*

Philo's analysis of government forms a significant though minor aspect of his apologetic. He indicates that traditional Greek and Roman forms of government are favored in the Bible, and he holds that democracy, approved by God, is the best, while mob rule is merely its counterfeit.[11] Indeed, the good Roman emperors were democrats. Augustus "led every state to liberty," but the subjects of the mad Caligula were "slaves of the absolute emperor."[12]

Prophecies and Politics

At the opposite extreme from apologetic stood prophets and apocalyptic authors who questioned Roman rule and predicted its end. They naturally flourished in the frontier provinces once held by older empires. From the East came the *Apocalypse of Hystaspes,* supposedly written by an ancient Persian king to predict that "the Roman name by which the world is now ruled will be taken off the earth and power will return to Asia, and again the East will rule and the West will serve."[13] The Christian apologist Justin reported that readers of books by Hystaspes were liable to the death penalty.[14]

Apocalyptic views were also expressed in the West. Just two hundred years after Rome decisively defeated the Iberians at Numantia, a priestly oracle, supposedly ancient, told how "sometime there will rise from Spain a prince and ruler of all."[15]

In the north, the barbarous Druids were famed for urging troops into battle against the Romans, who denounced their "dreadful cruelty." Various early emperors tried to keep Rome free of their cult,[16] while the Druids themselves viewed the burning of the Capitol in 70 as a sign of heavenly wrath against Rome. Tacitus says that in their "empty superstition" they believed that the fire "portended that the control of human affairs would pass to the peoples beyond the Alps."[17]

From Egypt, usually under full Roman control, there is no such explicit report. The "Potter's Oracle," written in Greek, foretells the downfall not of Rome but of Hellenistic Alexandria, the departure of gods thence, and the appointment of a king by the goddess Isis,[18] though conceivably readers could refer the oracle to the Roman empire. Second- and third-century papyri might suggest this possibility.[19]

The Egyptians were usually more cooperative than rebellious, however. By the reign of Domitian a permanent temple of Isis and Serapis had been erected in the Campus Martius, and at Corinth the Isiac scribe regularly prayed for "the great emperor, the Senate, the equestrians, and the whole Roman people."[20] To be sure, a section of the Hermetic treatise *Asclepius* states that the land of Egypt is the copy of heaven and predicts that the gods will go away from it,[21] but the prediction seems to have no political implications for the empire. Anti-Roman apocalyptic thus flourished on all the borders except the southern one.

Roman emperors did not welcome apocalypses or the attitudes they expressed, and frontier peoples like the Jews were suspect as the emperors attacked divination and even astrology if used by others than themselves. Augustus' agents collected and burned more than two thousand prophecies in Greek and Latin, keeping only the "authentic" Sibylline oracles.[22] Tiberius also investigated books containing divination and somehow differentiated worthless from genuine ones.[23] According to Justin, there was a death penalty for reading not only Hystaspes but also the Sibyl and even the Hebrew prophets. At the very end of the second century, the prefect of Egypt also denounced divination.[24] Because he had encountered many dupes of diviners, he ordered everyone to "abstain from this dangerous inquisitiveness." No one was to pretend to know matters beyond human ability or profess to know the obscure future, at any rate through oracles or the parading of images that gave oracular answers. A diviner would be subject to the death penalty, as would officials who failed to enforce the decree. Though Egyptian chronology for these years is chaotic, the decree must be related to an Egyptian visit of Septimius Severus and his investigation of secret books, which he locked up in the tomb of Alexander at Alexandria.[25]

Astrologers made similar difficulties.[26] Like their subjects, most emperors believed in astrology and therefore proscribed its use because dangerous to themselves. The phrasing of one such proscription and the reply resembles what was sometimes decreed for both Jews and Christians. The emperor Vitellius ordered that astrologers were to leave Rome and Italy by the Kalends of October, just as according to Acts 18:2 Claudius had ordered all the Jews to leave Rome.[27] In turn the astrologers put up an anonymous poster: "It would be good if Vitellius Germanicus were no longer anywhere by the same day of Kalends." Their point was that he should not be anywhere—that is, be nowhere, be dead. The formula is reflected and repealed in the edict of toleration issued by Galerius in 311, "that Christians may exist again." This evidently reverses an earlier decree which provided "that Christians should not exist (anywhere)."[28]

Both Jews and Christians were suspect in Roman eyes partly because of their concern for prophecy and apocalyptic prediction. For this reason Jewish and Christian apologists say little about the future. Philo gives exegesis of the Pentateuch, not of the prophets. Josephus downplays the importance of prophecy and treats apocalyptic leaders as unstable rebels against Rome, rightly suppressed by the military. Christian apologists explain that the prophets were moral teachers who made predictions almost entirely fulfilled in the history of Christ and the church.

Opposition to Jews and Judaism

In spite of apologies, upper-class Romans were often hostile toward Jews and Judaism. Cicero expresses their attitude in his oration *For Flaccus* when he calls it a "barbarian superstition" and says that "each state has its own religion; we have ours."[29] He adds that Pompey's capture of Jerusalem has shown with what disfavor the immortal gods regard the Jewish people. Tacitus reiterates this view when he says that Judaism is a superstition opposed to Greek morals.[30] The Greek anti-Jewish writer Apion had claimed that Jews kidnapped an occasional Greek and fattened him for sacrifice, "tasting his entrails and taking an oath to maintain hostility toward Greeks."[31] Indeed, they swore by "the god who made heaven and earth and sea" not to be friendly with any foreigner, especially Greeks.[32] "Misanthropy" was thus an accusation laid against Jews before Christianity arose, as was the charge of ethical indifferentism and that of cannibalism.

The Jewish Revolt and Apologetic

In spite of the efforts of kings and apologists, Palestinian Jews finally revolted against the Romans in 66 and fought them for more than four years. During the war, class tensions within Jewish society became acute, and a resistance party of "zealots" fought as much against the old Jewish establishment as against the Romans. The end came with the almost accidental destruction of the temple at Jerusalem in 70 and the reduction and leveling of the fortress at Masada in 73. The priestly general Josephus survived as a Roman prisoner and won influence by predicting the reign of the Roman general Vespasian on the basis of ancient prophecies. Later, on a pension at Rome he wrote books defending both the Flavian emperors and the Jews of his own class.

Flavius Josephus was born perhaps a decade before the death of Philo into a Jerusalem family of priestly ancestry. In his twenties he visited Rome and realized that revolt would be impossible, and at thirty as a general in Galilee he tried to moderate the extremists. He was captured by the Romans, who unsuccessfully used him as a mediator. In Rome he wrote a history of the revolt, published first in Aramaic for Babylonian Jews, then in a Greek version toward the end of Vespasian's reign. This work defended his role as a general and attacked the rebels, especially the "zealots." Under Domitian in 93–94 he completed his twenty-volume Jewish history based on the Bible, Jewish traditions, his own imagination, and the *Universal History* by the court historian of Herod the Great. The Herodian source inevitably resulted in a strong conservative emphasis. Josephus called it *Jewish Antiquities* in imitation of the twenty volumes of *Roman Antiquities* by Dionysius of Halicarnassus. Dionysius complains that the Greeks are ignorant of early Roman history and Josephus repeats the charge in relation to events from the creation onward.

Still later Josephus returned to the defense of his brief military career in an *Autobiography,* and in the two-volume treatise now known as *Against Apion* replied to anti-Jewish critics from the third century B.C. to the first century A.D. The original title of this work, known to both Origen and Eusebius, was "On the Antiquity of the Jews."[33] In this addendum to the *Antiquities,* Josephus denies the antiquity of the Greeks, explains the silence of their historians over Jewish affairs, proves the antiquity of the Jews from such oriental historians as Manetho and Berossus, and rejects a wide variety of anti-Jewish slanders.

The occasion of the apology lay in the situation of the Jews late in the reign of Domitian. After the revolt the *Fiscus iudaïcus* had been levied to rebuild the temple of Jupiter Capitolinus in Rome, and under Domitian tax evasion led to the investigation of circumcision, which was taken to imply liability.[34] Dio Cassius sets these investigations in the year 95.[35] Josephus therefore wrote because of hostility toward Jews as the emperor was trying to collect the tax "more rigorously than all the rest." He replied to the charge that Jews "wage implacable war on mankind."[36]

Josephus on Forms of Government

Like Greek authors under the Roman empire, including Philo, Josephus discussed monarchy, aristocracy, and democracy, and with the others he was trying to correlate native governments with the overarching Roman state. For this reason he did not finally favor democracy. He used the Bible for tracing the forms from aristocracy under Moses and Joshua through anarchy or tyranny to restoration under the judges.[37] Viewed another way, this last period was also a time of monarchy, confirmed under Saul.[38] The line of his successor David lasted until the exile. After that, oligarchy returned, only to be followed by Hasmonean kingship.[39] Alternatively, post-Davidic monarchy was followed by democracy and then Hasmonean oligarchy.[40] The Romans restored aristocracy in 59 B.C.[41] and again, after the Herods, under the prefects.[42] In such discussions he was trying to make Jewish history comprehensible to Greek readers.

Though Josephus used his categories inconsistently, they show that for him biblical institutions were mutable and had clear Greek parallels such as those provided in the sixth book of Polybius' *Histories.* His real preference was for "theocracy,"[43] which in practice meant rule by the priestly aristocracy to which he himself belonged. This theocracy could be accommodated to Roman rule and like Roman rule could be termed true democracy.[44]

Such discussions offered no precedents to the early Christians, who discussed nothing but kingship. Hippolytus agrees with others when he interprets Daniel's prophecy of a divided kingdom, partly strong as iron, partly feeble as clay (Dan. 2:40–43), in relation to the Roman empire.[45] He stands alone when he explains that the clay means "divided democracies."[46]

Response to Apologetic

Two decades after Josephus, Tacitus provided an ethnological and historical summary on the Jews which shows that he paid no attention to Jewish apologetic. He accepted the view that the religion of Moses is opposed to all others. The Sabbath rites are mere imitations of Egyptian religion or the cult of Saturn, while their other customs are "sinister and depraved" and their way of life is "absurd and debased." As for ethics, "among them nothing is illicit."[47] Tacitus was also aware of their threat to the empire and cited a prediction popular during the revolt of 66–70: "The Orient would grow strong and men from Judea would control the world."[48] Writing during the reign of Trajan, he criticized both Judaism and Christianity as oriental religions.

2
The Beginnings of Christian Apologetic

As the Christian church moved out from Palestine through Asia Minor to the West, its leaders came in contact not only with the Roman empire but with Greek and Roman schools and the culture they promoted. Christians began to analyze the relations between their own religious teachings and the religious-cultural attitudes inculcated by state and school. Some interpreted negatively, with apocalyptic emphases often leading to martyrdom. Others entered upon apologetic, which ideally led to discussion and exchange of views.

Paul and Political Theology

The most valuable early discussion of relations with the Roman state appears in the letters of the apostle Paul, who refers directly to Roman governmental authority. The key texts are to be found in 1 Corinthians 2:8 and Romans 13:1–7. The Corinthians text states that "none of the rulers of this age knew the hidden wisdom of God; had they known it, they would not have crucified the Lord of glory." This means that the crucifixion was an accident due to the ignorance of the rulers.

But who were the rulers? A sermon in Acts (4:27) interprets the "kings" and "rulers" of Psalm 2 "against the Lord and against his Christ" as Herod and Pontius Pilate. Marcion favored a Gnostic interpretation, treating them as the (demonic) servants of the lower creator-god.[1] Irenaeus refrained from mentioning the verse, and Clement of Alexandria did not explain it[2] or cite the passage from Romans, presumably because of the prevalence of Gnostic exegesis. Since for Gnostics the text had no political relevance, they kept the more orthodox from using it theologically.

In Romans, Paul insists on loyal obedience to the rulers.

Every person is to be subject to the governing authorities. For there is no authority except from God, and those that exist have been instituted by God. Therefore he who resists the authorities resists what God has appointed, and those who resist will incur judgment. For rulers are not a terror to good conduct, but to bad. Would you have no fear of him who is in authority? Then do what is good, and you will receive his approval, for he is God's servant for your good. But if you do wrong, be afraid, for he does not bear the sword in vain; he is the servant of God to execute his wrath on the wrongdoer. Therefore one must be subject, not only to avoid God's wrath but also for the sake of conscience. For the same reason you also pay taxes, for the authorities are ministers of God, attending to this very thing. Pay all of them their dues, taxes to whom taxes are due, tribute to whom tribute is due, reverential awe to whom awe is due, honor to whom honor is due. (Rom. 13:1–7)

It is true that Marcion probably deleted this passage from his edition of Romans,[3] but in the early church the text was usually understood politically. Polycarp of Smyrna informed the proconsul of Asia that "we are taught to pay fitting honor to the principalities and powers instituted by God if the honor does not harm us."[4] When Theophilus of Antioch synthesized New Testament teaching he laid emphasis on the passage from Romans. "The divine word gives us orders about 'subordination to principalities and powers' (Rom. 13:1–3) and 'prayer for them, so that we may lead a quiet and tranquil life' (1 Tim. 2:1–2); and it teaches us to 'pay all things to all men, honor to whom honor is due, fear to whom fear, tribute to whom tribute; to owe no man anything except to love all' " (Rom. 13:7–8).[5] Elsewhere he noted that the emperor must "be honored with legitimate honor," for "he is not God but a man appointed by God, not to be worshiped but to judge justly."[6] The emperor is not divine, but God appointed him. Irenaeus too insists that Paul spoke "not of angelic powers or invisible rulers, as some [Gnostics] venture to expound the passage."[7] Origen says that the passage has various interpretations but according to the ordinary one the rulers are emperors. Tyrants present a problem which he will discuss elsewhere.[8] (He has already favored tyrannicide.)[9]

There can be little question that the language of the passage is political,[10] perhaps uncritically devoted to the state. In order to correct Paul, Ernst Käsemann claims that this section of the letter is not really related to his basic ideas about Christ or the future, and can therefore be passed over, like his remarks about slaves and women.[11] He says Paul is merely reflecting "everyday life in the Hellenistic world" and cites a supposedly exact parallel from Josephus to prove it. The parallel is not bad: Josephus says that "sovereignty comes to no man unless God so orders matters." But the statement he cites is Essene doctrine,[12] set forth more fully in his *Antiquities.* There an Essene predicts that Herod will reign because he is worthy of God, while God's wrath will come upon him if he forgets justice and piety.[13] Indeed, Herod later did ascribe his reign to the will of God[14] but apparently forgot about justice and piety. Josephus himself did not forget, since he knew that when the rebels against Rome in 66–70 neglected justice and piety they brought destruction upon Jerusalem. All this shows that whether or not the ideas came from "everyday life in the Hellenistic world" the Essenes, Paul, and Josephus found them theologically meaningful.

At another point the apostle stands close to Greco-Roman political ideas and uses them in a theological-political context. His discussion of unity within the body of the church in 1 Corinthians 12 is based on language about the body of the state. Like the state the church is one "body," though made up of many members with different functions. If all played the same role the functions would be inadequately performed. There must be reciprocity. The inferior members cannot withdraw just because they do not have superior functions, and the superior ones cannot claim independence from the others.

The picture is remarkably similar to a popular Greco-Roman fable and like it insists on mutual care without discord, not democratic self-expression but cooperation by cohesive orders in the state. Ancient authors often used the comparison of the body politic to the human body, common in Greek thought after the early fourth century B.C. when Xenophon ascribed to Socrates a comparison of two brothers, made to serve each other, with pairs of hands, feet, eyes, made by God for mutual aid.[15] In Rome a favorite story was said to have been told by a senator to plebeians in 494 B.C.[16] He spoke of a conspiracy against the belly wrongly undertaken by hands, mouth, and teeth. The consequence was weakness throughout the body. Such a picture was popular in later times. Cicero used it to defend private property,[17] and echoes recur in Philo, Seneca, and Epictetus. Writing to the young Nero in 55/56 Seneca modifies the figure thus: "You are the spirit of your state, it is your body." He also explains that "from the head proceeds good health in all the members; all are vital and erect or hang down in weakness, in proportion as their spirit lives or fades away."[18] Similar ideas are expressed by Paul (1 Cor. 12:12–26; Rom. 12:4–5) and among Paulinists (Col. 2:19; Eph. 1:22–23; 4:16).

The Successors of Paul

Paul's loyalty to the empire was reiterated a generation later in 1 Peter and the pastoral epistles. The first text reads thus:

> For the Lord's sake be subject to every human institution, whether it be to the emperor as supreme, or to governors as sent by him to punish those who do wrong and to praise those who do right. For it is God's will that by doing right you should put to silence the ignorance of foolish men. Live as free men, yet without using your freedom as a pretext for evil; but live as servants of God. Honor all men. Love the brotherhood. Fear God. Honor the emperor. (1 Peter 2:13–17)

In essence this is the doctrine of Romans, now more explicit perhaps because of the persecution mentioned in 1 Peter 4:12–16 (Christians must suffer as Christians, not as criminals) and 5:9 ("the same experience of suffering is required of your brotherhood throughout the world").

In the Pastorals Paul is represented as urging prayer for a quiet church in a quiet empire. This is obviously the teaching of 1 Timothy 2:1–2 ("I urge that supplications, prayers, intercessions, and thanksgivings be made for all men, for kings and all who are in high positions, that we may lead a quiet and peaceable life, godly and respectful in every way") and Titus 3:1 ("Remind them [the Christians] to be submissive to rulers and authorities, to be obedient, to be ready for any honest work"). The morality of the Pastorals is sometimes called "bourgeois," but at this point it reflects Paul's political teaching.

To be sure, not everyone was a Paulinist. The New Testament now includes (though in antiquity it sometimes did not) the Apocalypse of John, in which there is no hint that Roman authority is derived from God. Instead, the author holds that all earthly power will end in the course of angelic invasions and battles. As judgment impends on Mount Zion, the earthly city with seven hills (Rome) will collapse, "the great city that has dominion over the kings of the earth," and finally Christ with his martyrs will reign for a thousand years; then there will be a new heaven and earth, and a new Jerusalem will descend from heaven. Nothing shows that pagan critics read such predictions, and the apologist Justin, who tells how John foretold a thousand years' stay in Jerusalem, says nothing about the collapse of Rome.[9]

The Pauline line is very clear, however, in a contemporary letter of advice to the church at Corinth from the church at Rome, with reflections of both Romans and 1 Corinthians. In an attempt to restore order and end sedition, the Roman church insists upon the divine origin of all order, comparing the Christian life to service in ideal armies of the Old Testament as well as the Roman legions. A prayer at the end is addressed to God the supreme master and director of all political life, both civil and religious. "Grant that we may be obedient to our rulers and governors upon earth. Thou, Master, hast given them the authority of sovereignty that we may be subject to them, in nothing resisting thy will."[20] For Clement, obedience to all constituted authority is essential. He is providing what is virtually a paraphrase of Romans 13. He does know that there were many martyrs under Nero (whom he does not name), but ascribes the martyrdoms to "jealousy," not to any conflict between church and state.

What is most conspicuous in the church-state statements of the post-apostolic age is firm loyalty to the Roman government and its provincial authorities as well. During this period the traditions about the death of Jesus were being adjusted to put less blame on the Roman authorities, more on the Jews, especially unpopular with Romans after the revolt of 66–70.

Thus Pontius Pilate came to be viewed not so much as an executioner as a figure linking the divine and human worlds. Tertullian finally describes him as "a Christian in his conscience."[21] We see this movement in the creeds: *crucifixus sub,* "under" (rather than *a,* "by"), *Pontio Pilato.* People came to believe that the Roman state could not have been responsible for the crucifixion.

Apologetic in Paul

The most important examples of apologetic argument in the letters of Paul are his defenses of the doctrines of creation and resurrection which anticipate the main lines of second-century apologetic.

Paul discusses creation in the context of his diatribe against pagan immorality in Romans 1:18–32. Since the pagans should have known better, the apostle digresses to explain that they could have known God but did not turn toward him. "Ever since the creation of the world his invisible nature, namely his eternal power and deity, has been clearly perceived in the things that have been made" (Rom. 1:20). Unfortunately mankind "exchanged the truth about God for a lie and worshiped and served the creature rather than the Creator, who is blessed forever" (1:25). What Paul describes is not exactly "natural" knowledge of the Creator, for in verse 19 he has already stated that "what can be known about God is plain to them, for God has shown it to them." But what God has shown can also be described as the kind of knowledge to be derived by inference from the creation. Those who did not make the inference "became futile in their thinking and their senseless minds were darkened" (1:21). Though this is not "natural theology" it points toward such theology.

Paul also moves toward apologetic when he argues over the nature of resurrection. He derives his basic arguments from the apostolic preaching and the Old Testament, but he also uses arguments we can only classify as apologetic. First, he claims that there must be a future resurrection because people are baptized for the dead, because he himself runs risks for the gospel and even fights with wild beasts, and because without resurrection one could be a libertine; and to reject the possibility he relies on a proverb-like line from Menander (1 Cor. 15:29–33). As for the difference between a resurrection body and an ordinary one, he relies on the diversity present among various seeds and fruits; in the "flesh" of men, animals, birds, and fish; between celestial and terrestrial bodies; and among sun, moon, and various stars (15:37–41). He is not trying to "prove" the actuality of resurrection so much as to explain how it will take place.

It is in *1 Clement* that the analogies are used as proofs. "The Master constantly shows us that there will be a resurrection." First comes the resurrection of Jesus, then the recurrence of seasons and day and night, the growth of fruits from decaying seeds, and the spontaneous generation of a phoenix from the decayed flesh of its predecessor.[22] It must be admitted that Seneca more reasonably used the seasons and day and night to illustrate "the round of the universe."[23]

Both creation and resurrection would remain the principal themes of Christian apologetic, in this reflecting its Jewish heritage.

Apologetic Sermons in Acts

It makes no difference whether the sermons ascribed to Paul in Acts 14 and 17 really come from him or not, for they undoubtedly reflect early Christian apologetic preaching. The first has a setting at Lystra in Lycaonia, where crowds hail Barnabas and Paul as Zeus and Hermes, and Paul urges conversion from the worship of idols.[24] He calls them to "turn to a living God who made the heaven and the earth and the sea and all that is in them. In past generations he allowed all the nations to walk in their own ways; yet he did not leave himself without witness, for he did good and from heaven gave you rains and fruitful seasons, satisfying your hearts with food and gladness" (Acts 14:15–17).[25]

The second sermon, at Athens, refers to God as creator and sustainer of mankind but goes farther by speaking of the unity of humanity as descendants of the first man and imbued with the desire to seek for God and find him.[26] As in the speech at Lystra, Paul says that God overlooked their times of ignorance. Now he adds that God demands repentance in view of the impending judgment, to be made by a man raised from the dead. Whether or not Paul ever delivered precisely such an address "in the middle of the Areopagus," it is clear that he could have done so, for he reminded the Thessalonians (whom he had visited before reaching Athens) that they had "turned to God from idols, to serve a living and real God, and to await his Son from heaven, whom he raised from the dead, Jesus who delivers us from the wrath to come" (1 Thess. 1:9–10). The themes of God's universal providence and humanity's search for him are to be found in Stoic sources and in Hellenistic Judaism. They belong to the apologetic tradition, as does the emphasis on creation and resurrection.

Finally, the apostle himself sets forth a universal standard of excellence in Greek terms when he writes: "Whatever is true, whatever is honorable, whatever is just, whatever is pure, whatever is lovely, whatever is gracious, if there is any excellence, if there is any praise, think about these things" (Phil. 4:8). The apologist Justin says nothing different when he claims that "whatever is well said by all belongs to us Christians."[27]

Greek Poetry in the New Testament

Apologists thus can cite the writings of authors outside their own group in order to show that their own tenets are not unique but universal. In the

Greco-Roman world with its popular system of literary education it was inevitable for outsiders of any kind to make use of the texts commonly taught in schools. Such texts, especially from anthologies of poetry, are present in various parts of the New Testament and, later on, very common among the apologists. Partly because of their transmission either as proverbs or in anthologies there is often something odd about the quotations. The meaning is likely to be more or less skewed.

Menander

The first quotation from Greek literature in the New Testament occurs when the apostle Paul warns his Corinthian converts against using the maxim "Let us eat and drink, for tomorrow we die" (Isa. 22:13). He counters this maxim with a tag found in the poet Menander: "Bad company ruins good morals" (1 Cor. 15:33), and adds an exhortation: "Come to your right mind and sin no more." The quotation from Menander stood in his *Thais,* now lost, and survives only in anthologies. In the fifth century the church historian Socrates wrongly ascribed it to Euripides,[28] and may have relied on a heading in such a book.[29] As a "one-liner" it was handed down in the *Monostichoi* of Menander.[30]

According to Athenaeus, Menander's play was about a prostitute.[31] Perhaps for this reason, only one fragment of consequence survives, describing someone, presumably Thais herself, in mock-epic terms: "Sing to me then, goddess, of such a one: bold and beautiful yet persuasive, doing wrong and locking her door, constantly asking for gifts, in love with nobody but always pretending." Early Christian authors naturally did not pick up these lines. And Paul himself—like Clement of Alexandria[32]—surely did not know the source of his quotation. He cannot have read the play or seen it performed.

Epimenides

Whoever wrote the epistle to Titus included a reference to the ancient philosophical poet Epimenides from Crete. "Titus" is supposedly having trouble among the Cretans, and the author of the epistle uses a quotation from "one of themselves, a prophet of their own" against them. This prophet, the ancient poet Epimenides, had said that "Cretans are always liars, evil beasts, lazy gluttons." To this statement the author of the epistle adds the comment that "this testimony is true" (Titus 1:12–13). Clement of Alexandria was able to identify his source.[33]

What was the testimony? Philosophers were well aware of the logical dilemma Epimenides presented, for as a Cretan he must have included himself among the liars he denounced, speaking either truth or falsehood. The problem was recognized by the anti-Aristotelian logician Eubulides and discussed by Aristotle's pupil Theophrastus, who wrote three books on it.

The Stoic Chrysippus wrote no fewer than six treatises on the subject. "If you say you are lying and you speak the truth, you lie; but you say you are lying and you speak the truth; therefore you lie."[34] The Hellenistic poet Philetas claimed on his tombstone that the problem had made him waste away.[35] (Bertrand Russell too was taken with the problem, but not to such an extent.) The author of the Pastorals was not interested in the logical intricacies and presumably thought he could cut the Gordian knot by declaring that the testimony was "true." In any case, he was somehow acquainted with this line from the *Theogony* or *Oracles* of Epimenides and used it in support of his own point.

The Christian apologists took no interest in logic but turned to a line in which Callimachus, not a Cretan, imitated the line at the beginning of his *Hymn to Zeus*.[36] "Cretans are always liars, for Cretans built your tomb, O King; but you did not die, for you are forever." In another fragment preserved on papyrus, Callimachus mentions the more reliable view of someone who "speaks true words and says he knows the Cretan tomb is empty."[37] Some Christian apologists agreed with Callimachus' Cretans and insisted that Zeus had died and was buried on Crete. Similarly Clement cites only the words "Cretans built your tomb, O King," in order to prove that Zeus died.[38] Athenagoras seems more original. He quotes the lines from Callimachus and criticizes him for believing in the birth of Zeus (mentioned in lines not quoted) but not in his tomb.[39] On the other hand, the pagan orator Aelius Aristides insists that the cosmic Zeus made everything, including himself, and denies the story about his infancy on Crete.[40]

Arguments pro and con continued to flourish. The pagan critic Celsus was well aware that Christians made much of the tomb of Zeus, while in reply to him Origen quoted Callimachus to show that "he relates that Zeus experienced what is the beginning of death; for the origin of death is birth." Since Callimachus thought that Zeus was immortal, he thus contradicted himself.[41]

Aratus

The third text appears in the course of Paul's sermon before the court of the Areopagus in Acts (17:28). He is proving that God is not far from each one of us, and he says that "in him we live and move and exist; as even some of your own poets have said, 'For we are indeed his offspring.' " And he goes on to point out that since we are God's offspring we should not imagine that the Deity is like an idol. It is clear enough that "We are his offspring" is from the Stoic poet Aratus.[42] It occurred toward the beginning of his *Phenomena* and passed thence into anthologies used by pagans and Christians alike. The poem was also a favorite among Romans just before Paul's time. Most of Cicero's translation into Latin survives, along with a few lines from that of Varro and much of the version by Germanicus Caesar, nephew of Tiberius. When Luke describes Paul as citing this poem he is referring to a widely read and valued text.

The point in Acts would be made if the text said what Paul or Luke says it said, but in fact it does not. The poem starts out thus:

> From Zeus let us begin; we mortals never leave him unnamed; full of Zeus are all streets, all men's markets, the sea and the harbors. We all always have need of Zeus. For we are also his offspring, and in his kindness to men he gives signs of favor and raises up the peoples to work.

Zeus does so by noting seasons through the "phenomena" he causes. Neither Paul nor Luke revered Zeus. They could use the text only by starting with "For we are also his offspring," without mention of the pagan god.

One way to avoid speaking of Zeus was provided by the Hellenistic Jewish apologist Aristobulus. He quoted the first nine lines of the poem but always substituted "God" for "Zeus," explaining that this name is what the poet meant to use.[43] Clement of Alexandria, on the other hand, quoted such lines in the original version with references to "Zeus," but agreed with Aristobulus that the poet really meant "God" when he said "Zeus."[44]

Later on, Origen said that Paul made the lines of the unnamed poet his own and like Clement cited the beginning of the poem as "From Zeus let us begin." Apparently he thought that Paul himself creatively reinterpreted the poem.[45] Pagans made similar reinterpretations: Aelius Aristides once refers Aratus' statement that "all things are full of Zeus" to Zeus himself, but on another occasion says that "all things are full" of Sarapis.[46]

Some scholars, ancient as well as modern, have supposed that the line just before the reference in Acts to "some of your own poets" comes from Epimenides: "In him we live and move and exist." The judicious discussion of the point by H. J. Cadbury should put an end to such a guess.[47] Moreover Origen, who as we have just seen was aware of the quotation from Aratus, says that "in him we live and move and exist" is Christian doctrine.[48]

3
The Reign
of Trajan

The New Testament does not refer to the persecution under Nero (though *1 Clement* refers to the martyrdoms of Peter and Paul without mentioning the emperor's name), and there was little contact between Christians and the Roman state even under Domitian. This emperor injudiciously asked courtiers to address him as "Lord and god," and his enemies in the Senate murdered him in 96. His successor was an aged and reliable caretaker named Nerva, who before his death in 98 adopted the Spanish-born general Trajan as his successor. Three years later the new emperor was able to celebrate a triumph over the Dacians and Scythians, and he soon turned Dacia into a Roman province. Later he made treaties with nearby foreign nations and began an extended war in the East (114–117), occupying Armenia, Assyria, and Mesopotamia and even stationing a fleet in the Red Sea. Revolts behind the lines, especially among the Jews, led to withdrawal from the new provinces, and in 117 he died on his way back to Rome.

Trajan and the Christians

Eusebius sets the martyrdom of Ignatius, bishop of Antioch, during Trajan's reign, while two letters (96–97) from the tenth book of Pliny's *Letters,* correspondence between Trajan and his legate in Bithynia/Pontus in 111–113, are concerned with Christians in those provinces. Eusebius believed that the martyrdom was somehow related to the letters and apparently tried to correlate Ignatius' journey to Rome to fight wild beasts with Trajan's animal shows at Rome. After the emperor returned from Dacia in 107 "he gave shows on 123 days, during which about 11,000 animals, both wild and tame, were killed, and 10,000 gladiators fought."[1] Eusebius had no way to date the letters of Pliny and therefore set them in the *Chronicle* just after Ignatius' martyrdom, in the *Church History* just before it. In fact, however, there may be no relation between the dates of Pliny and Ignatius.

The bishop may have been condemned after a violent earthquake at Antioch in 115. We have already cited a passage in which Tertullian explains anti-Christian passions as due to rivers too high or too low, lack of rainfall, and even earthquakes (see chapter 1).

In addition, at some time during Trajan's reign a bishop of Jerusalem was accused of being not only a Christian but also a descendant of David, hence potentially seditious, and was put to death, perhaps during the Jewish revolt of 115–117.[2]

Christians were obviously suspect during Trajan's reign, and the letters exchanged by Pliny with the emperor reveal the ambiguous impression Christians made on Roman officials. Their extravagant superstition was spreading into all levels of society *(omnis ordo)* and infected both town and country. It threatened other religions as well as the merchants who supplied animals for sacrifice. When Christians were arrested both temple attendance and animal sales improved. Pliny was uncertain how to deal with such people and therefore asked Trajan what was to be investigated and punished. Was it the name "Christian" or the crimes inherently related to the name? He described his interim procedure for testing people suspected of being Christians. He had them call upon the gods, offer incense and wine before Trajan's statue, and curse Christ. In his reply the emperor approved the punishment of these criminals; he neither identified their crime nor allowed search for them. He did permit pardon for those who recanted while allowing most of Pliny's tests; but he was not enthusiastic about the use of his own statue.[3]

Pliny and the Christians

It seems likely that when Pliny interrogated the Christians he had in mind the classical case concerning foreign religions with nocturnal rites.[4] The Bacchanalia, supposedly introduced to Rome through Etruria by a nameless Greek, were harshly suppressed for immorality in 186 B.C.[5] even though three centuries later they were enthusiastically accepted by prominent Romans in Campania (see chapter 9).

Pliny's account of the Christians' testimony contains striking parallels to Livy's account of the nocturnal rites of the Bacchanalia and their suppression.[6] In his basic commentary on Pliny, A. N. Sherwin-White described my views as "subversive" because I was discounting the evidence for what Christians did and thought.[7] He misunderstood my point. Pliny was not distorting some "real" picture of the Christians because of his memories of Livy or something similar. Instead, the tradition about the Bacchanalia gave him the kind of filter he needed for interviewing them and constructing his report. It helped him phrase questions and listen to answers.

We know that Pliny found Livy valuable reading. Thirty years earlier, when Vesuvius was erupting, he had been reading Livy and indeed had made extracts for future use.[8] We assume that then or later he read about the Bacchanalia and remembered something about the precedent-making case. He needed such a precedent, since as he informed the emperor Trajan he had never been present when such people were interrogated.

Cicero, whom Pliny greatly admired, already treated the suppression of the Bacchanalia as a precedent for the treatment of any nocturnal rites, and especially those involving women, like those practiced by Christians.[9] Pliny's description of the Christians may well contain echoes of Livy's "classical" account of the Bacchants. When he says that they sometimes met before dawn, took an oath but for good behavior, ate ordinary and harmless food, and accepted an immoderate superstition, he is presumably reporting the answers to questions inspired by the Bacchanalian precedent.[10]

Trajan's reply is interesting for what it says and does not say. The emperor explicitly discourages Pliny from hunting for Christians. He does not refer to any distinction to be made on the basis of age, sex, or rank and thus favors none. He does not mention Pliny's test of suspected Christians before the imperial statue. Prayer to the gods will suffice. Anonymous accusations, however, must never be accepted. They follow the worst precedent—that is, the reign of Domitian as recalled under Trajan[11]—one that is "not of our age." The expression "our age" obviously refers to the "new era" that began after the death of Domitian. The new justice of the new age conceivably encouraged Christians to hope for better times.

Is there a conflict between Christianity and the "cult of the emperor"? Charlesworth thought that Pliny followed a precedent set under Domitian when he asked for veneration of the emperor's statue,[12] but Pliny says he has never taken part in the investigation of Christians and more probably the idea is based on his own attitude toward the emperor.[13] In the *Panegyric* Pliny insists that Trajan is a man who worships the gods, though he will be deified after death.[14] In a letter from Bithynia he tells Trajan of his plan to build a temple with statues of various emperors and asks permission to include one of Trajan himself. Trajan agrees, but reluctantly.[15] Similar reluctance appears over Pliny's test for Christians with the emperor's statue. Still later, Pliny himself again recognizes the distinction between gods and emperor.[16] His vacillation suggests that using the statue for testing Christians was an ad hoc procedure of his own.

A more ominous picture of Christians appears in the *Annals* of Pliny's friend Tacitus. He knows that Christ, the "author of the name," was punished under Pontius Pilate in the reign of Tiberius, though the detestable superstition broke out again and reached Rome, the goal of everything vile and shameful. Accused of setting fire to the city, the Christians were burned alive not so much for that crime as for their "hatred of the human race." In turn, the mob at Rome hated them for their unspecified crimes.[17]

The account of the Christians may conceivably owe something to Pliny, since apparently the *Annals* were written after his term as legate. Some details, however, seem to come from the earlier *Histories* in which Tacitus had provided an unfriendly account of Judaism in relation to the fall of Jerusalem.[18] The parallels set forth in Appendix 3 illustrate Tacitus' procedure. He found little difference between Christians and Jews.

In the work of a third contemporary, Suetonius, there is nothing but rhetoric: "The Christians were punished, a race of men given to novel and harmful superstition."[19] Suetonius was in touch with Tacitus at the time the historian was writing about the Christians and may have derived his notice from him.

It is clear enough that these three authors saw the Christians through distorting glasses. They are important not for their information but as representing the attitude of significant Romans toward Christianity at the beginning of the second century, before the rise of apologetic literature.

Charges Against Christians

It is not clear whether or not there was a definite and specific law or decree forbidding the existence of Christians, even though one can argue that there should have been one. This is why the charges against Christians remained important throughout the second century and the apologists found it necessary to reply to them. Similar accusations had already been brought against Jews and answered by Jewish apologists like Josephus; they reappear in the earliest pagan notices about Christians, as when Pliny denies that they meet for immoral purposes and allows that their common meal is "harmless," while Tacitus claims that the Christians were "hated for their crimes." Christians were explicitly accused of sexual promiscuity at night, probably because of their common supper called the Agape or "love feast." Charges of ritual murder and cannibalism may have been based on slanders about the Eucharist. In addition, the less specific crime of "godlessness" meant that Christians refused to reverence the gods of paganism. The apologists devoted much time to explaining that the gods of paganism were demons or dead men or did not exist. In addition, they replied by developing their own philosophical and theological doctrines of God.

Attacks sometimes came from the highest levels of Roman society. The Latin apologist Minucius Felix cited a detailed and exotic account of the Christian "banquet" from Cornelius Fronto, consul in 143 and teacher of rhetoric to the emperor Marcus Aurelius.[20] Though around 177 the anti-Christian author Celsus did not refer to them,[21] the pagan mob at Lyons did so, and the apologists routinely responded to them from Aristides (17.2) onward.

Trajan, the Jews, and Christian Apologetic

Though the earliest Christians were Jews, at some point early in the second century the split between church and synagogue widened. As Trajan moved toward his Parthian war, another Jewish revolt broke out against Rome. Dio Cassius tells how in Cyrene, under their leader Andreas, Jews slaughtered both Romans and Greeks. Similar events occurred in Egypt, as well as in Cyprus, from which Jews were still banned a century later.[22]

The church historian Eusebius supplies a good deal of information about the revolt. It began in 114 or 115 when Libyan Jews took action in Egypt, Alexandria, Cyrene, and the Thebaid. Gentiles prevailed against them in Alexandria, however, and the next year the emperor sent Lusius Quietus to drive other Jewish rebels out of the new province of Mesopotamia. After he killed many in battle, Trajan made him procurator of Judea. On Cyprus in 116 Jewish rebels killed Gentiles in Salamina and took the city. This is the account found in Eusebius' *Chronicle.*

In the *Church History* he says his fuller report comes from "such Greeks as have handed down in writing an account of those times."[23] There are few differences from the *Chronicle,* but Eusebius now gives a date for the outbreak of revolt, names the Jewish "king" in Cyrene (Lucuas), and has the Romans forestall the revolt in Mesopotamia.[24]

Where did Eusebius get his accounts of the revolt? They are more detailed than one would expect. Few early Christians were interested in military history; indeed, the only exception seems to be the third-century polymath Julius Africanus. The church historian must therefore be using a source which found such items important. It could be a pagan source on secular history, but since he rarely uses such materials it is more likely to be the apologetic source he would also use for the Jewish revolt under Hadrian, whose author he names in the *Church History* as Aristo of Pella.[25] Aristo's work was certainly apologetic, for it laid emphasis on the decree banishing Jews from Jerusalem. It may well be Eusebius' primary source for the events under both Trajan and Hadrian, and probably was intended to show that Christians had nothing to do with unsuccessful Jewish revolts against these emperors.

Obviously, a religious group related to Judaism could suffer persecution under such circumstances, and at least two Roman writers of this period noted the connection of Christianity with the Jews. Tacitus reports that Christianity itself arose in Judea, while Suetonius tells how Jews at Rome constantly rioted "at the instigation of Chrestus" *(impulsore Chresto),* or possibly "over the messianic question."[26] Antipathy toward the "mother church" was transferred to the daughter, who became unwilling to stay at home.

The increasing tension between church and synagogue is marked in Hegesippus' stories about bishops of Jerusalem under suspicion as messianic claimants. It is also evident in the letters of Ignatius, bishop of Antioch and a prospective martyr around the time of the Jewish revolt. In Asia Minor Ignatius stopped at Philadelphia, east of Sardis, before passing westward, presumably through Sardis and Magnesia, to Smyrna, where he spent some time in touch with Polycarp before continuing his journey toward Rome.[27] Letters written to the Magnesians and the Philadelphians contrast "Christianism" with the Maccabean term "Judaism"[28] and urge Christians not to "live according to Judaism" or to "Judaize" or to listen to anyone expounding Judaism. Indeed, hostility toward Judaism occupies his mind more than the question why he is on the way to martyrdom. "It is primarily where Ignatius thinks of his martyrdom in the capital that a negative attitude toward those outside the church comes to expression."[29] Though he "attributes broad powers to 'the ruler of this age,' "[30] he does not identify him with the Roman emperor.

Evidently Ignatius was more deeply involved with rhetoric and theology than with political or even social ideas. Under circumstances like his there was no reason for apologetic to arise, any more than at Jerusalem as the bishop was being executed there.

4
The Reign
of Hadrian

Trajan's widow Plotina insisted that he had chosen Hadrian to succeed him, and after the Senate confirmed the appointment he returned from Syria to Rome to celebrate a triumph over the Parthians in Trajan's name. His changes in command led to the conservative "conspiracy of the four consulars," which ended when the Senate executed the leaders. When he visited Rome again he won popular favor by canceling debts due the treasury. He also discontinued Trajan's expansion into the East, though he set Roman colonies in Libya, devastated by Jewish rebels in 115–117.[1]

In 120 he began the grand imperial tour which lasted for eleven years, with coins of 121 announcing the beginning of the "golden age."[2] Even in the West his attention was drawn toward Athens. Trajan's widow asked for a favor concerning the succession in the Epicurean school at Athens, and an inscription contains her Latin letter of 121 to Hadrian as well as her Greek letter to "all the friends" on his favorable reply. She was happy to describe him as "genuinely a benefactor and director of all culture."[3] The geographer Pausanias says that Athens "flourished again when Hadrian was emperor."[4]

During the tour Hadrian naturally dealt with other areas such as the province of Asia. The proconsul there wrote about an inheritance problem in 119/120, and the emperor replied to his successor in September of the latter year.[5] Similarly Silvanus Granianus, proconsul in 121/122, wrote about the Christian problem and the emperor's answer was sent to Minicius Fundanus in 122/123. In his rescript Hadrian denounced informers, eager to blackmail their victims, and insisted that charges had to be proved in court, not simply initiated by petitions or popular clamor. His ruling, like Trajan's to Pliny, did not revoke the penalties against convicted Christians but did require orderly procedure. Apparently this was the only letter from Hadrian that Christians could cite.[6] Though Melito refers to Hadrian's letters "to many others besides" he does not name addressees or describe contents.

The First Visit to Athens

In 122 Hadrian traveled to Britain and founded "Hadrian's Wall" in the north on the 73-mile Solway-Tyne line. Returning southward, he passed through Gaul to Spain, thence to western Asia Minor and late in 124 to Athens.

The picture of Hadrian at Athens found in the *Chronicle* of Eusebius-Jerome seems quite reliable, even though it spreads the events of 124/125 over the years 122–127. The *Chronicle* says that at the Athenians' request Hadrian gave them a constitution based chiefly on the laws of Draco and Solon. This is an odd statement because Solon himself repealed all Draco's laws except one against murder,[7] and an inscription gives a better picture: the Athenians simply asked him for permission to "use the ancient laws of the city."[8] In addition, he forbade the export of all agricultural produce except oil. Again, an inscription provides some of his regulations on this export.[9]

Next Eusebius-Jerome discusses the inundation of Eleusis by the flooding river Kifissos. Hadrian built a bridge across it from Athens, thus showing his concern for the sanctuary and its processions. (Four arches remain.) The account continues with Hadrian's initiation, presumably into the Lesser Mysteries, in the autumn of 124.[10]

> When Hadrian was initiated in the rites of Eleusis he bestowed many gifts on the Athenians. Quadratus, a disciple of the apostles, and Aristides the Athenian, our philosopher, gave Hadrian books composed on behalf of the Christian religion.

The chronology of Eusebius or Jerome is erroneous. It treats the letter to Fundanus as Hadrian's response to the apologies, whereas it was really written two years before the visit to Athens. The events have nothing to do with each other. Perhaps Eusebius even made further errors in his chronology. It seems likely, however, that an Athenian Christian would seize the opportunity to present a petition at this time. He would be aware of the emperor's concern for law, Athens, and the Eleusinian mysteries.[11]

The Apologist Quadratus

Hadrian's rescript to Fundanus had shown that he would maintain the relatively impartial attitude of Trajan toward Christians. An Athenian apologist might therefore have pressed toward further concessions. Unfortunately we possess only one brief fragment from Quadratus, defending Christianity indirectly by pointing to its miraculous content.

> But our Savior's works were permanent, for they were real. Those who had been cured or rose from the dead not only appeared to be cured or raised but were permanent, not only during the Savior's stay on earth but also after his departure. They remained for a considerable period, so that some of them even reached our times.[12]

What is the context of Quadratus' argument? Two settings seem appropriate. First, he may be referring to an debate among Christians over the physical reality of the Savior himself and the actuality of his miracles. Later such a setting seems confirmed by Irenaeus' parallel language used in an attack on Gnostic views.[13] There was no sharp division between antiheretical and apologetic writing, and apologists like Justin and Theophilus also wrote against heresies. But why should Quadratus discuss such a topic when addressing the emperor? Why bring up the Gnostic problem?

Another setting may be equally important. Quadratus could be writing in the context of pagan religion, in which the Savior's miracles would naturally be compared with those of some deified son of a god. We supply a possible context in italics along with Quadratus' own words.

> *You may say that Jesus was a benefactor regarded as a god after his death—like Heracles, Asclepius or the Dioscuri.*[14] *But the works of leaders—especially those which are false—remain unaltered only while the leaders are alive, and are done away after their death. . . . Many were counted as gods during their lifetime but were despised after death.*[15] *On the other hand,* "The works of *our* Savior were ever present, for they were real. Those who had been cured or rose from the dead did not just appear to be cured or risen but were ever present, not just during the Savior's visitation but also after his departure they remained for a considerable time, so that some of them even reached our times."

The same arguments could thus be used inside against Gnostics and outside against critics of Jesus' deeds.

As for the evidence Quadratus cites, more than half a century later Irenaeus was still willing to speak of resurrections in Christian churches,[16] though Theophilus doubts that a pagan would accept even firsthand testimony.[17]

The Apologist Aristides

Eusebius says that, like Quadratus, the Christian Athenian philosopher Aristides presented an apology to Hadrian, and the Armenian fragments agree with this address. The whole apology survives only in Syriac, addressed to Antoninus Pius, though it was reused in the eighth-century Greek novel *Barlaam and Josaphat.* The Syriac was discovered by Rendel

Harris, while his friend Armitage Robinson found the Greek parallel.[18] Two fourth-century Greek fragments on papyrus turned up later,[19] neither of them bearing the title or the names of author or recipient.

Aristides' plan is quite simple. First he describes the true God, relying chiefly on the negative epithets typical of Middle Platonic philosophy; next he shows how Chaldeans, Greeks, and Egyptians presented false notions about gods; then he praises Jewish monotheism but criticizes failure to accept Christ; and finally he praises Christianity chiefly because of its (Jewish) morality.

Aristides' Doctrine of God and Gods

Both Greek and Syriac versions begin with a philosophical definition of God. "I call God him who made all things and sustains them, without beginning, eternal, immortal, without needs, above all passions and failings, such as anger, forgetfulness, ignorance, and the rest."[20] On the basis of his definitions Aristides proceeds to contrast pagan religions with Judaism and Christianity. The Greek version explains that only Jews and Christians properly worship the one God, while Chaldeans, Greeks, and Egyptians taught polytheism to the other nations.

His discussion reflects the widespread interest in the history of religions in the early second century. Philo of Byblos had translated the ancient Phoenician author Sanchuniathon, many of whose statements about religion have been confirmed by materials from Ugarit, and during Hadrian's reign widespread concern for oriental religions was met by such works as Plutarch's treatise *On Isis and Osiris* and the lost book of Pallas *On the Mysteries of Mithras*.[21] Hadrian himself used themes from Egyptian religion for his villa at Tivoli.

The Chaldeans worship heaven or earth, water, fire, the winds, sun, moon, and (presumably) stars. Next come the Greeks as worshipers of at least eight immoral and imperfect human-like gods and four goddesses, three with male consorts. Third and worst are the Egyptians, who worship not only Isis and her brother-husband Osiris but also many irrational animals. These three barbarian nations thus worship physical nature, humanity, and the animal world, none of them objects worthy of devotion.

Aristides and the Jews

In Aristides' opinion the Jews are nearer the truth than any of these nations. They worship one God alone and they imitate him in their concern for the poor and captives and the burial of the dead—a concern received from ancestral tradition and pleasing to God and men alike. They have gone astray, however, for they deny Christ.

Aristides and Christian Tradition and Morality

Christians, who are best of all, trace their genealogy back to "the Lord Jesus Christ, the Son of the highest God, who came down from heaven," was born of a virgin, and assumed flesh. He taught true theology, as well as the morality which Christians practice when they keep "the injunctions of Christ."

Aristides obviously regards his description of this morality (ch. 15) as the most important part of his apology. Christianity, for him as for other apologists, is essentially a new law. Presumably the forbidding of adultery, fornication, false witness, refusal to repay deposits, and desire for the goods of others are derived from an expanded decalogue, as is honoring father and mother. Christians, like Jews, love their neighbors and give just judgments. They do not make idols; they observe the negative golden rule; they do not eat foods offered to idols. The picture is obviously Jewish as well as Christian.

Aristides goes on to show how Christian actions support harmony in society when both men and women practice an austere sexual morality in the hope of a heavenly reward. They persuade their servants or children, if they have any, to become Christians and call them brothers [and sisters]. They do not worship strange gods. They practice humility and kindness, reject falsehood, and love one another. They care for widows and orphans and give generously to the poor, provide for the burial of poor Christians and supply the needs of Christian prisoners, especially those "punished for the name of Christ."[22] If they have no food for the poor, they fast for two or three days to obtain it.[23]

When one of them dies they give thanks to God and follow the corpse as if he were passing from one place to another. When a child is born they also praise God, and if it dies in infancy they praise God for the one who passed through the world without sin. Again, if they see that one of them has died in wickedness or sins, they weep for him and mourn because he is about to pay a penalty.

The apology thus combines a vigorous attack on the gods of paganism with an extended defense of Jewish and Christian morality. The combination gives the apology its power.

Is the Syriac Version Based on a Later Edition?

A possible reason for not dating the apologist Aristides under Hadrian is that in the Syriac version, not the Greek, he asks the emperor to admit that when Greeks blaspheme and revile Christians for homosexual acts and incest they refer to practices of their own (17.2; cf. 8.2). Such a request could hardly have been tactful if made of Hadrian, who had probably encountered his favorite Antinous in Bithynia in 124. Criticisms of Antinous come only from the reign of Antoninus Pius and later, when Christian apologists felt free to criticize his deification.[24]

The shorter Greek version, however, as well as the Armenian fragments, could well come from the reign of Hadrian,[25] and the relatively favorable picture of Judaism suggests a date well before 132.

The Preaching of Peter

Another apologetic work probably from the reign of Hadrian is the apocryphal treatise called the *Preaching of Peter*. It is hard to date but presents apologetic much like that of Aristides. Christian writers used it toward the end of the second century, when Clement ascribed it to the apostle Peter.[26] The Gnostic Heracleon too thought it came from Peter, and Origen therefore raised the question whether it was "genuine or not or mixed" in character.[27] No matter who wrote it, it is an important witness to early Christian apologetic.[28]

Like Aristides, the *Preaching* combines philosophical discussion of attributes with a biblical emphasis on God as Creator. He is "the invisible one who sees all things, the infinite who contains all, the one without needs whom all need and for whom they exist, the incomprehensible, everlasting, imperishable, uncreated, who made all things by the word of his power." A similar but less elaborate description appears even in the popular Christianity represented by Hermas.[29]

"Peter" like Aristides goes on to explain that God cannot be worshiped in the manner of the Greeks, who make idols and offer sacrifices to them, nor in the manner of the Jews.[30]

> They think they alone know God but do not know him. They worship angels and archangels, the months and the moon. Unless the moon shines they do not observe the so-called "first sabbath" nor observe the new moon or days of unleavened bread or the feast or the great day.

This criticism of Judaism is close to what the Syriac Aristides provides, probably relying on the *Preaching.* The author next explains that the prophets, pre-Christian Christians, really wrote about the coming of Christ, as well as about his death and suffering, all due to "the Jews." The gospel is presented most clearly by the apostles, who remained in Jerusalem for twelve years after the crucifixion but then began their mission to the Gentiles "so that no one might say, 'We have not heard.'"

The two aspects of the *Preaching* that immediately influenced apologetic were the primarily philosophical doctrine of God and the notion that Greeks worship idols while Jews worship angelic powers. Such a picture of three groups—Greeks, Jews, and Christians—was already present in the letters of Paul, notably in 1 Corinthians 1:24, while both of "Peter"'s basic themes recur in the *Apology* of Aristides. It is hard to tell whether "Peter" influenced Aristides or vice versa, but there must be some relation.

The temple of Zeus Olympios at Athens, with Parthenon behind

Though the booklet cannot be dated precisely, its concerns fit the religious melting pot of the reign of Hadrian, and either before or after the revolt it emphasizes separateness from Jews as well as Greeks. It is an important work because it shows doctrines expressed by the apologists being used inside the church, where the "preaching" might well be read.

Hadrian's Tour Continued

In 127 the emperor returned to Rome through Sicily but soon left for Africa to address the army. The second part of the imperial tour took Hadrian to Athens again late in 128 and the next year he was initiated into the Greater Mysteries at Eleusis,[31] an event which an Eleusinian priest recalled forty-six years later.[32] He then proceeded from Eleusis to Ephesus and thence to Caria, Cilicia, Cappadocia, and Syria. In 130 he made a voyage up the Nile, where his favorite Antinous drowned and was deified. He founded the town of Antinoöpolis in his memory and had statues of him erected throughout the empire.

Hadrian and Zeus Olympios at Athens

Not long afterward, Hadrian took part in the dedication of the great temple of Zeus Olympios at Athens and founded the Panhellenion or Greek League. An Epidaurus inscription refers to these events and is dated in 133/134: the third year after the events and the tenth year after Hadrian's first official visit to Athens.[33] The dedication therefore occurred in 131/132, confirmed by dedicatory inscriptions with dates equivalent to December 131/December 132.[34] The *Chronicle* of Eusebius-Jerome gives a similar date for the orator Polemo, who reached the peak of his career when he spoke on the occasion.[35]

The temple, south of the Acropolis, was the greatest in the world. Pisistratus had laid its foundations in the sixth century B.C. Its greatest benefactor had been Antiochus Epiphanes, the Hellenizing Syrian king (175–164), but he was unable to complete the work. Under Augustus the client kings of the East proposed to finish the temple and dedicate it to the Genius of the emperor,[36] but nothing came of their scheme. In 124 or so Hadrian gave orders to finish it, and by 128/129 he dedicated the cella. The consecration ceremonies ending in the spring of 132 were to point toward the religious and cultural unity of the Greco-Roman world, with its center in the Olympian Zeus and his earthly representative the emperor. In Polemo's dedicatory address he hinted that he himself had been divinely inspired.[37]

Another memorial of this time is the Arch of Hadrian, with inscriptions marking the line between the older "city of Theseus" and the new "city of Hadrian."[38]

The Jewish Revolt 132–135

This attempt to unite the empire religiously recalls the similar attempt made by Antiochus Epiphanes in the Seleucid empire, and it had a similar though more tragic result. Hadrian not only celebrated at Athens but laid plans to build a new city at Jerusalem with a new temple for Zeus. In 132 revolt broke out, led by a certain Simon ben Kosiba, who claimed to be a messianic king. The prominent rabbinic teacher Akiba apparently acknowledged him, and his followers called him Bar Kokhba, "son of the star," with reference to the rising star in Numbers 24:17.

Apparently Bar Kokhba first struck at Jerusalem and the Tenth Legion Fretensis stationed there. It is certain that he took the city, for land-sale contracts made at Jerusalem date from the second and the fourth years "of the liberation of Israel."[39] In addition, the rebels were issuing coins of their own, with those of the first year (131/132) bearing the date "Year One of the redemption of Israel" and those of the second dated "Year Two of the freedom of Israel."[40] Some of them point to the restoration of temple worship, with a temple portal, the lulab and the ethrog, and trumpets. Some also name "Eleazar the priest."

The Roman campaign against the guerrillas did not go well, and in 133 Hadrian himself visited Judea, accompanied by his legate Lollius Urbicus, formerly in command of X Gemina in Britain.[41] The rebels had fortified strongholds with mines and walls, connected by tunnels. The Romans could not deal with this guerrilla warfare. By the end of the year Hadrian sent for the governor of Britain, experienced in dealing with rebellious tribes.

> He did not venture to attack the enemy in the open at any one point, in view of their numbers and their desperation, but by intercepting small units, thanks to the number of his soldiers and junior officers, and by depriving them of food and shutting them up, he was able, rather slowly but with comparatively little danger, to crush, exhaust, and exterminate them.[42]

A reliable though apologetic source of Eusebius' *Chronicle* briefly describes the course of the war.

> The Jews took up arms and depopulated Palestine when Tinius Rufus governed the province. Hadrian sent him an army to put down the rebels. Cochba, leader of the Jewish faction, tortured and killed the Christians who refused to aid him against the Roman army. The Jewish war in Palestine came to an end with the condition of the Jews deeply depressed. From that time their liberty to enter Jerusalem was taken away, first by God's decree, as the prophets foretold, then by Roman prohibitions.[43]

Evidently Eusebius' source was the Christian apologist Aristo, who as we suggested also discussed the failure of the revolt under Trajan (chapter 3). Another Christian apologist, Justin, tells how "during the recent Jewish war, Bar Kokhba, the leader of the insurrection, ordered Christians alone to be executed if they would not deny and curse Jesus the Messiah."[44] And Tertullian cites Isaiah 33:17 to show that the prophets foretold Jews' seeing the city "from afar" when the Romans forbade them to visit the site.[45] More detail about the end of the war appears in the *Church History.*

> The war was at its height in the eighteenth year of the reign [134/135], round about Beth-ther, a small but very strong town not far from Jerusalem, where a protracted siege brought the rebels to utter destruction through hunger and thirst, and the instigator of their madness paid the penalty due him. From then on the whole nation was absolutely prohibited from setting foot on the country around Jerusalem, by a law of Hadrian with a decree and regulations forbidding them even to look from a distance on their ancestral home.[46]

Here he names Aristo of Pella, who presumably provided information not only about Hadrian's decree but also about events during the war.[47]

Obviously there was another significant break between Jews and Christians at this time. After the war the Jerusalem church, once Jewish, consisted only of Gentiles.[48] A vehement response appeared among the Gnostic leaders who during and after the Jewish war flourished in Christian churches and sharply separated themselves from Jews and indeed from "the God of the Jews." Basilides, who flourished during the reign of Hadrian (indeed, the *Chronicle* sets him in 132), rejected the basic Old Testament picture of the Creator and the creation. The names of his "prophets" Bar Kabbas and Bar Koph may be parodies of the rebel's name.[49] In addition, both Valentinus and Cerdo, Marcion's teacher, were at Rome in 140, early in the reign of Antoninus Pius. Harnack calculated that Marcion himself came to Rome in 137 and was expelled in 144.[50] Presumably in reaction against Bar Kokhba's revolt, Marcion rejected the Old Testament as inspired by a warlike and merely just god who was not the good Father of Jesus.

Hadrian's Last Years

After the war Hadrian lived in Rome, where he was constructing the Pantheon, the temple of Venus and Rome, and his mausoleum, now the Castel Sant'Angelo. His villa near Tivoli, with its many Egyptian motifs, was also important to him. Plots multiplied in his last years but before dying at Baiae in 138 he arranged for the succession of Antoninus Pius—who adopted Marcus Aurelius and Lucius Verus, thus ensuring the continuance of Hadrian's plans. Antoninus insisted on his deification.

5

Antoninus Pius
and the Christians

Historians of most second-century emperors rely on the third-century author Dio Cassius, but the Byzantine epitome of Dio's book 70 states that "the account of Antoninus Pius is not found in the copies of Dio, probably because the books have met with some accident, so that the history of his reign is almost wholly unknown." Such remains the case today, except for gleanings from fragments, the unreliable account in the *Augustan History,* the rhetoric of Aelius Aristides and Fronto and the meditations of Marcus Aurelius, along with a few bits from late chroniclers. It is very hard to obtain a clear picture of this reign. Our impression of tranquillity may be due to our ignorance.

The modern historian Paul Petit does not give much help in connection with Christian history. To be sure, Antoninus "showed himself a strict economist, counting the pennies of both government and governed, traveling very little, building almost nothing, loth to expand the machinery of administration," and surrounding himself "with senators from Latium and the highly romanized western provinces." His religious concerns were conventional and he preferred Latin cults to Greek. Though he revered the oriental goddess Cybele, she had been worshiped at Rome since republican times and had a temple near the Forum.[1]

The emperor's political and military ideas were not highly developed. Toward the beginning of his reign he built a new wall in Britain along the Clyde-Forth line, north of Hadrian's Wall but less substantial. It guarded a shorter line, but the emperor neglected political factors; "the rear of the Antonine Wall was never fully pacified, and its front remained unsecured." In consequence it could be held for little more than a dozen years when revolt broke out.[2]

We know practically nothing about the revolts that marred the emperor's peace. His wall in Scotland was built after his legate Lollius Urbicus (later a judge of Christians as prefect at Rome) suppressed a revolt by the Brigantes. Other revolts were put down in Mauretania, Germany, Dacia, and Judea—after the emperor perhaps forbade circumcision—as well as in Achaea and Egypt.[3] There were also plots that presumably originated in Rome itself.[4] Conceivably one or more of these revolts triggered Christian apologetic or contributed to triggering it. (For a more important cause see chapter 6.)

The Revised Apology of Aristides

During Antoninus' reign the apology of Aristides was revised and presented to the emperor, perhaps toward the beginning of his reign. This revision is reflected in the Syriac version, which shows Marcianus Aristides addressing "the emperor Caesar Titus Hadrianus Antoninus Pius."

The Syriac version adds a discussion of God as nameless and containing everything, and finally states that he is "Wisdom and wholly Mind, and through him everything has held together." Most of this is conventional Middle Platonic theology, though the words about "holding together" seem based on the Wisdom Christology of Colossians 1:17.

Other additions include the allegation that the Jews worship angels and not God when they observe Sabbaths, "new moons," passover, fasting, circumcision, and dietary laws (14.3), along with the undeveloped statement that Jesus was born of the race of the Hebrews and had twelve disciples and arose three days after his death and ascended into heaven (15.2). The new version says twice that homosexual acts (like those of Hadrian and Antinous) are immoral (8.2; 17.2).

Antoninus and the Christians

Antoninus agreed with the *Apology* of Aristides on homosexuality,[5] but little is known about his dealings with the Christians. Gnostic teachers freely visited Rome under the bishop Hyginus, and Polycarp of Smyrna could easily visit Anicetus of Rome around 155. No Roman bishop was a martyr under the Antonines, or indeed until the Decian persecution. On the other hand, Polycarp was certainly martyred in Asia soon afterward, after being sought for. He refused to say "Caesar is Lord" or offer sacrifice. The proconsul of Asia asked him to take an oath by the Fortune of the emperor (commonplace in the papyri of the time) and say "Away with the godless." He refused the oath, pointed at the pagan mob as the godless, and insisted that he was a Christian. He was then burned alive. Polycarp was basically accused and condemned for the name "Christian."

It may be that not long afterward Antoninus put water on the fire by writing letters forbidding "innovation" and maintaining the more moderate anti-Christian policy traditional since Trajan. The later apologist Melito lists some of the letters he wrote with Marcus Aurelius between 147 and

161, in which the emperor forbade such novelties, addressing the citizens of the eastern Greek cities of Larissa, Thessalonica, and Athens and, in addition, "all Hellenes."[6] The last letter was certainly written not to the Council of Asia, as Lawlor and Oulton supposed, but to the Panhellenic Council established by Hadrian at Athens in 131/132.[7] Antoninus wrote to towns in Macedonia, Thessaly, and Achaea as well as to the Panhellenic Council. A letter found on stone at Aezani in Asia, northeast of Sardis, was addressed by Antoninus "to the Panhellenion" in the year 157.[8]

The cities of Antoninus' letters were associated with the council. An Athenian inscription of 156 contains a dedication by the council of the Thessalians to the archon of the Panhellenion "because of his virtue and love toward the Panhellenion and the city of the Athenians."[9] Thus the emperor's letters on Christians were sent to closely related recipients proud of their Hellenism, perhaps after Justin wrote to him. It may be that such "Greeks" were especially hostile toward the Christian movement.

Christian Crimes?

Traditional charges against the Christians continued to flourish in Antoninus' time, and apparently were publicized by the rhetorician Fronto, consul in 143. The alleged promiscuity of both heretics and Christians brought unfavorable comment, as Justin admits in his *Apology* (1.26–29), and suspicions of sedition were aroused by their idea of a future kingdom to be given them by God. "If we expected a human kingdom," Justin replies, "we should deny in order not to be killed, and we should try to escape in order to attain what we expect" (1.11.2). He also insists that Christians pay taxes in obedience to the teaching of Jesus. Though they worship God alone, they are glad to serve the emperors, whose authority they acknowledge while praying that "reason" may accompany its expression. They even find the cross, potentially a subversive symbol, in the standards and trophies of the Roman legions (1.55). On the other hand, Justin does warn of possible punishment in eternal fire for rulers who persist in injustice.

Against All Heresies

In the *Apology* Justin refers to an earlier work, perhaps from around 140 or so, in which he denounced all the heresies that the demons had aroused among Christians. This work was itself apologetic, for he wanted to blame the heretics for the behavior that led to pagan attacks on Christian morals. He was well equipped to write it, for he originated from the homeland of two heretics and apparently was teaching in Rome in the time of a third.

Simon Magus

Since Justin came from Samaria (see chapter 6) he was able to discuss Simon's nondescript origins. This heretic came from "a village called Gittae"[10] but, by means of demon-inspired magic, advanced from this humble beginning to receive honors that the Roman Senate voted him during the reign of Claudius. Justin lays emphasis on a statue erected on the Tiber Island "between the two bridges." He probably saw at least the inscription, which he says read in Latin SIMONI DEO SANCTO.

There were sanctuaries of Asclepius, Iuppiter Iurarius, Veiovis, Faunus, Semo Sancus, and Tiberinus on the island, but no architectural remains have survived.[11] The Simonians related themselves to the shrines of Iuppiter and Veiovis when they identified Simon with this god.

Justin's political point is that the Roman Senate has honored a charlatan while not recognizing the virtue of Christians. He asks for the removal of the statue.

Simon and Archaeology

The Roman Senate certainly erected no such statue to a Gnostic hero and redeemer, but there was some justification for the Simonians' boast. An inscription[12] found on the Tiber Island in 1574 reads thus:

A Roman inscription to Semo Sancus (Vatican)

SEMONI
SANCO
DEO FIDIO
SACRUM
SEX[TUS] POMPEIUS SP[URII] F[ILIUS]
COL[LINA TRIBU] MUSSIANUS
QUINQUENNALIS
DECUR[IAE]
BIDENTALIS
DONUM DEDIT

The dedication refers to the old Sabine god Semo Sancus as identified with Dius Fidius, and the dedicator insists on his own official status.

How could the Simonians get DEUS out of DIUS and SIMONI out of SEMONI? In inscriptions as in manuscripts, I could be written for E, or E for I, because these vowels were pronounced alike. The DEUS of the inscriptions is the "Dius" of literary sources, and SEMONI could be interpreted as "Simoni." But what of Justin's SANCTO? The word turns up in inscriptions that refer to Semo not merely as SANCUS DEUS but also as SANCTUS DEUS. There are at least two of them. One[13] reads as follows:

SANCO SANCTO SEMON[I]
DEO FIDIO SACRUM
DECURIA SACERDOTUM
BIDENTALIUM RECIPERATIS VECTIGALIBUS

Another,[14] now in the Vatican, is even closer to Justin's text:

SEMONI SANCO
SANCTO DEO FIDIO
SACRUM
DECURIA SACERDOT[UM]
BIDENTALIUM

In both cases the stonecutter has added SANCTUS to SANCUS.[15] Presumably Simonians preferred an inscription with SANCTUS to attest the holiness of their cult hero.

Thus in the Simonian explanation Justin knew, "Deus" was not "Dius" but was used to identify Simon as the "holy god." Later on, Irenaeus (perhaps following Justin) says that the Simonians have an image of Simon made in the likeness of Zeus and one of Helen in the likeness of Athena, and they worship these.[16]

Justin does not refer directly to these images but his words about Athena suggest he knew about Helen as Athena. He refers to "a certain Helen, who wandered about with him then and was a prostitute earlier." Before that, she was "the first Thought *(ennoia)* produced by him."[17] Justin supposes that such a view is self-evidently false. In another passage he ascribes to "them," presumably followers of Simon, the notion that Athena the daughter of Zeus was not born in human fashion but "when the god thought of making the world through a thought, Athena was the first Thought." This time he explains why the idea is wrong. It is "ridiculous for the image of the Thought to bear a female form."[18]

Whether or not mediated by Simonians, this is the traditional philosophical-rhetorical explanation of Athena's birth from the head of Zeus. We find it, for example, in writings of the Stoic Chrysippus (in fragments preserved by Galen) and the rhetorician Aelius Aristides. We shall meet it again in chapter 19.

In this context Justin also refers to statues of Kore (Persephone) set up at fountains, and says that the demons were imitating the picture in Genesis of the Spirit of God borne above the waters when they called Kore the daughter of Zeus. Porphyry speaks of naiads as nymphs presiding over waters and says that, according to Justin's contemporary Numenius, the "Spirit of God borne above the waters" (Gen. 1:2) refers to souls settling upon the divinely infused water.[19] Justin's notion may somehow be related to Pythagorean precedent, but it is not clear how.

Menander

Justin also denounced Simon's disciple Menander, who taught and practiced magic at Antioch but came from a Samaritan village named Kappareteia. He persuaded his followers that they would never die, and "(even) now there are some followers who agree to this."[20] Obviously others do not; they are dead.

Marcion

Finally, the treatise against heresies follows Marcion's rupture with the Roman church in 144, since he is described as "still" teaching his sect.[21] Although Justin's language about "recent" events—they include not only the Jewish revolt of 132–135 and the death of Hadrian's favorite Antinous in 130, but even the life of Christ, whose crucifixion took place "in our time"—Marcion's break seems to have been fairly recent.[22] He falsely taught that there is a god greater than the Creator, and because of demonic aid he has followers everywhere.

Presumably this antiheretical work identified Justin as a reliable spokesman for the Roman church when an apology to the emperor and his adopted sons was needed.

6

Justin's Conversion and Works

The most important second-century apologist was Justin "the Martyr." He was born into a Greek-speaking non-Jewish family at Flavia Neapolis (Shechem) in Samaria, famous for the old Samaritan temple on nearby Mount Gerizim as well as for the newer temple of Zeus Hypsistos rebuilt by Hadrian and Antoninus Pius.[1]

Justin's father bore the Greco-Latin name Priscus, while his grandfather's name was Baccheius. Both names arouse interest. In Justin's own time Priscus was the name of a consul and of a college patron at Ostia; a little earlier, of a centurion and of a gladiator.[2] Baccheius was an appellation of the god Dionysus in poetry and a cult name at Corinth. This name could be borne by Jews, for a Roman denarius from 54 B.C. refers to "Bacchius Iudaeus"—though presumably this Baccheius was not one of Justin's ancestors. Diognetus, a teacher of the young emperor Marcus Aurelius, urged him to study philosophy and hear the lectures of another Baccheius.[3] The names thus suggest that Justin's family was fully attuned to Hellenism. His "Samaritan connection," possibly reflected in odd comments about exegesis and chronology, was not so important, though he gave details about two Samaritan heretics in his *Apology* and was willing to call himself a Samaritan in his *Dialogue* (120.6).[4]

The Quest for Truth

Justin was originally converted to Platonism, perhaps in his late teens or twenties. He was "taking delight in the doctrines of Plato" when he heard the Christians accused of immorality, but after he witnessed Christian bravery in the face of death he could not believe the charges against them (2.12.1). Later he became a convert to Christianity. Like other apologists, he describes his conversions in a rather stylized literary manner. This is not surprising, for his philosophical hero had been Plato, renowned for his literary style. In addition, he was aware that the account of his conversion could serve as a model for pagan readers to follow. It is odd, however, that he tells about it not in his *Apology* but in his *Dialogue.*

Other second-century authors such as Lucian and Galen described their pilgrimages from one philosophical school to another before their final arrival at the true solution. Justin himself explains that he first tried a Stoic who proved unable or unwilling to discuss theology. The classical Stoic curriculum, as set forth by Chrysippus and reported by Plutarch, began with logic and ethics and ended with physics, with teaching about the gods as its final part.[5] Justin wanted to begin at the end. Next he turned to a Peripatetic, stereotyped as too subtle and too fond of money. Then he approached a Pythagorean, who insisted on prerequisites Justin did not possess: music, astronomy, and geometry. Last of all he found a Platonist, recently arrived in "our city" (perhaps Ephesus), with whom his studies advanced every day. "The knowledge of the incorporeals and the vision of the ideas gave wings to my understanding, and I hoped to have the vision of God in the near future: for this is the goal of the philosophy of Plato."[6] Justin's reach exceeded his grasp, as he found out when, not far from the sea, he encountered a mysterious old man who cross-examined him on contradictions in Platonism. The old man finally forced him to admit not only his own ignorance but that of Plato himself and, when Justin asked for a higher religious authority, pointed him toward the Old Testament prophets, older and better than philosophers. A fire was lighted in his soul, along with love for the prophets and the friends of Christ.[7] He became a Christian, though not a cleric, turning toward teaching as his Christian vocation.

With him he brought a general picture of the history of philosophy and its decline from unity to multiplicity. The first philosophy, "sent down to men," was one. No sects or schools existed; they were founded later by individual teachers who no longer investigated truth.[8] The sketch looks like a simplified version of what the Middle Platonist Numenius said in his treatise *On the Infidelity of the Academy Toward Plato.* Divisions arose because Plato's successors "did not hold to the primitive heritage but rapidly divided, intentionally or not."[9] As a Christian, Justin used this historical precedent to explain the rise of heresy when he treated heretics in chronological sequence in his treatise *Against Heresies.* Christ and his disciples had delivered the true teaching before the rise of the first heretic, Simon Magus, the predecessor of Menander and Marcion. Later on, Irenaeus would take his "genetic" idea of heresy from Justin.[10] Apparently the originator of the analysis was Numenius.

Later Justin took part in controversy with Jews at Ephesus. He says that one of them hailed him as a "philosopher," and this notice may have given rise to Eusebius' assumption that he regularly wore the philosopher's garb.[11]

When Justin was a pagan Platonist and "rejoiced in the doctrines of

Plato" he already heard the usual charges of immorality levied against the Christians, but when he saw "that they were unafraid before death and all the other supposed terrors" he "considered it impossible for them to be living in wickedness and hedonism." He thus contrasts not only supposed vice with actual virtue but also hearsay evidence with observation, presumably his own.[12] He soon learned that those who lived in "wickedness and hedonism" were Gnostics, not Christians, and he wrote a book against them.

Justin's Authentic Works

The authentic works we still possess from Justin are the two *Apologies*—if really two—and the *Dialogue with the Jew Trypho*. These are preserved, along with inauthentic works, in one manuscript of the year 1364 (Cod. Paris. gr. 450), presumably copied as the Greek church continued discussions with Rome about the meaning of early tradition, in order to close the breach made in 1054 (see chapter 23). Eusebius had access to materials better than our present manuscript, for he preserves a portion of the "second apology" now lost from it and somehow knows that the original dialogue with Trypho took place at Ephesus.[13]

The apology is addressed to "the Emperor Titus Aelius Hadrianus Antoninus Pius Caesar Augustus, and the son Verissimus, philosopher, and Lucius, philosopher, by birth son of [L. Aelius] Caesar and by adoption son of Pius and a lover of culture," as well as to the sacred Senate and the whole People of the Romans. The address is not quite correct. In official documents from Egypt during the reign of Antoninus his sons are not associated with him, but Justin makes his purpose clear by calling both Marcus and Lucius "philosophers." Later he addresses them in the plural and asks them to prove that they are "pious and philosophers and guardians of justice and lovers of culture" (1.2.2). The name "Verissimus" applied to Marcus Aurelius is a nickname used by Antoninus, not a real name, even though it is found on Greek coins.[14] Evidently Justin wrote after 147, when Marcus was closely associated with Antoninus, though not as a co-emperor. Egyptian papyri do not give dates based on years of his reign before 161, though he stood close to the throne.

Date of the Apology

Justin gives a date for the apology when he says that Jesus was born under Quirinius, "a hundred and fifty years ago" (1.46.1; cf. Luke 2:2). Sulpicius Quirinius was legate of Syria in A.D. 6–7, after the removal of Herod's son Archelaus. If Justin or a source wanted to find his date, he could have read Josephus, who carefully dates the beginning of Herod's thirty-seven-year reign in 40 B.C. and has his son deposed in his tenth year.[15] The *Apology* thus comes from around 156, a date confirmed by the mention of "Felix" as a recent prefect of Egypt (29.2–3). Papyri date the regime of Munatius Felix as early as November 11, 148, and show that his successor, Sempronius Liberalis, held office on August 29, 154. On the latter date the prefect's edict referred to troubles now past—almost certainly a revolt in the countryside—and ordered strangers to return home.[16] Scholars have reasonably claimed that the revolt took place under Liberalis' predecessor.[17] Conceivably Justin points to Christian loyalty in Egypt when he tells of a Christian youth who remained celibate after Felix denied permission for him to be castrated. He may be showing that Christians obeyed civil authority.

The two strands of evidence related to Quirinius and Felix point to a date for the *Apology* around 155–157 and make possible a correlation with the martyrdom of Polycarp.[18]

Occasion of the Apology

The occasion for the apology must have been given by the martyrdom of Polycarp, which took place in 155 or 156. This aged bishop of Smyrna was well and favorably known at Rome, where he had visited the new bishop Anicetus about 155.[19] The account of his martyrdom was sent to Rome and "all the sojournings of the holy Catholic Church in every place." It showed that he had been the object of a search, forbidden by both Trajan and Hadrian, that the mob had clamored for his execution (a practice forbidden by Hadrian),[20] and that the proconsul of Asia, the famous sophist Statius Quadratus,[21] had threatened to burn him if he did not recant. Polycarp replied thus: "You threaten the fire that burns for a time and is quickly extinguished, for you do not know the fire that awaits the ungodly in the future judgment and eternal punishment."[22] Within a short time the bishop was burned to death.

Justin begins his *Apology* by attacking the unfairness of Roman prosecution (1–2) and the lack of genuine investigation (3–8). He ends this section with a reference to Plato's teaching on punishment after death for five hundred years;[23] Christians, however, believe that the punishment of the wicked will be perpetual. More than that, Justin frequently insists—twenty times in both apologetic works—that the punishment will be by fire. No doubt he is influenced by the Synoptic Gospels, but what motivated him must have been his knowledge of the fiery martyrdom at Smyrna.

Another special feature of Justin's apology is his description of the Eucharist and his echoes of eucharistic prayers (see chapter 7). Polycarp and his martyr-acts provided a similar emphasis, for the bishop was above all a man of prayer. Before his arrest he prayed constantly for the churches throughout the world[24] and on the pyre he paraphrased the eucharistic prayer of the church.[25]

There was even an apologetic context in the *Martyrdom of Polycarp.* The proconsul had suggested that he should "persuade the people." Polycarp replied that he would have been glad to discuss the subject with him as an official appointed by God, but making a defense to the mob would have been pointless.[26] This proconsul was a sophist who could "argue extempore on abstract philosophical themes."[27] It is noteworthy that unlike other apologists Justin insists that the emperors must examine the sayings of Christ, which "were short and concise, for he was no sophist, but his word was the power of God" (1.14.5). He tells the emperor and his sons that he has now done his best to persuade them and is "free from reproach even if you disbelieve" (1.55.8). He thus criticizes the proconsul and supplies the argument which Polycarp had no opportunity to set forth.

It appears that the specific occasion for Justin's apologetic work, especially his emphasis on eternal fire, was the martyr death of Polycarp at the stake.

Apology and Rhetoric

Though Justin criticizes rhetoric, all the apologists used it. He himself called his work a *prosphōnēsis* or "address," or what Eusebius called a *prosphōnetikos logos.*[28] It is described by the rhetorician Menander as "a speech of praise to rulers spoken by an individual," with special emphasis on such virtues as justice, and including "humanity to subjects, gentleness of character and approachability, integrity and incorruptibility in matters of justice, freedom from partiality and from prejudice in giving judicial decisions."[29] These are just the themes with which Justin deals as he contrasts the unfair treatment of Christians with what it should be (1–7).

His work deals with other matters as well and he calls it an *enteuxis,* "petition," and an *exēgēsis,* "explanation."[30] He intends to prove that Christianity alone is true and prior to paganism; that Jesus Christ was the only Son of God; and that demons inspired pagan myths (23.3).

After digressions in chapters 24–29, Justin gets back to his very long *apodeixis* or "demonstration" on prophecy and the life of Christ, who was not a magician because the prophets foretold what he would do (30–60). At the end he describes Christian worship (61–67) to show that it is not immoral, and concludes a peroration (68) with a copy of Hadrian's letter to Minicius Fundanus, proconsul of Asia in 122/123.

It is hard to tell whether or not the so-called *Second Apology* is really part of the so-called *First Apology.* Eusebius differentiates two apologies and says that Justin delivered "a second book to the rulers already mentioned." These are Antoninus Pius, Marcus Aurelius, and Lucius Verus.[31] In a list of Justin's works, however, he speaks of a *logos prosphōnetikos* addressed to Antoninus Pius, his sons, and the Roman Senate (this agrees with the preface to the *"First Apology"*), as well as a second work addressed to

"Antoninus Verus" (the name he uses for Marcus Aurelius).[32] The manuscript presents the *"Second Apology"* first, entitling it "To the Roman Senate," but this is probably based on a misunderstanding by Eusebius or a source of his. The work is clearly a *libellus* or "petition" addressed to more than one Roman emperor.[33] We conclude with W. Schmid that there was originally one petition,[34] though with him and Millar we have to admit some uncertainty.[35]

If the two "apologies" are really one, or based on one, the so-called *Second Apology* is not an appendix to the first, nor are the two of them really "apologies."[36] The whole work is a *syntaxis* or "composition," more specifically a *biblidion* or "petition," with the second part inspired by recent events in Rome under the urban prefect Urbicus, evidently Q. Lollius Urbicus, prefect at a highly uncertain date. The work gradually becomes more favorable toward philosophy—there is hardly any Christian theology toward the end of it—perhaps because Justin was aware that the "philosophers" addressed at the beginning were soon to be the successors of Antoninus.

7
Justin: Church, Bible, and Theology

Justin was not simply a philosopher or theologian, whether biblical or philosophical. He was a churchman who shared in Christian worship, beginning with baptism and going on to the regular Sunday Eucharist, "in which it is right for no one to participate except the one who believes that what is taught by us is true, and has been washed in the bath which is for remission of sins and rebirth, and lives as Christ delivered the tradition."

Christian Liturgy

The *First Apology* therefore ends by describing this worship. Indeed, Justin prefaced his earlier account of Christ's teaching with a statement about our

> sending up solemn prayers and hymns for our creation and all the means of health, for the variety of creatures and the changes of the seasons, and sending up petitions that we may live again in incorruption through our faith in him.[1]

Such prayers are also echoed in his *Dialogue:*[2]

> We give thanks to God for having created the world with all that is in it for the sake of man, and for having freed us from the vice in which we lived, and for having completely brought to naught the principalities and powers, through him who became subject to suffering according to his will.

There is another liturgical echo in the *Dialogue:* "Let us glorify God through the King of glory, through the Lord of the powers."[3]

The most important passage is found in the *Apology,* however, with its description of the baptism of "those who are persuaded and believe that what is taught and said by us is true, and promise to be able to live accordingly." They proceed to prayer and fasting before entering the water of dedication to God and rebirth, "in the name of God the Father and Master of all, and of our Savior Jesus Christ, and of the Holy Spirit." This rite of washing is also called "illumination."[4] Obviously it is for catechumens, not for infants.

After the washing comes the baptismal Eucharist with common prayers. The "president" (presiding elder or bishop) is given bread and a cup of water mixed with wine, and offers praise and glory to the Father through the Son and the Holy Spirit. After the people say "Amen" the "deacons" transmit the bread and wine to those present and take them to the absent. Justin explains that the Eucharist is not common bread or drink. Instead, "the food consecrated by the word of prayer that comes from him . . . is the flesh and blood of that incarnate Jesus."

He also tells about the regular Sunday Eucharist with readings from the memoirs of the apostles or the writings of the prophets,[5] a discourse by the president, common prayers, and the eucharistic prayer and meal.

> Those who prosper and so desire by their own free will give what each wishes, and the collection is deposited with the president. He looks after orphans and widows, those who are in need because of ill-health or some other cause, those who are in prison, and resident aliens—in short, he is the guardian of all in need. This eucharistic offering expresses the common concerns of the Christian group through the agency of the bishop and his deacons. The liturgy is performed on Sunday, the first day of the week, when God changed darkness and matter and made the universe and when Christ rose from the dead.[6]

Justin does not supply much theological interpretation of these liturgical actions. They come to him from traditional usage at Rome and in the other churches he has encountered. He is speaking not just for himself but for the Christian community. His purpose, as always, is twofold. He wants to set forth the real nature of Christian life, and he wants to do so to refute the slanders of pagan critics. Neither purpose could be achieved apart from the other. And of course he *was* concerned with philosophy.

Justin and the Bible

When Justin was converted to Christianity he was introduced to the writings of the prophets, who lived long before the philosophers and by divine inspiration foretold the future. They did not write to provide logical demonstration but were witnesses to the truth and performed works of power. Since this language echoes 1 Corinthians 2:4–5, it implies that the prophets were essentially Christians.[7]

These prophets made predictions in remote antiquity: Justin says that some predicted Christ's coming 5,000 years before him, some 3,000, some 2,000, some 1,000, and some 800.[8] He is relying on something like Josephus' statements that Jewish history covers a period of 5,000 years and that the legislator of the Jews was born 2,000 years before his own times.[9] Perhaps following another source he immediately forgets Adam and states that Moses was the first prophet.[10]

Justin knows that under one of the Ptolemies Old Testament writings were sent to the Alexandrian library and translated into Greek. Unfortunately he thinks that Herod was then king of the Jews.[11] This error may point to Justin's use of a Christian source. When he quotes Old Testament texts *in extenso*, as in the central section of the *Apology* and in the *Dialogue*, he uses two different kinds of materials: texts quoted from "testimony sources" based on Christian versions and texts quoted from the Septuagint found among Jews. Generally speaking, he quotes testimonies in *Apology* 32–54 and Septuagint texts in the *Dialogue*. He regards the former version as the true text, the latter as having been transmitted and modified by the Jews. When he complains in the *Dialogue* that Jews have removed prophecies of Christ from their text he is comparing it with his own book of testimonies. The Jewish text, he believes, originally referred to Christ as born of a virgin and as God and man and crucified and dying. The Jews, however, have read Isaiah 7:14 as "Behold, the young woman will conceive" and refer the announcement to Hezekiah. They have deleted a mention of "this passover" as "our Savior and refuge" from (Pseudo-)Ezra and a couple of passages from Jeremiah. Here he clearly relies on his testimony source to criticize the Septuagint.[12] The whole situation becomes more complicated in the *Dialogue* when Justin uses "testimony" texts as if they came from the Septuagint and, in addition, relies on a still extant "Jewish, Hebraizing recension of the Septuagint" for the Minor Prophets.[13]

Such use of testimony sources in the earlier *Apology* confirms the view that Justin was converted not by reading the Old Testament as such but by reading it in a Christian manner with Christians.

Justin and the "New Testament"

Among even more specifically Christian works, Justin certainly knew "the reminiscences of the apostles" or "Gospels," read at the Eucharist and available for quotation.[14] It is also clear that he used a "harmony" of the Gospels, not necessarily complete, like the one his pupil Tatian later published. Bellinzoni has shown that he was relying on handbooks and liturgical texts in which Gospel texts were already harmonized, often in relation to the Old Testament testimonies.[15]

Justin also knew the Apocalypse produced by "John, one of Christ's apostles,"[16] and it is virtually certain that he knew the Gospel of John. For example, he says that Christ "was Only-Begotten of the Father of all, properly begotten of him as Logos and Power, and later became man through the virgin, as we learned from the reminiscences of the apostles." It is hard to restrict what the apostles taught to the virgin birth. Presumably there is an echo of the prologue to John.[17]

The point is even clearer in the *First Apology*. "Christ said, Unless you are born again, you will not enter into the kingdom of the heavens." When

Justin adds that "it is obvious that those once born cannot enter their mothers' wombs" he is following the line of argument in John 3:3–4.[18] I hesitate to invent a common source and prefer to agree with E. J. Goodspeed that when Justin refers to Gospels composed by Jesus' apostles and by their followers,[19] he has two of each class in mind. He was certainly opposed to Marcion's notion of a single Gospel.

His attitude to the epistles is ambivalent, to say the least. He speaks of reminiscences that came from Peter—apparently the Gospel of Mark—but not of any epistles written by him.[20] He never mentions Paul or his epistles, although he uses patterns of exegesis that are certainly Pauline in origin. Presumably the church in his time, still baffled by Marcion's stringent criticism of Paul's letters, was unable to make much use of them, and did not find them helpful for apologetic. Clement of Rome, sixty or seventy years earlier, had referred to 1 Corinthians and used Romans,[21] but he was using them as authorities for Corinthian Christians who knew and admired Paul.

In his *Dialogue,* though not in the apologies, he cites the book of Revelation as composed by John, "one of the apostles of Christ," and goes out of his way to claim that his millenarian doctrine is orthodox.[22]

Doctrine of God

As the first Christian philosophical theologian, Justin went well beyond Aristides and juxtaposed his special interpretation of divine transcendence (based on Middle Platonic philosophy) with biblical and traditional Jewish and Christian ideas of God. He makes this point when he explains that Plato used the creation narrative in Genesis for his doctrine that God fashioned the world out of preexistent matter.[23] He also uses philosophical language when he identifies the God whom Christians worship as "most true and Father of justice and temperance and the other virtues, not involved with wickedness." Justice and temperance are two of the four cardinal virtues esteemed by Platonists and Stoics alike. And he goes on to speak of reverencing and worshiping "the Son who came from him and taught us these things, and the army of the other good angels who follow and resemble him, as well as the prophetic Spirit." It is odd to find the angels mentioned before the Spirit, and Justin does not refer to them when he numbers Christian thanksgivings, first to the immutable and eternal God and, "in the second place, Jesus Christ who was crucified under Pontius Pilate, . . . the Son of the real God himself; and in the third rank the prophetic Spirit." Here the underlying formula must be baptismal: Justin says that the Christian "washing" takes place "in the name of God the Father of all and Master, and of our Savior Jesus Christ, and of the Holy Spirit."[24] Presumably his reference to Christ's angelic army is due to his special Christological concerns, as we shall presently see.

The basic points of the philosophical doctrine are these: God is "the eternal, immovable, unchanging Cause and Ruler of the Universe, nameless and unutterable, unbegotten, residing far above the heavens, and is incapable of coming into immediate contact with any of his creatures, yet is observant of them although removed from them and unapproachable by them."[25] The key passage is *Dialogue* 127.2. "The Father never descended on earth or appeared to man, but remained always in the highest heaven." He adds that no one with even minimal intelligence would venture to say that the Maker and Father of all left the whole region above heaven and appeared in some slight part of the earth.[26]

In some respects this doctrine is that of Justin's contemporary Numenius, who held that the First God was simple and existed in himself; he took no part in any activities but was King of all. The second was the Demiurge, and the third was what was fashioned. The first is stable, while the second is in motion.[27] Numenius' triad is not Justin's, however, for Father, Maker, and Creation are obviously different from Father and Maker, Logos, and Holy Spirit. For God as both Father and Creator, Justin may have relied on the philosophical tradition derived from Philo, not the similar Stoic version mentioned by Diogenes Laertius.[28] He certainly read the book of Genesis, which depicts God as the active Creator and Ruler.

In addition, as in both Gnostic and philosophical thought, Justin argues that the titles he bears, such as Father, God, Creator, Lord, and Master, refer to his activities, not to his essence.[29]

Doctrine of Sophia-Logos

Justin does not have much to say about Sophia ("Wisdom") as God's agent in creation and revelation. The notion never occurs in the apologies, where indeed we learn only that "because of *sophia* Jesus was worthy to be called Son of God."[30] Presumably this refers to Jesus' own *sophia,* occasionally mentioned in the Synoptic Gospels. In the *Dialogue,* however, Justin relies on Proverbs 8:21–36 to tell how God generated a certain rational *(logikē)* power out of himself as a "beginning" before all created beings. The Holy Spirit, inspirer of scripture, calls this power "Glory of the Lord," "Son," "Sophia," "Angel," "God," "Lord," and "Logos." He called himself "Chief General" when he appeared to Joshua in human form (Josh. 5:14).[31] If he is "Chief General" and "Angel," he must be general of an army of angels, and we have seen that such he is.

Justin explains that the Logos originates as human speech does: when we emit a word *(logos)* we generate it and do not emit it by abscission *(kata apotomēn)* as if the reason *(logos)* in us were diminished. Similarly one fire can be lighted from another.[32] Comparison with a lamp or fire appears in the fragments of Numenius,[33] but Justin's fundamental basis is biblical. He implicitly refers to Proverbs when he says that the Logos was the "first thing generated by God."[34]

His doctrine of the Logos was based on a doctrine of Sophia developed within Hellenistic Judaism but not taken directly from Philo òf Alexandria. Indeed, it contrasts sharply with one of Philo's doctrines. When he once cites Proverbs 8:22 Philo states that God was the Father of the universe, Sophia its mother and nurse. Elsewhere he alludes to the passage merely in reference to the wisdom of Moses, though he occasionally speaks of Sophia as the daughter of God.[35] There is no trace of such familial exegesis in Justin, for whom Christ was essentially Logos and Son, not Sophia.

In the *Dialogue,* arguing with Jews, Justin insists that there is a "second God" and that this is Christ. The supreme God is "Lord of the Lord on earth, since he is Father and God and the cause for the existence of the Mighty One, Lord, and God."[36] Verbally, we are in the realm of Numenius, who spoke of a First God, a Second, and a Third, sometimes assimilating the Third to the Second.[37] Even in Justin's thought the Second and the Third are sometimes identified, as when he speaks of the conception of Jesus by a "spirit and power from God, none other than the Logos, which is the firstborn of God."[38] Justin may be indebted to Numenius for some important phrasing used in his theology, though not for the doctrines themselves.

The Incarnate Christ

Justin does not hesitate to speak of the incarnation of the Son of God, and this is one reason why he was Irenaeus' favorite apologist. The philosophical problems involved in the doctrine did not disturb him, and he worried only about the resemblance of the Gospel story to myths about Greek gods.

> When we say that the Logos, the first begotten by God, was born without sexual intercourse as Jesus Christ our teacher, and that he was crucified and died and rose again to ascend into heaven, we bring forward nothing new in comparison with those whom you call sons of Zeus.[39]

Justin proceeds to provide an exercise in comparative religion. Hermes too was the hermeneutical Logos and teacher of all; Asclepius was a healer and though killed ascended into heaven; Dionysus was torn asunder. Heracles in flight from pain gave himself to the fire. Further evidence for ascended gods comes from astronomy or astrology. The name of the constellation Dioscuri refers to sons of Leda, while Perseus was son of Danaë and the human Bellerophon ascended into heaven on the Horse, later called Pegasus.[40] Justin goes on to mention "Ariadne and those like her set among the stars,"[41] and then ridicules those who swear that dead emperors have also ascended.

After deriding the behavior of the gods, especially Zeus and his sons, he calls them evil demons, not gods, but has to note similarities between such sons of the gods and Jesus. He recalls that Hermes too was called Logos, that sons of Zeus suffered, that Perseus was born of a virgin, and that Asclepius worked cures like those of Jesus. "But Jesus Christ alone was truly born to God as a son, since he was his Logos and Firstborn and Power, and by God's will he became man and taught us these things for the conversion and restoration of the human race."[42]

In order to prove that Jesus was not like these sons and was not a magician, Justin has to go through Old Testament predictions that point forward to Christ. He devotes nearly half his apology (chs. 30–60) to this effort. It is hard to imagine a Roman emperor, or even a secretary dealing with petitions, finding this kind of material convincing or impressive. Presumably it was developed for use within the Christian community itself, where it was especially suited for controversy with Jews.

The Cross in the Creation

Justin defends the cross of Christ by arguing that the cross occurs in scripture, in nature, and in human society. Plato read about it in Numbers 21:8–9, where Moses set a bronze serpent upon a pole to protect the Israelites from snakebite, but he thought this meant that the Demiurge "impressed the shape of an X in everything."[43] Justin went on to find the shape of the cross in a ship's mast, a farmer's plow, even the human frame with arms outstretched or the face with the nose crossing the eyebrows. (He corroborates the last point from Lamentations 4:20: "Breath before our face is Christ the Lord.") Indeed, even the Roman legions testify to it with their standards, symbols of authority and power, but wrongly bear images of dead and deified emperors on them.[44]

Doctrine of Spirit

In the *Apology,* especially in a section on prophecy (chs. 30–53), the Spirit is essentially "prophetic spirit" (20 out of 23 instances). This is why Justin could place the "army of angels" ahead of the "prophetic spirit," as we have seen: for him the Spirit was not precisely personal.

Toward the end of the *First Apology* he cites an enigmatic passage supposedly from Plato.[45] He leaves out the first sentence: "All things are about the King of all and exist for him, and he is the cause of all that is good," but cites what comes next: "The second things are about the Second and the third about the Third," interpreting the words in relation to Father, Son, and Holy Spirit (the spirit borne above the waters in Genesis). Plato's text was much used in early Christian philosophical theology. It appears in both Athenagoras and Clement. The anti-Christian author Celsus cited it, and Hippolytus said that the Gnostic Valentinus used it when he invented his Pleroma.[46] Once more, their proximate source was probably Numenius, who seems to have used the words in relation to his system of three gods.[47] Since Numenius also allegorized the words of Genesis 1:2 about the Spirit of God,[48] it is likely that Justin was following in his footsteps.[49]

The *Dialogue* provides no fuller analysis than the *Apology*. The Spirit is the prophetic spirit (10 times), or the holy prophetic spirit (twice), or the holy spirit (19 times). Its functions remain the same, but now Justin emphasizes the Gospels and speaks of its activity in relation to the birth, baptism, and death of Jesus.

Angels and Demons

Earlier Christians had discussed both angels, usually viewed as good spirits, and demons, viewed by Christians as bad. Angels are frequently mentioned in the New Testament, less often among the apostolic fathers. *1 Clement* echoes the language of the epistle to the Hebrews about angels, while Hermas sometimes refers to them, calling Michael "the great and glorious angel."[50] Ignatius uses the noun and the related adjective once.[51]

The word "angel" occurs fifteen times in Justin's apologies but eighty times in the *Dialogue*. Obviously it reflects a Jewish setting like that of the Synoptic Gospels. It is also important because Justin finds the Logos in appearances of angels in the Old Testament.

As for demons, the word *daimonion* is common in the New Testament, though Paul does not use it.[52] It becomes rare in the apostolic fathers, where Ignatius uses it once (Ignatius *Smyrnaeans* 3.2) and Hermas three times. The term *daimōn,* more respectable among philosophers, appears only in Matthew 8:31.

In Justin the more popular *daimonion* occurs only four times in the apologies but twenty-seven times in the *Dialogue,* while *daimōn* appears fifty times in the apologies, only four times in the *Dialogue*. The Jewish setting of the *Dialogue* must have influenced the choice of terms, even though Justin may have read Xenocrates in his Platonic school and thought this philosopher made some form of demonology respectable.

The notion of *daimones* as standing between God or the gods and humanity was apparently developed by the Platonic philosopher Xenocrates. He held that the supreme god was Zeus, while the world soul was Hera. Heaven was also a god, and the fiery stars were the Olympian deities, while there were other "invisible sublunary *daimones*" or demigods.[53] Plutarch's treatise *On Isis and Osiris* (chs. 25–27) shows that this notion was ascribed to Plato and Pythagoras and associated with Xenocrates and the Stoic Chrysippus. Schmid reasonably suggests that in *Apology* 1.18, where Justin seems to refer to "Empedocles and Pythagoras, Plato and Socrates"[54] as authors who taught that souls remain conscious after death, he wrote not "Socrates" but "Xenocrates."[55] But the Jewish setting is more important than whatever philosophical connections Justin may have in mind.

In his teaching about angels and demons Justin is close to the Jewish-Christian tradition. He explains that the leader of the evil demons is called "Serpent and Satanas and Devil, as you can learn by searching our scriptures." Christ taught that he will be sent into fire to be punished eternally with his army and the men who follow him.[56] In the *Dialogue* he cites authorities. Moses called him Serpent (Gen. 3:1), Job (1:6) and Zechariah (3:1) called him Devil, and Jesus addressed him as Satanas (Matt. 4:10). In Justin's opinion the name Satan "in the language of Jews and Syrians" means "apostate," while Nas means Serpent.[57] According to a fragment in Irenaeus, Justin held that before the coming of Christ Satanas did not know that he was heading for eternal fire; it was Christ who told him.[58] Justin differentiates him from the other angels.

In the *Second Apology* (ch. 5) Justin refers to the myth about these other angels which is found in *1 Enoch* and based on Genesis 6.[59] God entrusted the care of mankind and the world to the angels, but they abandoned their rank, "were overcome by intercourse with women," and generated sons who are called demons. These demons became the gods of the pagans. Justin's idea is quite different from that of Philo, who held that the beings whom Moses called angels were called *daimones* by "other philosophers."[60] His account simply reflects Jewish-Christian tradition as expressed, for example, by Papias of Hierapolis. "God gave some of them (the angels) rule over the created world and commanded them to rule it well; but their place came to nothing."[61]

The Kingdom of God

In the setting of Justin's theological and apologetic ideas there could be little room for a doctrine of the kingdom of God on earth. He was well aware of the failure of two Jewish revolts, and while he accepted the apocalyptic prediction of the millennium at Jerusalem after the resurrection of the flesh,[62] he also insisted that the expected kingdom was "with God" and not merely "human."[63] Similarly, according to Hegesippus, the grand-nephews of Jesus maintained that the kingdom of the Messiah was "not of the world or earthly, but heavenly and angelic" and would appear at the end of the world.[64]

Gnostics also held that the kingdom of the Father or of Christ was not political. Marcion, for example, claimed that "in the Gospel the kingdom of God is Christ himself."[65] We find obscure parables of the kingdom in the Gospel of Thomas, whose author says that the kingdom is "inside you" and "outside you" (saying 3), while Basilides used the term "kingdom" for the rational state of the soul.

Later apologists did not mention the kingdom, though they may have interpreted it in relation to the Roman empire. We shall see that Melito viewed empire and church as providentially growing up together, while Theophilus believed that God had given the Romans their power.

8
Justin on Moral Questions

According to Justin, he was deeply impressed, when a pagan, by Christian martyrs, "fearless unto death," and could not believe they were guilty of the charges brought against them. Such men were incapable of hedonism or licentiousness (2.12.1–2). He insists that such charges are false and mentions them only in relation to Gnostics or possible slander by some Jews, not others (1.26.7).[1] The accusations influenced the way he presented Christian morals in his apologetic works.

The Christian Way of Life

Justin sets forth the Christian way of life in chapters 15–19 of the *First Apology*,[2] relying on "what Christ taught," especially in the Sermon on the Mount. He arranges this teaching by topics, following the example of Greek anthologists. Naturally the topics are chosen in support of his apologetic. Thus he begins with the heading "on chastity," quoting Jesus on adultery, lust, and eunuchs. Both acts and inner motives are important; most important of all is conversion from unrighteousness. The next topic is "on loving all," with sayings on love of enemies and, beyond that, "on sharing with those in need and doing nothing for vain glory." Further selections illustrate the themes "on being blameless and servants of all and free from anger" as well as "on not taking oaths," while longer passages enjoin worshiping God alone and living in accordance with Christ's teaching. An apologetic note deals with the payment of taxes (but not worship) to imperial officials, and explains that Christians expect a heavenly kingdom, not one on earth.[3] The whole section ends with discussion of the eternal fire which will come upon the wicked after the resurrection.

Eternal punishment is related to the belief in eternal life which Christians share with pagan philosophers (notably Plato), oracles, and poets, though their doctrine goes farther since it involves the recovery of bodies. Nothing is impossible for God. Such resurrection is no more incredible than the generation of human beings from "some tiny drop of human seed" would be if it had not taken place. God created and can recreate. "It is better to believe in things impossible by their own nature and to men, since we know that our teacher Jesus Christ said, 'Things impossible with men are possible with God' and 'Do not fear those who kill you and afterwards cannot do anything, but fear him who is able to cast soul and body into Gehenna after death' " (1.19.6–7).

The Pagan Way of Life

Justin's whole apology shows his determination to refute the charge of sexual immorality made against Christians. This was his concern at the beginning, the middle, and the end. He suggests that the accusations might properly be assigned to Simonians and other heretics.[4] Later on, Irenaeus would discuss such charges, suggest that the Carpocratian Gnostics might be blamed, and add that a Carpocratian woman named "Marcellina came to Rome under Anicetus [c. 155–c. 166] and destroyed many."[5] Presumably she arrived after the period when Justin wrote, for he never referred to Carpocratians.

Like his pupil Tatian, Justin insists upon the immoral behavior of pagan sculptors who make statues of the gods; "they usually seduce the slave-girls who work with them" (1.9.4). Clement of Alexandria shows how several sculptors used their own favorites as models, while Origen too refers to the immorality of sculptors.[6] Justin also denounces pagans for "exposing" unwanted children, likely to be picked up by those who maintain "herds of boys" (Tatian liked this expression)[7] for prostitution, as well as females, hermaphrodites, and others involved in unnatural intercourse. The Roman state accepts their taxes and fees,[8] while it ought to eradicate them. Christians are accused of incest, but obviously there is a high risk of that in Roman brothels. Again, they prostitute their children and wives,[9] while some are castrated for homosexual abuse and offer the "mysteries" to the Mother of the Gods. All this is to illustrate the viciousness of contemporary pagan society (1.27).

Ordinary Christian Morality

Contrasting with such behavior is that of Christians, many of whom have maintained their chastity from infancy to the age of sixty or seventy, that is, since the year 80 or 90 A.D. (1.15.6). Just so, the Roman church's official letter of the first century *(1 Clement)* refers to Christians "who have lived among us without blame from youth to old age" (63.3).

Justin is the first author to say that Christians marry only for the procreation and nurture of children (1.27; 29.1). He thus shares the view of the

Roman Stoic Musonius.[10] Later on another apologist, Athenagoras, would insist that Christians abstain from intercourse with pregnant wives, "for with us the measure of lust is fecundity."[11]

Christians also practice practical charity. "We who have property care for all in need, and we are always together." More specifically, "each person who is prosperous gives by free choice what he wishes of his own, and when collected it is deposited with the presiding officer. He cares for orphans and widows, and those who are in want because of disease or some other cause, and those who are in prison, and resident foreigners—to sum up, he is in charge of all in need" (1.67.1 and 6–7). Similarly *1 Clement* 38.2 speaks of the support given by rich to poor. The idea is widespread. Tertullian echoes the theme, while Ignatius contrasts Christian charity with Gnostic lack of love.[12]

Sex and Marriage

Because of pagan accusations Justin is intensely concerned with sexual matters and illustrates his ascetic teaching by two case histories illustrating Christian attitudes on the subject.

The most influential early Christian attitudes were strongly ascetic. In the New Testament the apostle Paul denounced pagan eroticism, fiercely attacking pagans who dishonored their bodies and entered into unnatural sexual relations (Rom. 1:24–27), while among the apostolic fathers the *Epistle of Barnabas* (ch. 10) explained that some of the animals rejected in Moses' dietary laws symbolized sexual immorality.

Beyond such details, the basic Christian attitude toward sex was generally ascetic because of the expectation that the world would soon end. Paul thought that "men who have wives should live as though they had none" (1 Cor. 7:29), and the book of Revelation even referred to 144,000 men who would be "redeemed from the earth" because they "have not defiled themselves with women, for they are chaste" (Rev. 14:3–4).

Such an attitude may well underlie what Justin says about erotic topics in his apologetic work. It is true that around his time interest in such themes seems on the rise in some pagan circles. A. Henrichs finds it in a contemporary Greek romance from the East.[13] But Christian tradition adequately explains his concern. His two case histories involved a young Alexandrian who wanted to be a eunuch and a Roman matron divorced after she turned toward Christian behavior. In addition, he denounced literature he considered pornographic.

The Would-be Eunuch of Alexandria

In Justin's recital of Christ's teachings, he quotes a famous if difficult Gospel saying. "There are some who were made eunuchs by men; there are those who were born eunuchs; there are those who made themselves eunuchs because of the kingdom of heaven; but not all receive this" (1.15.4; Matt. 19:11–12). Presumably the many "chaste" old men and women he mentions were eunuchs in a spiritual sense. Sometimes asceticism went farther, apparently when pagans like Christians became incensed by rumors of their opponents' immorality.

Justin defends Christians against rumors that in their assemblies they extinguish lamps and turn to promiscuity and cannibalism (1.26.7). In reply, he attacks pagan immorality and praises Christian marriage, then offers his most telling example of asceticism.

> One of our people, in order to persuade you that promiscuous intercourse is not a sacred rite *(mystērion)*[14] for us, recently presented a petition at Alexandria to the prefect Felix, asking permission for a physician to remove his testicles, for the physicians there said it was forbidden for them to do this without the prefect's permission. When Felix was quite unwilling to agree, the youth remained firm in his opinion but was content with the approval of his own conscience and that of his fellow believers.

The story ends rather indecisively, but the prefect's impression of the youth and his friends cannot have been favorable. Two emperors, Domitian and Hadrian, had explicitly forbidden castration.[15] Indeed, Hadrian even forbade requests for the operation: "No one, free or slave, involuntarily or not, is to castrate anyone, nor is anyone to offer himself voluntarily for castration."[16] After Hadrian forbade circumcision as well, Antoninus Pius allowed it for Jews but not for others.[17] Papyri from that time and afterward show that prospective Egyptian priests had to get official permission to be circumcised.[18]

Justin denounced men publicly castrated for homosexual purposes who offered the mysteries to the Mother of the Gods. In his view the youth's intentions were quite different. Presumably he knew that he was an "orthodox" Christian rather than a Gnostic. The youth may have thought he would become a eunuch for the sake of the kingdom of heaven, but half a century later a bishop of Alexandria would "marvel exceedingly" at a rash act of this sort.[19]

Few admired eunuchs in any case. Theophilus, following a chronologer who was a freedman of Marcus Aurelius, said that the vicious king Tarquin the Proud was "the first to exile Romans and corrupt boys and make eunuchs of natives."[20] Many Roman authors denounced them." In addition, people were generally aware that castration was not a cure for lust.[21]

Justin was obviously defending Christians against charges of immorality. Secondarily he may have been trying to defend the Alexandrian youth. If so, the defense was rather inept.

The Woman of Rome

Just as the case of the youth at Alexandria provides a focal point for the opening chapters of the first or larger apology, so the *Second Apology* shows that Christians are not treated justly and reasonably by Roman judges and begins (in ch. 2) with a marital scandal at Rome.[22]

"Only ,esterday," says Justin, Christians were martyred at Rome during the period when Q. Lollius Urbicus was urban prefect (before 162). He gives an unusually full account of the events, some of which seem related to his denunciation, in the *First Apology,* of pagans who "prostitute their own children and wives" (1.28.4).

> There was a woman who was married to a licentious husband, and at first she too was licentious. But when she came to know the teachings of Christ she learned chastity and tried to persuade her husband to be equally chaste. She cited the teachings, which predicted punishment in eternal fire for those who do not live temperately and by right reason.

All the language in these sentences is characteristic of Justin and cannot be taken as literally historical. Indeed, it depicts the normal course of conversion as he describes it.

> But when he remained in the same licentious practices he alienated his wife through his actions. She considered it sinful to lie with her husband from then on, since he insisted on procuring passages for pleasure contrary to the law of nature and to what is right. She wanted a divorce. When her own people urged her to wait in the hope that her husband might sometime change, she forced herself to stay. But when he went to Alexandria and it was reported that his practices were yet more vicious, she decided she could not be a partner in his offenses and ungodly acts by remaining in the marriage and sharing his board and bed. She therefore gave him what you call a *repudium* and was divorced. That brave and true husband of hers should have been glad that she had stopped doing what she used to do recklessly with the servants and the hired men, when she took pleasure in getting drunk and in all evil, and glad that she wanted him to stop doing the same things. Instead, he accused her of leaving him without his consent and added that she was a Christian. She presented a petition to you, the emperor, to request permission to set her estate in order and then be allowed to make a defense against the accusation. You gave your permission. Her ex-husband, unable to say anything against her for the present, turned against a certain Ptolemaeus, who was her Christian teacher.

Justin is basically concerned with the moral situation. The marriage was by no means an old-fashioned Roman union, in which according to Marcus Cato a woman "is severely punished if she has drunk wine; if she has done wrong with another man she is condemned to death." (Significantly, the comment comes from a speech *On the Dowry.*)[23] Such a woman who "appeared to have drunk more wine than was required for the sake of her health, without her husband's knowledge," could be "fined the amount of her dowry."[24] We shall soon see that dowry questions were important in this case.[25]

The moralist Musonius Rufus, whom Justin admired, asks the rhetorical question, "Would it not seem completely intolerable not only if the woman with a lawful husband had relations with a slave, but even if a woman without a husband should have them?"[26] The woman in Justin's story had misbehaved not with slaves but with servants, but moral judgments would be the same. Artemidorus explains that a mistress's dream of intercourse with a servant is not propitious because "it means being despised and harmed by the servant."[27] Clement of Alexandria tells of dangers when mistresses bathe with such people.[28]

When she came to the teachings of Christ, presumably guided by the catechist Ptolemaeus, she must have encountered something like Justin's own collection in chapters 15 to 17 of the *First Apology,* a collection prefaced by the statement that "we who once rejoiced in sexual immorality now welcome chastity alone." Such an emphasis is taken for granted in the pastoral epistles and even more strongly asserted by Musonius. "Above all a woman must be chaste and self-controlled; she must, I mean, be pure in regard to unlawful love, exercise restraint in other pleasures, not be a slave to desires, and not be contentious, lavish in expenditure, or extravagant in dress."[29] Similarly Clement, perhaps directly following Musonius, condemns "whorish pleasures" related to "unseemly embraces" as "assaults upon marital self-control."[30] This was a prime aspect of second-century morality both Christian and pagan.

The woman's attitude was strongly influenced by an ascetic rigor that recalls the story of the Alexandrian youth previously mentioned. She has come to espouse chastity, right reason, the law of nature, what is right. She is against license, vice, and pleasure. Her attitude is close to ordinary Stoic morality, but unlike Stoics and like Justin she fears punishment in eternal fire. And Justin learned this lesson on chastity from Christ. "If your right eye offends you, cut it out, for it is better for you to go one-eyed into the kingdom of heaven than to be sent with two eyes to the eternal fire" (1.15.2; Matt. 5:29; 18:8–9).

Such points (apart from the fire, which as we have seen is especially emphasized by Justin) also recall the *Sentences of Sextus,* an anthology slightly revised from a Pythagorean base and used by Alexandrian Christians in the latter years of the second century.[31] There we find attitudes and precepts like Justin's. Sextus commends chastity and, if necessary, self-castration. He favors right reason and what is right, and he denounces license and, especially, pleasure.[32] What does Sextus lack? Only an appeal to the law of nature in regard to sex, and Christian teachers could find this in Romans 1:26–27.[33]

The matron's new attitudes were encouraged by the teachings of Christ as assembled at Rome in her time, by Stoic philosophy as admired and taught there, and perhaps by a popular ascetic Pythagorean treatise used by Christians, as well as several verses from Paul's letter to the Romans, which Roman Christians considered authoritative.[34]

Her newfound way of life required her to remain with her husband, at least for a time, in the hope of converting him to chastity. "Her people," perhaps Christians, urged her to take this course. Paul and Hermas provided precedents. In 1 Corinthians the apostle urged Christians to remain married to pagan partners provided some compatibility was left. A pagan husband could be "sanctified" by a Christian wife; he might be converted as well (1 Cor. 7:13–15). We do not know, however, that by this point she had become a Christian. If she had, she could have heeded the counsel of the Roman Christian Hermas, who urged couples to remain married unless the adultery or pagan practices ("acting as the heathen do") of one would make the other a "partner" in the spouse's sin. The injured party should live alone in the hope that the other will repent.[35] In the present case, however, the wife finally divorced her husband so that she would not be a partner in his crimes. Again Musonius had something to say on the subject.

> Where each partner looks only to self-interest and neglects the other or, worse still, one of them is so minded and lives in the same house but fixes his attention elsewhere, unwilling to pull together or agree with his mate, then the partnership is doomed to disaster and affairs go badly though they live together. Eventually they separate entirely from each other or have a life together that is worse than isolation.[36]

In general, however, classical authors were sympathetic toward errant husbands who claimed to respect their more restrained wives. Plutarch writes that "if an ordinary man is licentious and dissolute in his pleasures and sins a bit with a prostitute or a servant, his wife should not be indignant or angry but should reckon that out of respect for her he transfers his drunken behavior, license, and lust to another woman." An even more ordinary man, however, "fond of pleasure," might make his wife "meretricious and licentious";[37] and seemingly this was the goal of our matron's husband.[38]

Her husband demanded "unnatural" modes of intercourse. These were not forbidden by Greek or Roman law, and poets and satirists often found, or claimed to find, them acceptable.[39] Some rabbinical teachers approved; others disapproved.[40] Christians like Justin and Clement who found the purpose of marriage in procreation inevitably disapproved.[41] The wife's criticism also reflects the attitudes of philosophers like Musonius, who criticized "shameful embraces," and Epictetus, who praised the guidance of nature.[42]

At this point the husband left for Alexandria. Old-fashioned Romans did not think much of the city of his dreams. Greeks and Romans refer to the flexibility of Alexandrian morals.[43] When news of his activities there got back to Rome, his wife decided not to remain his accomplice and sent him a "bill of divorcement," refusing to share bed or board with him. *Symbiōsis,* life together, the essence of marriage, was at an end.[44] The sole requirement for divorce was that one party give or send a bill of divorcement to the other.[45]

A different problem arose at once, however, when ill will between the parties inhibited the husband from returning the wife's dowry and one or both parties began making accusations. Earlier Greek marriage contracts in Egypt usually stated that husbands were not to have children by other women or drive their wives out, insult them, or treat them badly, while the wives were not to put their husbands to shame. Penalties were to be levied if the dowry was not returned immediately after divorce. Later contracts do not discuss matters so precisely. In one case the couple is to live "blamelessly."[46] But Roman examples show that the return of the dowry was related to the moral turpitude of one party or the other.[47]

The wife's petition to the emperor shows that dowry matters were involved. Apparently the husband was unable to reply adequately to her accusations and therefore charged that she was a Christian. The kind of petition she offered was common just in the reign of Antoninus Pius.[48] What she wanted first was to administer her own estate, presumably including the marital dowry she expected her husband to repay. Her request seems to imply that there had already been some delay, possibly because he had first accused her of immoral behavior. He was not likely to accuse her of adultery, however, since in that case he should have divorced her earlier. Presumably he intended to retain at least a part of the dowry.

A case described by both Valerius Maximus and Plutarch shows how this might work.[49] The story shows that an "aggrieved husband" might hope to keep a large part of a dowry but was by no means assured of doing so. We may compare a legend about Marcus Aurelius, whose wife Faustina (daughter of Antoninus Pius) was said to cohabit with sailors and gladiators. He said, "If we divorce our wife we must also return the dowry"—that is, the empire.[50] The request for the dowry was the first part of the matron's petition.

The second part contained two requests: first, for a delay,[51] and second, for permission to defend herself against the charge of being a Christian. The delay was therefore not the stay of execution sometimes offered by Roman judges to declared Christians. Obviously the emperor's answer to the first part of the matron's petition would implicitly judge her morals. At a later date she could proceed to argue either that she was not a Christian or that the charge was unjust. Had she answered in the latter manner, presumably she would have been among the early Christian apologists or martyrs.

Obviously Justin's story is not simply erotic or even antierotic. Its characters are deeply embedded in legal conflicts with which the apologist is not really concerned. He tells about them only to anticipate his account of some early martyrs at Rome. Along the way, however, the sexual problems come to the fore.

Justin on Pornographic Literature

Toward the end of the *Second Apology* Justin says that anyone can read the doctrines of Sotades, Philaenis, Archestratus, and Epicurus, but not Christian books. It looks as if he knew nothing directly about this erotic literature but derived it from the anti-Epicurean blasts of the prolific Stoic philosopher Chrysippus.[52] Like Justin, in one breath Chrysippus mentioned Philaenis, authoress of a sex manual, and Archestratus, author of a gourmet cookbook, both of them so that he could lambaste Epicurus.[53] Since the apologist praises Stoic teaching on ethics, there is little reason to doubt that Chrysippus provided him with his information, such as it is, about writers on food and sex.

The beginning of Philaenis' work has turned up in Oxyrhynchus Papyrus xxxix.2891,[54] and it does not seem quite as dangerous as Justin supposed. "Philaenis daughter of Okymenes, a Samian, wrote this for those who want . . . life . . . and not incidentally. . . ." What must be the first chapter discusses "approaches" to women. "He who makes approaches must be unadorned, with uncombed hair, so that he may not appear too dressed up to the woman. . . ." In another fragment Philaenis recommends terms of endearment for calling some woman (perhaps rather large) "godlike," an ugly one "lovable," and an older one—here the text becomes illegible.[55] The next section is "on kisses," but the text is lost. No early Christian author would have commended a book of this sort.

9

Marcus Aurelius
and the Christians

The principal opponents of Christianity during the reign of Trajan were closely interrelated, and their common prejudices provided a setting for anti-Christian activities (see chapter 3). Under Antoninus Pius and Marcus Aurelius such officials were not so closely related, but there was a demonstrable continuity among their religious attitudes in Italy and Asia.

Urban Prefects and Christians at Rome

We begin with the reign of Antoninus Pius, and look briefly at Q. Lollius Urbicus, the judge before whom the Roman matron's Christian teacher appeared. He had been a suffect consul under Hadrian, then governor of Britain, where in 142 he built the Antonine Wall from the Forth to the Clyde. Apparently he became prefect of the city of Rome after 157 or so. The date depends on Justin's apology. Urbicus simply followed law or tradition and ordered the execution of the Christian Ptolemaeus. Another Christian who was present denounced the sentence as without foundation and unworthy of Antoninus Pius, his son Marcus Aurelius, and the Roman Senate. Urbicus condemned him to death as well, along with a third man who confessed voluntarily.

Not many years later, perhaps in 167 after the outbreak of the plague,[1] Justin himself appeared before another urban prefect at Rome. He had aroused the animosity of a Cynic philosopher who attacked both Justin and his pupil Tatian by accusing them of godlessness and immorality.[2] With six disciples, not including Tatian, he came before the urban prefect Q. Iunius Rusticus, formerly a tutor of the emperor, consul for the second time in 162 and probably urban prefect in the same year. Since the successor of Rusticus seems to have been L. Sergius Paullus, consul for the second time in 168, who became prefect after Galen's first stay in Rome (which lasted from 162 to 166),[3] Justin's martyrdom must have taken place between 162 and 168.

According to the martyr-acts, Justin lived "above the baths of Timo-thinus," a private establishment not now identifiable. Seneca, not Justin, tells us what living over baths meant.

> My lodgings are right over the public baths. Imagine all the different noises I have to listen to—loud enough to make me hate my own ears! For instance, when the muscle-man is exercising with the barbells, either working hard or putting on a good act, I can hear every grunt, and the asthmatic panting when he lets his breath out. . . . On top of this, some drunk or pickpocket being hauled off by the police.[4]

This was not the kind of life, or the aspect of Greco-Roman culture, with which Justin wanted contact. On the other hand, he was probably not eager to meet a prefect either. He was often in danger of being "hauled off by the police" if outsiders invaded his school and demanded worship of the gods. If he and his disciples did not acquiesce, they would be taken before the tribunal, accused of opposing the "decree of Caesar," and condemned to death.[5]

Rusticus shared Justin's overall attitude toward life and culture. He was resolutely opposed to "oratory, poetry, and preciosity" and favored simplicity in writing. He urged Marcus to comprehend "the need for reform and therapy in morals." But he was part of the Roman system, not the Christian church. He was one of three people the emperor met for whom he later thanked the gods.[6] Obviously he was going to judge Christians severely.

He began the proceedings by inquiring about the morals of Christians but rapidly moved to doctrine and the meetings at Justin's lodgings. The basic problem, however, was simply membership in the Christian community. "Are you a Christian?" The answer "Yes" brought the death penalty, and this was imposed on all the witnesses. Thus Justin ended his life after a significant career for the church.

He was essentially an individual teacher. At his trial he said that he had paid two visits to Rome and now lived above the baths. He also stated, "I have known no other meeting place than here. Anyone who wished could come to my abode and I would share the words of truth with him." Presumably he was not giving away the location of other assemblies or of the church officers he mentions in the *Apology*.

Attitudes of Proconsuls of Asia

Just around this time we hear something more about the religious or rhetorical connections of several proconsuls of Asia and can draw inferences about anti-Christian attitudes in high Roman circles. We have already mentioned the rhetorician Statius Quadratus, consul in 142 and the proconsul of Asia who sentenced Polycarp of Smyrna (see chapter 6). It should be noted that he was consul just a year before the emperor expressed his devotion to Greek and Latin rhetoric by appointing both Herodes Atticus and Cornelius Fronto suffect consuls.

Cornelius Fronto

At some point in his career Cornelius Fronto, suffect consul in 143 and tutor to Marcus Aurelius, produced a speech in which he dredged up the old scandal about incest at Christian worship.[7] He would have become proconsul in Asia about 158—that is, soon after Quadratus—had his health permitted. A letter to Antoninus Pius expresses his regrets.

Sisenna Rutilianus

P. Mummius Sisenna Rutilianus was suffect in 146 and became proconsul of Asia about 162/163; his uncle had held the same office a dozen years earlier. At about sixty he had the misfortune to fall into the clutches of the false prophet Alexander of Abonuteichos, a charlatan who gave oracles only after dismissing skeptical Epicureans and Christians who might disrupt his seances.[8] Alexander sent oracles to the superstitious proconsul, and ordered him to marry the daughter of himself and the moon.[9] Through Rutilianus he made contacts at Rome and went to Italy himself, claiming that he would protect cities against the plague and even that he could defend the empire against the Marcomanni and the Quadi in 167. His oracle asked for two lions to be thrown into the Danube, but when they swam across to the enemy side the barbarians killed them and in a counterattack destroyed twenty thousand Roman troops.[10]

When Alexander captivated Rutilianus he made an important catch. In his rite of "sacred marriage" the "very pretty woman" who took the part of the moon was the wife of an imperial procurator, and her name was Rutilia. Presumably she was a relative. Obviously friends of Alexander were foes of Christianity.

Squilla Gallicanus

A religious concern is also evident in the family of M. Gavius Squilla Gallicanus, consul in 150 and proconsul about 165. His father had been consul in 127 and his son would be consul in 170. His wife, Pompeia Agripinilla, owed her name to her ancestor Theophanes of Mitylene, who as political adviser and biographer of Pompey took his name. She was the patroness of a Bacchic group of about four hundred men and women near Rome, most of them with Greek names. She is best known for the statue-base now in the Metropolitan Museum, with its list of members arranged by categories and beginning with family names related to Gallicanus: a "hero," a torch-bearer, seven priests, and two priestesses.[11] Such a family was not likely to favor Christians.

Marcus Aurelius Himself

Such officials and their families formed a rather solid phalanx of hostility toward Christians, and to it we must add the emperor Marcus Aurelius himself. His view of the Christians requires some comment. Farquharson thus translates his words on the question of suicide: "This resolve must arise from a specific decision, not out of sheer opposition like the Christians, but after reflection and with dignity, and so as to convince others, without histrionic display."[12] The Christians thus sought death out of "sheer opposi-

The emperor Marcus Aurelius (Louvre)

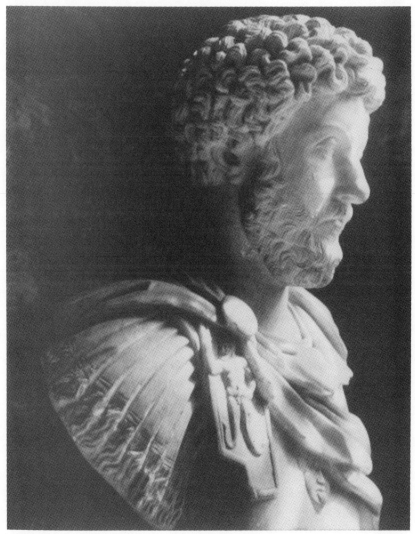

tion" *(psilē parataxis).* [13] The word has connotations of conflict and conspiracy, matters with which the emperor was concerned as Roman statesman if not as philosopher. Another key to the passage lies in the reference to "histrionic display" or "tragedy." Elsewhere Marcus speaks of a person who "strikes a tragic attitude" instead of relying on his own intelligence (3.7). He also calls on his reader to be "neither a tragic actor nor a prostitute" (5.28). And he wants to be sure that the great men of the past really followed Nature, instead of "playing the tragedy-hero" who does not deserve imitation (9.29). Originally, he believes, tragedies taught the audience about the nature of life, though apparently they no longer do so (11.6). In Marcus' view the Christians are tragic in the sense that they are immature and insincere. It is hard to imagine an apologetic that could change his mind.

Celsus expresses something like the emperor's attitude toward their suicidal drive when he ridicules the cross and suggests that had Jesus died otherwise, Christians "would have spoken of "a cliff of life above the heavens or a pit of resurrection or a rope of immortality.""[14] A later proconsul of Asia found them hard to handle for a similar reason (see chapter 16).

Perhaps undue emphasis has been placed on Marcus Aurelius' concern for philosophy, not enough on his care for the empire. G. R. Stanton observes that more than half the legal texts related to him deal with women, children, and slaves—categories which play very modest roles in his book. His philosophy seems to have no special relation to his practice, since he was "basically a Roman rather than a Stoic."[15]

Years of War and Revolt

The emperor's seemingly endless campaigns on the northern and eastern frontiers of the empire led to unrest and disorder in several regions.

During the year 171 Christian leaders in Phrygia recognized the existence of an apocalyptic movement in the rural hill country, with predictions that the new Jerusalem would soon land nearby, though wars and anarchy would come before the end.[16] We shall discuss the movement in chapter 10 in relation to its opponent Apollinaris of Hierapolis.

In 172 a priest with the native name Isidorus led a revolt in Egypt after he had been able to kill two Roman officers and swore in his followers over their cannibalized corpses.[17] His boldness nearly won Alexandria, but Avidius Cassius, legate in Syria, arrived in Egypt and restored peace by dividing the rebels from their leaders.[18]

Also in 172 great storms on the Danube led to the defeat of the Quadi, who had surrounded Roman troops and kept them from getting water. The storms gave water to the Romans but lightning and hail drove off the barbarians. (Again, see chapter 10.) Afterward, the Roman soldiers hailed Marcus Aurelius as *imperator* for the seventh time,[19] and he began to make

A coin of Marcus from 173: RELIGIO AVG, with Hermes (photo: Special Collections, University of Chicago Library)

peace with the Quadi and other tribes. It is noteworthy that an Egyptian priest accompanied him on the Danube.

The Revolt of Avidius Cassius

The continuing campaigns produced a crisis, however, in the winter of 174/175. The empress Faustina had come to fear that her ailing husband, in camp on the frontier, was approaching death, and she was well aware that Commodus, the only heir to the throne, was "adolescent and rather simple-minded." She therefore urged Avidius Cassius, now legate in the whole East, to seize power.[20] His revolt began in Syria and rapidly spread along the coastal routes to Cilicia and Egypt.[21] It was frustrated in Cappadocia, however, when another eastern strongman, Martius Verus, stood fast for the emperor with his two legions XII Fulminata, soon given the honorific title *certa constans,* and XV Apollinaris, with the title *pia fidelis.*[22] Martius Verus himself won rapid promotion, becoming legate of Syria, then consul for the second time with Commodus in 179.

The situation was so serious that at first the emperor kept news of the revolt from the army, and later he rejected aid offered by barbarian tribes because they "should not know about troubles among Romans."[23] Religious fanaticism was also involved. The jurist Ulpian says that "the divine Marcus relegated to the island of Syros a man who during the revolt of Cassius made predictions and said much as if inspired by the gods."[24] Obviously he was punished for favoring Cassius and obviously he was not inspired by the gods. If Christians favored the revolt they too discredited their religion.

An odd tale in the *Augustan History* reflects either this situation or a similar one earlier. "A man kept climbing a fig tree on the Campus Martius" in order to predict fire from heaven and the end of the world. This would arrive "should he fall from the tree and turn into a stork." He was arrested when "at the appointed time he fell and released a stork from his bosom." Out of clemency the emperor pardoned him.[25]

Indeed, Marcus was supposedly so clement that after the death of Avidius Cassius he asked the Senate for a universal amnesty and put no one to death, whether obscure or prominent, or at least none of the senators. Dio does admit that a few "others" were executed.[26] His attitude may have suggested to Christians that he could offer them similar treatment. Certainly Athenagoras complained that unlike those who admired the gentleness and mildness of Marcus and Commodus and their peaceful and humane attitudes toward all, and enjoyed equality before the law as well as profound peace, Christians alone were being persecuted.[27] But Marcus wanted security for the empire, on his terms, not simply the practice of philosophical virtue.

The Imperial Tour of 175–176

A few months after the revolt ended, the emperor and his wife Faustina took Commodus and their daughters with them on a tour of the eastern empire, where rebellion had won support. Much of the journey can be confirmed from coins and inscriptions.[28] Coins of 175–176 speak of Fortuna Dux and Fortuna Redux, while at some point a port officer at Ostia dedicated an altar to Isis and Sarapis "for the health and safe return of the emperor Antoninus Augustus, Faustina Augusta, and their children."[29] An Alexandrian coin shows the emperor riding on horseback,[30] while a dedication by an unnamed tribune of the legion II Traiana Fortis in Egypt is intended to suggest that this legion had been, or would be, loyal to the emperor.[31]

Marcus and his party traveled from the base at Sirmium as far as the village of Halala in Cappadocia, where Faustina suddenly died of blood poisoning or, Dio thinks, by suicide.[32] A late Victorian author from Boston knows a good deal about her: "Her face, as it has come down to us on coins and in busts, is itself the witness alike to her beauty and her insincerity."[33] In any event, Marcus asked the Senate to offer amnesty to all former rebels, whatever their rank might be, and to deify his wife; he erected a temple in the village, renamed Colonia Faustiniana or Faustinopolis.[34] A letter to

The empress Faustina the Younger (Louvre)

Herodes Atticus comes from a winter army camp *(cheimadia).* In it Marcus laments his wife and speaks of his impending visit to Eleusis.[35] Presumably he wrote from Halala. Later the imperial party passed down through the Cilician Gates, where the pass had been closed by snow until mid-April,[36] then east to Tarsus.[37]

During a visit to Palestine, recently Cassius' stronghold, he commented on "malodorous and rebellious Jews," comparing them unfavorably with his barbarian enemies on the Danube.[38] He went to Egypt before turning back to Asia Minor and probably sailing either to Lycia[39] or to Cappadocia. Inscriptions may mark his route. A reference to a "high priestess of the goddess Augusta Faustina" comes from Iotape in Cilicia, just east of Side and Perge.[40] To the northwest, a priest of Termessus in Pisidia is named as "sent out as guide to the supreme emperor Caesar Marcus Aurelius Antoninus, victor over Armenians Parthians Medes [Dacians] Germans."[41] This inscription suggests that the emperor was taking the road up into the mountains, where Dio indicates the officials had remained loyal to him.[42]

Presumably the emperor passed from Iotape to Perge and then turned inland to Termessus where he acquired his guide into the mountains. Eventually he reached Smyrna, where he was greeted at a special festival called Theoxenia and had the privilege of hearing speeches by the orator Aelius Aristides.[43] To get from Termessus to Smyrna he would almost certainly have passed through Laodicea, with a possible side trip to Hierapolis.[44] Christian apologists must have seized the opportunity to present petitions to him. We shall examine their efforts in the next three chapters.

10
Apollinaris of Hierapolis

Hierapolis, now Pamukkale, in Phrygia stands at the top of a high plateau from which limestone in the springs has created a stalagmite cover.[1] The city was "among the prosperous cities of Asia," says Philostratus,[2] and it owed much of its prosperity to close commercial links with Rome. An inscription tells of a merchant of Hierapolis who undertook no fewer than 72 voyages to Italy,[3] and there was a significant group of Roman citizens living in the city who formed a *synedrion* or *conventus*.[4] These people were engaged in business, as inscriptions from other Asian cities indicate, especially one from Ephesus: *conventus civium Romanorum qui in Asia negotiantur*.[5] At Hierapolis the winner of a certain contest, perhaps Roman Augustan games, erected an altar to Gaius Caesar as *princeps iuventutis* (hence after 5 B.C.) and the goddess Roma.[6] Other cities shared this attitude. For example, a much lengthier inscription from Sardis mentions sacrifices and prayers for Gaius around the same time.[7] Loyalty to Rome was especially flourishing at Hierapolis, however, and was expressed in the imperial cult with a temple from the time of Claudius.[8]

The Apology of Apollinaris

The Christian bishop Apollinaris became famous for the apology he wrote in 176 to claim for Christians the rainstorm on the Danube that had given water to Roman troops and struck the enemy with lightning. It was due to the prayers of a whole Christian legion from Cappadocia.[9] Obviously both Apollinaris and the legion were loyal to the emperor and his army. The apology expressed the bishop's adherence to conservative loyalty and orthodoxy in both state and church.

It was evident that some god had defended the Roman army by sending lightning upon the enemy and rain upon the parched Romans. The events are depicted on the column of Marcus Aurelius in the Piazza Colonna in

Rome, where the giver of rain is identified as some deity with rain dripping from his wings. Modern studies of Dio Cassius and the column have suggested the date 172 or 174.[10] Dio Cassius says that the miraculous victory was a divine gift to the emperor but adds that some believed the rain fell because "Arnuphis, an Egyptian magician accompanying Marcus, invoked various deities *(daimones),* especially Hermes, god of the air."[11] Marta Sordi separates the Roman official picture of the pious emperor aided by Jupiter from accretions of a later period.[12] These accretions include the story about Arnuphis as well as the ascription of the miracle to the theurge Julian, an expert in Chaldean magic.[13] Certainly the emperor did not accept the claims of the Egyptian and the Chaldean. His tutor Diognetus had taught him to reject the assertions of magicians.[14]

The story about Arnuphis portrayed an Egyptian priest not as rebel but wearing Roman battle dress like the Egyptian gods in the Vatican and British Museums. Similarly, the Chaldean (like the Palmyrene god in the

The rain miracle on the column of Marcus Aurelius (Piazza Colonna, Rome)

British Museum) showed that Romans had nothing to fear from the predictions of the Chaldean Hystaspes, who supposedly foretold the destruction of the Roman empire (see chapter 1).

Apollinaris Christianizes the pagan theme, ascribing the storm to the prayers of the Christian Twelfth Legion from Melitene in Cappadocia, which because of the lightning received the title *fulminata.* His statement that the title was first given on this occasion is false. The whole Twelfth cannot have been active on the Danube or manned by Christians. In 70 Titus had removed it to Cappadocia because it had lost its eagle to the Jews,[15] and it had been called *fulminata* since the reign of Augustus.[16] Presumably a unit or two fought on the Danube in 172 or 174 and Christian legionary soldiers from Melitene were in service at the time. Apollinaris was proud of them and eager to show how the true God, answering their prayers, had defended the empire and the emperor. He used some of the traditional topics discussed by the rhetorician Menander.[17] Because of the king, says Menander, we do not fear barbarians or enemies. "Seasonal rains and cargoes by sea and the produce of fruits turn out well for us because of the justice of the emperor." Just so, Apollinaris could write of the miraculous storm by the Danube that saved the day for Rome because of the prayers offered by a Christian legion. Marcus Aurelius was the ideal just king for the bishop and his readers.

Finally, Apollinaris was probably answering widespread criticisms which were found in Celsus' anti-Christian work. If everyone refused military service as the Christians did, the emperor would be left isolated while "earthly affairs would come into the power of the most lawless and savage barbarians." Moreover, even if the Romans were to call upon the god of the Christians, he would not come down and fight on their side.[18] Apollinaris answers both complaints. Christians do serve in the army and God does hear their prayers. Two decades later, Tertullian still spoke of the rain miracle achieved "by the prayers of Christian soldiers." Probably he also reflected Apollinaris' circumstances when he stated that no Christians took part in the revolt of Avidius Cassius.[19]

The precise occasion of the apology, addressed to Marcus Aurelius as emperor in late 175 or mid-176, was the emperor's eastern tour, when political circumstances encouraged a Christian like Apollinaris to insist on the loyalty, ratified by God, of the Christian soldiers from Melitene. We suggest that he presented it to Marcus Aurelius in Hierapolis or nearby Laodicea.

Apollinaris as Hierapolitan Christian

Other works by Apollinaris reflect his situation in Phrygia as a loyal subject of the Roman emperor and a loyal collaborator with the Roman church. We begin with his two books *Against the Jews.*[20]

Apollinaris and Jews at Hierapolis

One might wonder what Apollinaris' books *Against the Jews* had to do with his political situation. To be sure, the Jewish community at Hierapolis was important and the church had once been in some form of communication with it. Inscriptions point to the strength of the Jewish community when they state that indemnities for tomb violation are to be paid to "the people of the Jews," presumably identical with "the colony of Jews dwelling in Hierapolis" which had a special "archive of the Jews" for copies of legal documents.[21] A wealthy Jew left an endowment for special donations at "the festival of unleavened bread" and "at the festival of Pentecost."[22] The name Maria in three inscriptions is presumably either Jewish or Christian in origin.[23] We thus see that while Jews were prominent they were also separate from other Hierapolitans, and by the end of the second century a Christian might not wish to be associated with their "festival of unleavened bread" (see below).

Christians and Jews must have been closely related in Hierapolis at the beginning, though we lack precise evidence. The church there is mentioned in the letter to the nearby Colossians (Col. 4:13), and the city is referred to in the *Sibylline Oracles.*[24] The Apocalypse of John mentioned only nearby Laodicea, and Ignatius of Antioch did not write to this church or refer to it in his letters, perhaps because its Christianity was closer to Judaism than he liked.

Certainly such closeness is evident in the fragments from the bishop Papias, who early in the second century produced five books of *Exegesis of the Dominical Oracles* in a relatively clear Greek style. He was concerned with literary matters but also devoted to sources of oral tradition, and credulously accepted Jewish apocalyptic. He asked Christian travelers about what the disciples of Jesus had said, for as he said, "I did not suppose that information from books would help me as much as that from a living and surviving voice."[25] Perhaps he was avoiding the apocryphal acts and gospels beginning to be produced in the names of such apostles. Among his informants were the daughters of Philip, who apparently told him about the recent resurrection of a corpse and the immunity of Justus Barsabbas (Acts 1:23) from poison. The Montanists of Phrygia later appealed to these prophetesses as spiritual ancestors.[26]

Papias stood close to apocalyptic Judaism. He took a prediction of miraculous fertility from the Jewish apocalypse called *2 Baruch* and ascribed it to Jesus.[27] Other early Christians used this work; two quotations from it appear in the contemporary *Epistle of Barnabas.* It is surprising, however, that Papias traced his "tradition" back from it through John to Jesus. Such a fusion of Jewish apocalyptic with Christian tradition again points ahead toward Montanism, as does Papias' preference for "living" oral tradition over books. In addition, it may be that his concern for "oracles," if that is what *logia* means, anticipates the Montanist quest for similar inspired utterances.

We do not know what Papias' attitude toward Rome was, but his apocalyptic enthusiasm, close to Judaism, cannot have encouraged him to admire the Roman state or church. The different views of Apollinaris may be due in part to very recent Roman precedent. In 176 as the emperor passed through Palestine on his way to Egypt he commented unfavorably on Jews, presumably former supporters of Avidius Cassius (see chapter 9). Doubtless his remarks circulated widely.

The Problem of Montanism

We have already noted that around 171 Jewish apocalyptic played an important part in the rise of Montanism in the rural hill country of Phrygia. Now we shall examine the "Phrygian sect" in a little more detail to see what attitude Apollinaris took toward it.

Montanus, a recent convert, used to go into trances and utter oracles predicting the imminent descent of the heavenly Jerusalem at the village of Pepuza. He urged devotees to assemble there, practice rigorous fasting, and offer money. In his oracles he said, "It is I, the Lord God almighty, who am present in a man," and "Behold, man is like a lyre and I hover over him like a plectrum; man sleeps but I watch; behold, it is the Lord who makes men's hearts ecstatic and gives them [new] hearts." Apparently he meant that God was using him as his instrument of revelation. Two oracles express his rigor: "The church can remit sins, but I will not do so lest others also sin," and "Do not hope to die in bed nor in abortion nor in languishing fevers, but in martyrdom so that he who suffered for you may be glorified."

Two prophetesses, Maximilla and Prisca or Priscilla, joined him to receive the Spirit. Maximilla herself claimed inspiration: "The Lord sent me as a devotee, revealer, interpreter of this labor and promise and covenant; I was forced, willing or not, to learn the knowledge of God" (cf. 1 Cor. 9:16). She delivered apocalyptic messages: "There will be wars and revolutions" and "After me there will be no more prophecy, but the end." The anti-Montanist Anonymous replies that in thirteen years after her death there have been no wars; she therefore died before the reign of Commodus (180–192). She aroused controversy: "I am driven from the sheep like a wolf; I am not a wolf but utterance, spirit, and power," though her admirers prevented orthodox exorcists from attacking her. Priscilla uttered "saving words, as clear as they are mysterious." She attacked the orthodox for being "flesh but hating the flesh." Her vision of Christ was all-important. "Appearing as a woman clothed in a shining robe, Christ came to me; he put wisdom into me and revealed to me that this place [Pepuza] is sacred and here Jerusalem will come down from heaven." Details of this oracle come from apocalypses. John supplies the shining robe and the new Jerusalem from heaven (Rev. 19:7–8; 21:2), while 2 Esdras provides the woman with shining face, replaced by the new Zion which is a sacred place with a city, and perhaps the identification of Zion with Ardab.[28]

An anonymous critic calls the movement a "heresy derived from schism" and criticizes Montanus as coming from a remote village in Phrygian Mysia, and for being a neophyte so strongly affected by "unbounded desire for the highest rank" that the devil entered into him (as into Judas Iscariot) and he went mad. He and the prophetesses "blasphemed" the universal church for not accepting the "spirit of false prophecy."[29]

The movement was religious in origin but the conflict soon became political as Montanus struggled with the bishops for "the highest rank" and claimed that unlike them he possessed the spirit of prophecy. The innovations of the movement undermined the authority of local churches and governors and of the Roman church and empire. The prophet and the prophetesses urged Christians to become martyrs. They traced their spiritual ancestry not through the major apostles but through the prophesying daughters of Philip, two of them buried at Hierapolis in Phrygia.[30]

Papias had been devoted to bizarre apocalyptic and strange sayings of Jesus, but the Montanists seem not to have spoken of him, preferring to mention the prophetess Ammia of Philadelphia. A mysterious inscription at Hierapolis reads thus: "For Ammia and As[k]lepius, the . . . of Christians."[31] One might supply ekklēsia, "church," or even synagōgē, "synagogue," with the feminine article and the word "Christians," in reference to the early prophetess. She came from Philadelphia, however, and few early Christians admired Asclepius. Justin found the stories of his healings rather embarrassing.[32]

It was Apollinaris of Hierapolis who led the "Roman connection" to try to suppress Montanism at a very early date. He wrote "while Montanus with his false prophetesses was just taking the first steps in his error."[33] He intended to prove that Montanism was "abominated before the whole [Christian] brotherhood in the world" by citing the testimonies and signatures of various Asian and Thracian bishops, presumably recorded at the "frequent synods in many parts of Asia" at which they "tested recent utterances, pronounced them profane, and rejected the heresy."[34] One bishop signed as a martyr. Another told how a colleague tried to exorcise a prophetess but was checked by "the hypocrites." Apollinaris' account of anti-Montanist decisions enjoyed wide circulation and was later used by Serapion of Antioch.[35]

Before that, however, the Montanists themselves appealed to Eleutherus of Rome against the excommunication of their leader.[36] In turn Apollinaris and others must have sent news to the imprisoned confessors of Lyons and Vienne, where confessors and martyrs had ties with Asia. Around 177 the confessors sent letters to "Asia and Phrygia and Eleutherus the then bishop of the Romans, for the peace of the churches."[37] The Asian addressees obviously included the bishop of Ephesus, those in Phrygia the bishop of Hierapolis. The confessors also described their sufferings in a letter to the non-Montanist "brothers in Asia and Phrygia who have the same faith and hope of redemption as we do."[38] For this reason they insisted that the Spirit was within themselves[39] and reserved the title "martyr" for those who had been put to death.[40] Eusebius says that their judgment was "pious and most orthodox,"[41] that is, in agreement with Apollinaris.

Rome joined in condemning the Montanists. Tertullian claims that a later Roman bishop, presumably Zephyrinus, "was already recognizing the prophecies of Montanus, Prisca, and Maximilla and by that recognition was bringing peace to the churches of Asia and Phrygia," when a certain Praxeas suddenly arrived from Asia and "by false assertions about the prophets and their churches and by defending the decisions of his [the Roman bishop's] predecessors forced him to recall the letters of peace already issued and withdraw his proposal to accept the gifts of grace."[42] Zephyrinus' two predecessors were Eleutherus and Victor, and if Tertullian's "predecessors" is exact, Eleutherus, influenced by Apollinaris and the Gallicans, refused to recognize the Montanist movement.

The Montanist schism in Phrygia was hostile to the Roman order. Indeed, a pre-Montanist Phrygian was conspicuous as a voluntary martyr just before Polycarp was put to death around 156, and the *Martyrdom of Polycarp* explicitly states that "we do not commend those who give themselves up, since the gospel does not teach this."[43] Apollinaris too stood against such doctrine.

Apollinaris and Synods on Easter Observance

Another controversy in which Apollinaris sided with Rome concerned Easter observance. The problem had arisen because the Asian churches were relying on the Jewish calendar in order to relate Easter to the date of Passover, when Christ was crucified. At Rome Easter was always observed on a Sunday; the matter had been discussed but not resolved when Polycarp of Smyrna visited Anicetus at Rome about 155. Disagreements also existed within the province of Asia itself, and at the end of the second century Victor of Rome urged synods to convene "throughout the world." Such synods met in Palestine, at Rome, in Pontus, in Gaul, at Jerusalem with the bishops of Caesarea and Jerusalem as presidents; at Rome under the bishop Victor; in "Osrhoene and the cities there," at Corinth, and in Asia.[44] Eusebius, who lists these synods, says that outside Asia they unanimously agreed that Easter should always be observed on a Sunday. He does not cite any evidence from Phrygia.

Obviously the unanimity was incomplete, for the Asians did not agree with the others. In addition, Eusebius seems to have misunderstood his excerpt from the letter of the Palestinians. They discussed their own apostolic tradition about the Passover and ended with this warning: "Try to send copies of our letter to every church, so that we may not be responsible for those who readily lead their own souls astray. We inform you that also in Alexandria they observe the same day as we do; for documents are exchanged between us so that we observe the holy day in agreement and together."[45] The Palestinians were trying to give publicity to their own minority report, evidently without success. Perhaps the stand taken by Narcissus of Jerusalem explains why he was mysteriously slandered and mysteriously disappeared from the episcopate, though later restored to reach the age of 116.[46] As for Alexandria, a fragment from Irenaeus was addressed "to an Alexandrian to the effect that it is right, with respect to the Feast of the Resurrection, that we should celebrate it upon the first day of the week."[47] The Alexandrian evidently did not celebrate the feast on a Sunday. Polycrates of Ephesus may have claimed the Palestinians and the Alexandrians for the Quartodeciman side, which celebrated Easter on the fourteenth of the Jewish month Nisan.

He also claimed "Philip of the twelve apostles, who sleeps at Hierapolis" as a Quartodeciman. Presumably the present bishop Apollinaris stood with Rome against other Asians.

Other Works by Apollinaris

We do not know what Apollinaris included in his five books *Against the Greeks* or the two *On Truth.* In view of his references to John on the paschal celebration, his point of departure for the last topic may have been the question raised by the Roman prefect Pontius Pilate, "What is truth?" (John 18:38), but we cannot be sure. In any case, he did not have historical truth in mind.

Christ's Human Soul

A final theological point may reveal Apollinaris siding with Rome once more. The church historian Socrates lists him along with Irenaeus, Clement of Alexandria, and Serapion of Antioch as a witness to the human soul of Christ.[48] Since he identified the water and blood that came forth from Jesus' side at the crucifixion (John 19:34) as Logos and Spirit, he must have held that the "spirit" that Jesus "gave up" (John 19:30) was his soul. And since both Irenaeus and Serapion stood close to Rome,[49] this may be one more example of a view shared with that church. We recall that Serapion used Apollinaris' treatise against the Montanists.

A Contemporary Apologist: Miltiades

Little is known about another apologist of this period, Miltiades, who closely resembled Apollinaris in that he wrote against Montanists, Greeks, and Jews, and "addressed to the rulers of this world a defense of the philosophy which he followed."[50] Later he was clearly regarded as orthodox,[51] and though confusion has arisen over his name in the text of the *Church History,* he was not a Montanist but an anti-Montanist who held "that a prophet should not speak in a state of ecstasy."[52] Presumably Tertullian opposed both him and Melito in his lost treatise *On Ecstasy.*

The anti-Montanist Anonymous used his work around 193 and Eusebius set him under Commodus, recently dead. His opposition to Montanism and the resemblances of his book titles to those of Apollinaris suggest that he wrote around the same time, probably with a content like that of Apollinaris and Melito. Jerome proposed that he addressed Marcus Aurelius and Commodus, thus between 176 and 180.[53] Valesius, cited by Salmon, supposed that he wrote to the provincial governors, while Salmon himself suggested that Marcus Aurelius and Lucius Verus were in view.[54] This last suggestion seems wrong because of chronology. Valesius' hypothesis is better, especially with Barnes' conjecture that by addressing provincial governors Miltiades prepared the way for Tertullian's apology.[55]

His use of *kosmikoi archontes* when addressing rulers might recall the denomination of the devil as the "ruler of this world" in the Gospel of John or the "ruler of this age," often in the letters of Ignatius. More significant, however, is 1 Corinthians 2:6–8: "None of the rulers of this age [who are passing away] understood this [secret wisdom of God]; for if they had, they would not have crucified the Lord of glory." Non-Gnostic early Christians interpreted such *archontes* in Romans as earthly rulers. We find this to be the case in the *Martyrdom of Polycarp* (10.2), two apologists,[56] and Irenaeus.[57] We assume, therefore, that they would be so interpreted in 1 Corinthians.[58] But then who were they? Acts 4:27 definitely identifies such "rulers" as Herod and Pontius Pilate—obviously provincial governors. Miltiades thus offered such transient rulers his explanation of the divine wisdom. Presumably he was more conciliatory than Tatian. His allusion to 1 Corinthians, however, shows that he was not as conciliatory as Apollinaris, Melito, or Athenagoras.

11

Melito
of Sardis

From Laodicea, Marcus Aurelius would have gone on to Smyrna through either Ephesus or Sardis. A monument to the deified Faustina and at least two of her daughters presumably points toward a visit to Ephesus: "To the divine Faustina and to Fadilla and [Annia] Faustina the emperor's daughters."[1] Perhaps he also visited Sardis, where as at Pergamum there is a dedication to the deified Faustina.[2]

In any event, loyalty to the emperor was often expressed on stone at Sardis. A second-century inscription refers to a "priest of the Augusti and [hierophant] of the mysteries."[3] Somewhat later the city is termed "autochthonous and sacred to the gods, first city of Hellas and metropolis of Asia and all Lydia, keeper of the two *koinon* temples of the Augusti."[4] Such loyalty brought rewards. The proconsul of Asia considered it "most just" that the attitude of certain citizens "should receive the recognition of a subsidy toward their loyalty toward the Augusti *(eusebeian tōn Sebastōn)*."[5] The subsidy does not mean that their loyalty was not genuine.

Another example of loyalty may be found in regard to the Hellenistic temple of Artemis at Sardis. When it was finally rebuilt in the late second century it was rededicated to Antoninus Pius and his wife Faustina. Part of a colossal head of this emperor has been found there. Conceivably the temple was dedicated when the emperor Lucius Verus visited the city in 166 and apparently dedicated the gymnasium next to the synagogue.[6]

A pedestal inscription set up in 212 for the athlete Marcus Aurelius Demostratos Damas includes mention of his victories at Sardis in the Chrysanthinon and at Pergamon in the Augusteia before stating that "at Rome in the victory games of our lords the emperors Antoninus and Commodus he was crowned with a golden crown and received a prize of gold." These games took place at the end of 176 after the emperors' visit to Asia. In addition, he was "honored by the god Marcus and the god Commodus with the native citizenship of Alexandria and with the athletic presidencies named below." These include the assembly of Asia at Sardis, the assembly of Asia at Tralles, and the Alexandrian citizenship. He seems to have been a citizen not only of Sardis and Alexandria but also (among others) of Nicomedia, Ephesus, Smyrna, Miletus, and Pergamum in Asia.[7] At the least, the inscription shows how closely the official world of western Asia related itself to Marcus Aurelius and Commodus.

The Apology of Melito

The summer of 176 is the most likely date for the petition to the emperor by Melito, the Christian bishop of Sardis. The most important fragments of the petition are preserved in the *Church History* of Eusebius.[8] The bishop held the thesis that since Christianity originated around the same time as the Roman empire and was somehow responsible for its success, the emperors could preserve themselves by protecting it. Melito's synchronism surely owes something to Luke's mention of "a decree from Caesar Augustus" at the time of Jesus' birth, though his interpretation is wrong.[9]

The occasion of the petition is what Melito calls "new decrees throughout Asia" or "this new ordinance, not fit to be employed even against barbarian enemies." It was common at this time to refer to enemies of Christianity as barbarians; thus the *Acts of the Gallican Martyrs* insisted that the devil was stirring up "wild and barbarous tribes" in Gaul (see chapter 13).[10] The author, perhaps Irenaeus, knows that barbarians live at Lyons; Irenaeus himself definitely states that he lives among Celts and usually speaks a barbarian language.[11] Melito's complaint also answers an appeal like that of Celsus to help the emperor against barbarian enemies. He replies that Christians themselves are being treated like barbarian enemies. Just so, the Gallican martyrs were being treated like enemies of the state, and as in Asia informers were trying to seize the property of Christians.[12] Tatian then uses the term of himself and others. (The question of "barbarians" will be discussed in chapter 13.)

Melito wonders if "this new decree" can come from the just emperor, especially since informers are relying on it. Hadrian, he points out, had forbidden "innovation" or novelty in attacks on Christians.[13] Is he blaming the new proconsul of Asia, whoever he was? The proconsul necessarily took orders from the emperor.

What is the "new decree" or "ordinances"? Apparently some important change is taking place, and the older prohibition of search or popular denunciation of Christians (Trajan, Hadrian) is being abandoned. Thus in Gaul mob action was to run unchecked, with a definite search for Christians.[14] The anti-Christian writer Celsus says that Christians may wander in concealment but they are hunted down under penalty of death.[15] A few years later the *Acts of Apollonius* state that by decree of the Senate "there are not to be Christians."[16]

Apparently there was some hunting for Christians after, and perhaps because of, the revolt of Avidius Cassius. Dio insists on the mildness and benevolence of Marcus Aurelius toward the conspirators and their families, though on the other hand he insisted on the death penalty for Roman citizens arrested as Christians in Gaul.[17] Conceivably in 176, with coins bearing the inscription CLEMENTIA AUGUSTI, Christians still hoped for a conciliatory response. The hope vanished when the Gallican martyrs were put to death.

Like Apollinaris and Athenagoras, Melito expresses firm loyalty to the emperor and his successor. This is a rhetorical topic of the time. Menander Rhetor offers counsel to "say a prayer requesting God that his kingdom should continue for a very long time, be given in succession to his sons and handed on to his family."[18] The kind of speech Menander had in mind was the *Roman Oration* by Aelius Aristides, delivered in 143, and it ends thus: "Let all the gods and children of the gods be invoked to grant that this empire and this city flourish forever . . . and that the great governor and his sons be preserved and obtain blessings for all."[19] The "great governor" is Antoninus Pius and the "sons" are Marcus Aurelius and Lucius Verus, adopted in 138.[20]

Similiar expressions occur in inscriptions, especially in Asia Minor, and reveal the same attitude in every period of the empire. An inscription from 5 B.C. mentions prayers to Augustus "on behalf of the sons."[21] Prayers are offered "for the safety of the rulers and gods and the perpetual continuance of their rule."[22]

The orator Aelius Aristides (Vatican)

In Melito's time there was a special reason for emphasizing the succession. He notes that Marcus Aurelius has "become the successor whom men desired" and expresses the hope that such he "will continue to be, along with the boy."[23] The boy must be Commodus, and presumably Melito has in mind the revolt of Avidius Cassius. Both Melito and Athenagoras refer to Marcus Aurelius and his one heir, but while a little later Athenagoras explicitly addresses the two rulers in the plural, Melito writes to Marcus alone and speaks of his son's future reign with him. The mention of future joint rule thus points to a date after the revolt of Avidius Cassius but before November 27, 176, when Commodus became co-emperor.

Melito approaches the succession by emphasizing history, another theme of rhetoric. Menander commends discussion of the emperor's family and its achievements.[24] Melito praises all the legitimate emperors and treats them as related by family ties. He speaks to Marcus of "your forefather Augustus" and notes that "from that time Roman power grew into something great and brilliant." The correlation impressed later theologians, and we find it again in Hippolytus' *Commentary on Daniel* (4.9) as well as Origen's treatise *Against Celsus* (2.30) and the works of Eusebius. Theophilus too ascribes the rise of Roman power to God, but presumably after some pagan source sets it under the last of the kings.[25]

Melito is modifying the common Roman view that Roman piety had led to Roman power, which appears in Posidonius, Polybius, Dio of Halicarnassus, Livy, and the Augustan poets, not to mention Plutarch, Pliny, and Aulus Gellius.[26] He boldly claims for Christianity what others claimed for pagan religion. The Christian religion is not natively Roman, but it has supported Rome. Though this "philosophy at first flourished among barbarians," it entered the Roman world in the time of Augustus and flourished along with the empire. The emperors honored Christianity "as they did the other religions," and "since the principate of Augustus . . . all things have been splendid and glorious in accordance with the prayers of all." There may be an allusion to the prayers of the Christian legion, but Melito is generalizing after apologists for pagan piety and refining with rhetoric. Even his critic Tertullian noticed his "elegant and declamatory mind."[27]

Melito cannot avoid the tradition that Nero and Domitian were persecutors, but he blames their "evil advisers," not the emperors themselves. In this respect he is less critical, or more tactful, than Marcus Aurelius was.[28] His praise of "your grandfather Hadrian" and "your father" (Antoninus Pius) shows that the emperor and his ancestors deserve the praise he is glad to supply. It also takes up a note often sounded in the inscriptions of Marcus Aurelius when they trace his legitimate ancestry back to Nerva.

Judaism at Sardis

In the third century, and presumably in the second, there was a large and important synagogue in the civic center of Sardis. The third-century building contained a marble table, evidently used as a lectern, with large Roman eagles, taken from some other edifice, on each side. By the third century, and perhaps earlier, the Jewish community thus expressed its loyalty to the emperor and his armed forces.

Envy of this synagogue, obviously highly favored in the city, may help explain the vehement hostility of the Christian bishop Melito toward the Jewish people, as set forth in his *Paschal Homily*. In its present form the synagogue is obviously too late to have influenced him.[29] Presumably the third-century building did not suddenly appear, however, but emerged from an older establishment which Melito may have found oppressive. Melito did not join the contemporary apologists Apollinaris and Miltiades in writing treatises against the Jews, but his *Paschal Homily* is so hostile that it more than makes up for the lack.

Christianity at Sardis

Christianity first appears at Sardis in one of the letters to "the seven churches of Asia" in the Apocalypse of John (Rev. 1–3). These were sent to three churches on a road northward by the Aegean Sea (Ephesus, Smyrna, and Pergamum) and four on the road from Pergamum to the southeast (Thyatira, Sardis, Philadelphia, and Laodicea). The church at Sardis has "the name of being alive" but is really dead, except for "a few names" of people who are undefiled by sin. John's charges are too vague for exact exegesis.[30]

We do not know why Ignatius of Antioch, who passed through Asia on his way to Troas and Rome, did not write a letter to the church at Sardis. He did write to both Philadelphia and Smyrna but did not even mention Sardis, which lies between the two cities. When Sardis comes on the Christian stage, however, its literary culture is already highly developed and its bishop is an important personage in the church of Asia.

Melito and Montanism

Like Apollinaris, Melito took an active part in church life, as fragments of his writings prove. Tertullian in his lost Montanist treatise *On Ecstasy* criticized Melito's "elegant and rhetorical mind" but admitted that many non-Montanists viewed him as a prophet.[31] The passage shows that Melito was hostile toward Montanism but renowned for rhetoric, perhaps primarily of the kind found in his paschal homily. The idea that he was a prophet might well come from his rhetorical habit of speaking in Christ's name in sermons.

The Controversy Over Easter Observance

Melito was also involved in the Easter controversy, but on the Asian side opposed to Apollinaris. Polycrates of Ephesus lists him among the "great stars" who observed the 14th day (of Nisan) for the Passover, "in accordance with the Gospel." He was named as "Melito the eunuch, who in every respect lived in the Holy Spirit, who lies in Sardis awaiting the visitation (of Christ) from the heavens when he will rise from the dead."[32]

Two more fragments come from Eusebius. From a treatise *On the Passover* we learn that "under Servilius Paulus proconsul of Asia, at the time when Sagaris was a martyr, there was much discussion in Laodicea over the Passover, which fell at the right time in those days, and this was written."[33] Unfortunately Servilius Paulus (if the name is right) is one of the few unknown proconsuls of Asia, and Eusebius' excerpt itself leads nowhere.[34] Clement of Alexandria wrote a work *On the Pascha* in which he quoted both Melito and Irenaeus, but it is lost.[35]

Other Writings

The other Eusebian fragment shows that Melito visited Palestine and obtained a list of "the books of the old covenant" from which he provided six books of "extracts" related to "our Savior and our whole faith."[36] They consist of five books of Moses, Joshua, Judges, Ruth, four books of Kings, two of Chronicles, the Psalms, then three books by Solomon ("Proverbs also called Wisdom," Ecclesiastes, Song of Songs), Job, the prophets Isaiah, Jeremiah, the Twelve in a single scroll, Daniel, and Ezekiel; and Esdras. P. Katz argues rather convincingly that Melito intended to list 22 books and must have meant that Samuel, Kings, and Chronicles were one book each, as in a similar list by Origen.[37] Origen adds Esther and combines Ruth with Judges, like most other witnesses counting 22 books.[38] It may be significant that Melito did not inquire about the books at the Jewish synagogue in the center of Sardis.

Fragments of Melito's other writings from Origen are not highly informative (see chapter 21), though he does refer to Melito's work "That God is corporeal," perhaps the same as what Eusebius calls *On the Corporeal God.*[39] The term "corporeal" may refer to the incarnation.[40]

Possibly more significant is a fragment *On Baptism.*[41] Poetry is closer than philosophy to the fragment, for like all Melito's work it is the product of a rhetorician who was prone to allude to the poets. Such a possible setting favors the genuineness of the fragment, as does the parallel from Theophilus to which we shall presently turn.[42]

Melito argues that Christ was bathed in the river Jordan because of the parallels in all nature for such beneficial dipping or bathing. (1) Metals are brightened or smelted with water. The earth bathes in rains and rivers. Egypt is flooded by the Nile. The air is bathed by rain. The rainbow bathes as well. (2) Similarly both sun and moon are "baptized" when they take baths in the ocean. The sun sets into the cold water and rises refreshed. Moon and stars follow the sun. (3) All this is true of Christ. "King of heavens and Captain of creation, Sun of rising who appeared to those in Hades and to mortals in the world, he also alone arose a Sun from heaven."

The first group of analogies is highly similar to what Theophilus says about chrism (at baptism) when he points out its usefulness for boats, towers, houses, babies, athletes, works of art, and the air, "anointed, so to speak, by light and wind."[43] Both authors are creating encomiums in the form prized by rhetoricians: Lucian wrote one on the common fly. Melito supplies what Tertullian, perhaps with reference to this very work, criticizes as "praises of water."[44] The use of such rhetorical examples parallels the general practice of second-century writers.

Finally, there is Melito's famous paschal homily, long known only from fragments but published from papyri in 1940 and thereafter. It is important not only for its vigorous use of rhetoric but also for its Christian content and its hostility toward Judaism. A slogan of his was later to be famous: "God has been murdered, the King of Israel has been slain by an Israelite right hand" (sec. 96). Apart from this overheated rhetoric, one wonders how many aspects of Christian thought and practice are not fully represented in the writings of the apologists. Perhaps they neglected important aspects of their beliefs as they wrote the extant apologetic texts.

The theology Melito expresses in the homily, as Hall has pointed out after Campbell Bonner, is "naive modalism" notably in "God has been murdered." That is to say that Christ is God more fully than even Ignatius of Antioch thought. Melito certainly calls Christ "Son," but he also calls him "Father" (sec. 9). We find this kind of emphasis in a passage that has formal parallels in Theophilus, though the theological meaning is quite different. Melito refers to Christ the kinds of appellations Theophilus uses of the ineffable God the Creator. Theophilus calls God "all things," while Melito uses the expression in speaking of Christ.[45]

Such Christological expressions are remote from Justin or Theophilus, though perhaps not from Tatian. They allow us to see the diversity among the apologetic theologians of the second century. In addition, Melito was a Quartodeciman and did not keep Pascha with the bishops of Rome and Hierapolis.

It may be, however, that Melito was not very unorthodox. Clement of Alexandria shows us how such terms as his could be based on scripture, citing Isaiah 9:6 for the names "wonderful Counselor, mighty God, eternal Father, Prince of peace," and exclaims, "O the mighty God, O the perfect child: the Son in the Father and the Father in the Son." The paradoxes of the prophet are to be understood in relation to the paradoxes of the Fourth Evangelist.[46] In addition, a Roman writer of the late second century cites him with Irenaeus as proclaiming Christ as God and man.[47]

Related to the theological diversity is the literary diversity reflected in the titles of Melito's works as given by Eusebius. Unfortunately, as Hall notes, there are errors in Eusebius' text and we are rarely able to tell what Melito wrote about. One exception is the work *On the Devil and the Apocalypse of John,* in which he discussed this Asian book that had mentioned Christians in Sardis and explicitly identified "the great dragon, the ancient serpent," as the one called "Devil and Satan" (Rev. 12:9; 20:2, 7).

Considering the differences between the theologies and politics of Melito and Apollinaris, it is impressive that they could unite in appealing for the favorable treatment of Christians. This issue must have been more important in the lives of Christian leaders than details of the theologies still being worked out.

12
Athenagoras of Athens

From Asia the emperor Marcus Aurelius and his children went on to Athens, where like Hadrian (and Lucius Verus)[1] he was initiated into the Eleusinian mysteries by the priest L. Memmius and the *hierophantis* Eisidote,[2] perhaps with the aid of Herodes Atticus. He also established endowed chairs for philosophers, to be chosen by Herodes, and rhetoricians.[3]

At this time another Christian, Athenagoras, may have presented a *presbeia* or "embassy" to him and Commodus,[4] and thus renewed the approach of Quadratus and Aristides to Hadrian. Hadrian too had toured the empire and had been initiated into the mysteries at Eleusis when Christians approached him. There are two reasons for setting Athenagoras' *Embassy* at this point in Marcus' journey. First, the Arethas manuscript of 914 calls Athenagoras "an Athenian Christian philosopher." Second, the work itself is addressed to "the emperors Marcus Aurelius Antoninus and Lucius Aurelius Com[m]odus, victors over the Armenians and the Sarmatians, and, above all, philosophers." Similar titles appear in Egyptian papyri dated between 176 and 179 in which both emperors are called victors over "Armenians, Medes, Parthians, Germans, and Sarmatians." Presumably a later scribe omitted the three middle epithets.[5] Father and son share the kingdom, and Christians pray that the son will succeed to the father's throne (37.2; cf. 18.2). It seems likely, as Barnes suggested, that the "embassy" was presented to the emperors at Athens in the early autumn of 176. Neither of them is called Augustus, a title both bore after the new year. To be sure, Commodus was first hailed as Imperator at Rome on November 27, 176.[6] Presumably Athenagoras either anticipated the event or revised his preface after it.

The *Embassy* expresses a conciliatory loyalist approach close to that of Apollinaris and Melito. It reflects slight acquaintance with predecessors or contemporaries, and in turn it finds no echo before Methodius in the early fourth century. Such neglect is not unique, for the *Meditations* of the emperor too are not mentioned before the fourth century.[7] Athenagoras writes after Melito, for he insists that hostile crowds are going beyond robbery to the murder of Christians (1.3). As a loyal subject of the emperors he asks them for a rescript ordering judges (normally provincial governors) to examine the conduct of Christians and "not pay attention to meaningless labels or to false charges from the prosecution" (2.3). His adulation of the emperors goes beyond Melito's when not only does he say that "all things have been subjected to you, father and son who have received your kingdom from above," but he compares their reign with that of God and his inseparable Logos-Son, praying "that the succession to the kingdom may proceed from father to son, as is most just, and that your reign may grow and increase as all become subject to you" (18.2; 37.2).

Such statements are typical of patriotic oratory, as we have seen when discussing Melito (chapter 11). Athenagoras may even have suspected that he would be competing for the emperors' attention with the famous Aelius Aristides, who had just spoken before them at Smyrna and the next year would ask them to help Smyrna after an earthquake. Aristides begins that oration by calling the Augusti "greatest of kings," while later he compares petition to "the most divine rulers" with prayer to the gods.[8] The rhetorician Menander refers to Aristides' address when he describes the *logos presbeutikos* or "ambassador's speech." Like the "crown speech," it is an encomium on the emperor, but it should

> amplify at every point the topic of the emperor's humanity, saying that he is merciful and pities those who make petition to him, and that God sent him down to earth because he knew that he was merciful and a benefactor of mankind.

The speaker refers to "the present misfortune, how the city has fallen to the ground" (because of earthquake) and asks the emperor to restore it in response to "the children and the women, the adult men and the aged," who "pour forth their tears and plead with you to be compassionate." The description ends thus: "Ask him to deign *(neusai)* to receive the decree."[9] Millar claims that Athenagoras himself provided the title *presbeia* or "embassy" to show that he was adhering to this form of speech, since he refers to petitioners before the emperors and at the end asks them to "nod *(epineusate)* your royal heads in assent" (16.2; 37.2).[10] It is barely possible that something remotely resembling the address was presented before Marcus Aurelius and Commodus.

Another political aspect of his praise of the emperors may be due to historical circumstance as well as rhetorical convention. Menander certainly recommends treating them as lovers of learning and philosophers but mere convention may not explain Athenagoras' six references to imperial intelligence *(synesis)* and two to their devotion to scholarship *(philomathe-statoi)*. Perhaps he was acute enough to know that even Faustina had expressed doubts about the wit of Commodus, though he did not discuss her recent deification. With similar discretion he refers to the deification of Hadrian's favorite Antinous and tactfully explains it as due to "the philanthropy shown by your ancestors to their subjects" (30.2).[11] By adoption Marcus was Hadrian's grandson, as we have seen from Melito's discussion of him. Thus Athenagoras not only looks forward to the future of the succession but backward. He is willing to praise all the Roman emperors, or most of them.

Still more must be said about Athenagoras' notion that

> as all things have been subordinated to you, father and son, who have received the kingdom from above—"for the king's life is in God's hand," says the prophetic Spirit—so all things have been subjected to the one God and the Word from him, known to be his inseparable Son. (18.2)

This is not only rhetoric but theology. The quotation from the prophetic Spirit comes from Proverbs 21:1, while the rest of the passage echoes the New Testament. First Corinthians 15:25–28 teaches the eschatological subordination of everything to the Son and the Father, while in Matthew 28:18 the risen Christ states that "all power in heaven and on earth" has been given him. The emperors' power is also of divine origin, however, not only according to Romans 13 but more specifically in John 19:11, where Jesus says, "You would have no power over me if it had not been given you *from above.*" Clearly, then, Athenagoras is willing to use Christological terms in reference to the imperial father and son. He thus anticipates the ideas of Eusebius in the fourth century.[12]

Athenagoras says he is writing a defense of Christian teaching against three charges: atheism, Thyestean feasts, and Oedipean intercourse (2.6–3.1).[13] He devotes chapters 4–30 to theism and atheism, 31–37 to the more sinister accusations. It has been claimed that the charges about infanticide and promiscuity first arose around this time, out of an oration by the emperor's old (and deceased) tutor Fronto as reported in the *Octavius* of the later apologist Minucius Felix (9.5–7).[14] What Minucius Felix ascribes to Fronto, however, includes only comments about the Christians' incestuous banquet, not their practice of infanticide. Their meal was the object of criticism as early as Justin's *Apology* (1.26.7), probably even from the time of Trajan.

The *Embassy* as a School Text

The environment of the third apologist of 176 lies in the school rather than the church. Athenagoras writes as a "philosopher," not as a bishop, although he has a good deal to say not only about Christian doctrine but also about Christian morals. The theological content of his *Embassy* is arranged in a scholastic manner, which A. J. Malherbe analyzed in relation to the *Instruction* of the Middle Platonist Albinus.[15] This introductory manual begins with a discussion of philosophy as such and continues with dialectics (4–6 = Athenagoras 4–6), theoretics (7–26 = Athenagoras 8–10; cf. 13), and ethics (27–36 = Athenagoras 11–12). Athenagoras' refutation is thus arranged in relation to the same topics. This kind of treatment is what we expect from an apologist devoted to philosophy and literature. He interprets Christianity as a philosophy for a philosopher-emperor.

Athenagoras and Pagan Culture

Proverbs

Athenagoras has studied philosophy, but he is essentially a grammarian, proud of his erudition. Greek education began with proverbs, and it is natural to find them in Athenagoras. One is a tale from the *Iliad:* "Sleep and death are twins" (12.3); another is a "sentence": "Those who test the quality of honey and whey can tell if the whole is good by tasting one small sample" (12.4). In one instance a proverb is identified as such: "The harlot presumes to teach the chaste woman," and in the same passage adulterers and pederasts are said to live "like fish" because "they swallow up whoever comes their way, the stronger possessing the weaker" (34.1, 3). Athenagoras' usage is typical of the late second century. The *Meditations* of the emperor are full of proverbial expressions, often repeated from one book to another. Lucian and Tatian, as we shall see, use them too.

Poets

Like other apologists, especially after Justin, Athenagoras offers frequent quotations from the poets and allusions to them. Most of his quotations come from Homer, seventeen from the *Iliad* against only three from the *Odyssey,* and two of the three are closely connected.[16] There are also two from the Orphic literature (see below), three from Hesiod, and four from unidentified tragedians; one apiece from Aeschylus, Pseudo-Sophocles, and Pindar; and eight from the more popular moralist Euripides. Because of his serious purpose Athenagoras quotes nothing from the comic poets. Like Marcus Aurelius, he probably thought that much comic poetry was vulgar.[17]

Literature of and on Religion

He also provides six lines from the Jewish *Sibylline Oracles* (3.108–13). Conceivably he was aware that in 162 the emperor Lucius Verus had visited, or was expected to visit, the temple of the Sibyl at Erythrae, not far from Smyrna.[18] Perhaps Marcus Aurelius and Commodus followed in his footsteps after fourteen years.

Finally, he cites the theosophical literature of his time for pagan ideas about the gods and the beginning of the world. He is the first known author to mention Hermes Trismegistus, who like Alexander the Great "links his own family with the gods" (28.6), for example in the popular tractate *Asclepius,* where the "four men" Hermes, Asclepius, Tat, and Hammon are in "the divine presence of God." More important, he shows definite acquaintance with one or more of the Orphic rhapsodies, with their mythical portrayal, older than Homer, of the origin of the universe.[19]

Historians on Religion

Athenagoras' use of Herodotus is especially interesting. Like Tatian he cites the historian for the date of Hesiod and Homer (17.2), but he also uses him as an authority on Egyptian religion. Eight quotations and three references come from Herodotus' study of Egypt in his second book and serve chiefly to show that the Egyptian "gods" were human. Such direct use was unusual, but Athenagoras was relying on Herodotus because of his critical attitude toward Egyptian religion. Perhaps he knew that an Egyptian magician had accompanied the emperor by the Danube.

He mentions but does not quote "Alexander the son of Philip in his letter to his mother" for the Egyptian doctrine that "the gods were once men" and that Alexander "links his family with the gods" (28.1, 6). The letter was usually ascribed to a certain Leon of Pella, mentioned by the second-century Christians Tatian, Clement, and Tertullian, and later by Minucius Felix.[20]

Athenagoras also appeals to "Apollodorus in his book *Concerning the Gods*" for Egyptian theology, and Geffcken supposed that this was his ultimate source for nearly all his "history of religions" materials (28.7).[21] It seems likely, however, that Athenagoras could refer to Apollodorus without stealing his sources.

Historians of Art

Several of the apologists have something to say about art history. Tatian, as we shall see, found Greek sculpture objectionable and used literary sources to attack the models used by sculptors. Athenagoras seems less hostile but when he lists the originators of various arts he is trying to show how recent and artificial Greek ideas about the gods are (17.3–4). He explains how "tracing out shadows" led to painting and relief modeling, which then were followed by sculpture and molding, and he finally provides a brief list of sculptors who made famous statues of gods and goddesses.

There are errors, of course, as Geffcken insisted after Förster and Kalk-mann,[22] and Athenagoras' statements are not as valuable as those supplied by Pliny in the 35th book of his *Natural History*. Both authors agree (Pliny says "all agree"), however, that "painting began with the outlining of a man's shadow," that Cleanthes of Corinth was very early, and that the role of "the maid of Corinth" was important.[23] Variations in names prove not Athenagoras' ignorance but his use of variant tradition.[24]

He also knows something about art in his own time, for he refers to gilt bronze statues of a contemporary Neryllinus as adorning the city of Troy, while there are statues of Alexander (of Abonuteichos) and (Peregrinus) Proteus at Parium. His basic interest lies not in art, however, but in attacking images (26.3–5). As Sciveletto pointed out, he uses the erudition of a grammarian to denigrate Hellenism.[25]

Philosophers

Athenagoras certainly knows something about philosophy from his reading of Plato, but he does not hesitate to use secondary literature. In his discussion of the doctrine of God in chapter 6 there is an explicit reference to *Doxai* or "opinions" of philosophers, one of the collections of opinions edited by Diels in his *Doxographi Graeci*. He uses such a work for the views of Aristotle and the Stoics. It is barely possible that an echo of the doxography underlies a textual error. Athenagoras is quoting a couple of lines from Empedocles which also occur in the doxography of Aetius and in Sextus Empiricus. The doxography discusses Epicurus just before Empedocles, and this may help explain why the text of Athenagoras reads not "Nestis, who with her tears fills the springs *(teggei krounōma)* of mortals" (a line from Empedocles) but the nonsensical *t' Epikourou nōmai*. If there is anything to this suggestion, the error must have been made by Athenagoras himself, nodding over his text (22.2).[26]

He also relies on a doxography for the early Pythagoreans Philolaus, Lysis, and Opsimus (6.1).[27] It is not the work by Aetius which the apologists usually employ but a Pythagorean numerological treatise. To show that "from time immemorial, and not only in our own day, evil has habitually opposed virtue" he begins with the example of Pythagoras, burned to death with three hundred companions, and then adds Heraclitus, banished from Ephesus; Democritus banished from Abdera and accused of being mad; and Socrates, put to death by the Athenians (31.2).[28] Justin had already insisted that Socrates and Heraclitus were Christians, even if regarded as godless, and later added the name of Musonius Rufus to those who were "hated and murdered"—he should have said "exiled."[29] Athenagoras does not regard them as Christians but describes the situation more accurately, perhaps relying on Pythagorean sources.

The Church and the World

Athenagoras tells nothing about the church of Athens, though it had drawn the attention of Dionysius of Corinth only a few years earlier. This bishop, obviously more prominent than his Athenian colleague, claimed that Dionysius the Areopagite, converted by Paul (Acts 17:34), was the first bishop of Athens.[30]

He says little about the society around him except as he denounces pagan religiosity. On the other hand, he does speak apologetically about the social life of Christians, whose lives are so completely free of lust that in liturgical ceremonies they exchange only one kiss; more might be "pleasurable." Marriage is exclusively for procreation, as Justin had said, but many Christians avoid sexual intercourse entirely and regard a second marriage as "respectable adultery" (32–33). They view pagan prostitution as disgusting and reject cannibalism as based on murder. Those who accuse them of such crimes are lying, and

> if someone asks them whether they have seen what they report, none has the effrontery to say that they have. Further, we have slaves, some many, some few, and it is impossible to escape their observation; but not one of them has ever told such monstrous lies about us.

Christians do not attend gladiatorial shows or fights with wild beasts, nor do they practice abortion or the "exposure" of unwanted infants (34–35).

Two of Athenagoras' main claims could have been questioned. First, Justin states that under torture slaves did accuse Christians of crimes, as was later the case for the martyrs of Lyons and Vienne.[31] Second, while Tatian and Theophilus also denounce gladiatorial shows, Valentinian Gnostics were willing to witness them.[32] Presumably, however, Athenagoras did not count such heretics as Christians.

It is possible that what he says about marriage has been influenced by the Montanist movement, which had spread as close to Athens as Thrace.[33] But while Montanists forbade second marriages and commended continence, ordinary Christians often upheld the same views.

Athenagoras' Doctrine of God

Athenagoras' theology was deeply influenced by the popular Platonism which he knew well. Like Albinus he conveniently summarizes: God is "uncreated, eternal, invisible, impassible, incomprehensible, and infinite." He "can be apprehended by mind and reason alone." He is "encompassed by light, beauty, spirit, and indescribable power." He created and adorned the universe and now rules it (10).

He was not the first apologist to identify God as Mind. Philo sometimes spoke about God as "the active cause, the most pure and unsullied Mind of the universe,"[34] and the Christian apologist Aristides called him "wholly Intellect."[35] According to Clement such a doctrine is Platonic.[36] Others did not make this identification. In the *Corpus Hermeticum* (2.14) we read that "God is not Mind but the cause of the existence of mind," and Theophilus said, "If I call him Mind, I speak (only) of his intelligence" (1.3). They thus tried not to be unduly precise.

A remarkable feature of Athenagoras' discussion of God is the proof he provides for the existence of only one God (ch. 8). The two preceding chapters have cited one spurious text from Sophocles and the philosophers who favored this belief, from the Pythagoreans onward. Now he provides "the reasoning that supports our faith." The argument seems to go as follows:

> Two gods (or more) would have to be in (1) the same category or (2) different categories. (1) As gods, uncreated, they could not belong to the same category. (1.1) Against Platonic doctrine: created things belong to the same categories because made after models; uncreated things are dissimilar. (1.2) God is not composite and divisible into complementary parts (i.e., gods). Against Stoic doctrine: he is "uncreated, impassible, and indivisible." (2) As gods they could not be independent. (2.1) The Maker of the world is above and around the spherical creation and governs it, and therefore there is no place for other god(s). (2.1.1) Such a god could not be in the world since it belongs to God. (2.1.2) Such a god could not be around the world since God is above it. (2.2) Such a god could not be above the world and God, in another world and around it. (2.2.1) For if he is in or around another world, he is not around us, since the Maker rules our world, and (2.2.2) his power is not great, since he is in a limited place [so he is not God]. (2.3) And if he is not in or around another world, he does not exist, since there is no place for him or anything for him to do. Therefore there is one God, the Creator of the world.

The argument apparently contains echoes of chapters 3–4 of Pseudo-Aristotle, *On Melissus Xenophanes Gorgias,* an eclectic treatise from the Roman period.[37] The chapters printed by Diels under "Xenophanes" begin with the assertion that "what comes into existence must come either from like or from unlike" and move on to conclude that God is eternal. Then "if he is most powerful of all, he must be one. For if there were two or more, he would not be most powerful and best of all." The author then considers motion and shape (spherical) in regard to God, though not the "place" on which Athenagoras lays emphasis. There is no reason to suppose that the teaching goes back to Xenophanes, but it is one more link in the chain that binds the name of this pre-Socratic philosopher to early Christian monotheism.[38] Later on, a simplified version of the argument appears in Irenaeus and Tertullian.[39]

The Logos

Athenagoras calls the Son the Mind, Logos, and Sophia of the Father and claims that he is "united in power" with him "yet distinguished in rank." For him, as for Justin, the Son is the "first being begotten by the Father." The expression may reflect a doctrine of a primal Logos-Sophia, based on what "the prophetic Spirit" said in Proverbs 8:22: "The Lord made me the beginning of his ways for his works" (24.2; 10.2–5).

The Son is Logos of the Father "in ideal form *(ideai)* and energy *(energeiai)* in relation to the creation." Here Athenagoras' terms recall the Platonic *idea* and the Aristotelian *energeia,* as Schoedel notes. The language is derived from philosophical doctrines.

Does Athenagoras really have a Christology? It is hard to say, since there is only one possible allusion to the incarnation. "If a god assumes flesh by divine dispensation, is he then a slave of lust?" Probably such a God, the Logos, did assume flesh; but while Athenagoras cites teaching from the Gospels he does not ascribe it to Jesus (11.2; 21.4; 32.2).

The Spirit: No Relation to Montanism

We have seen that there is no reason to relate Athenagoras' ideas of marriage to the Montanist movement, which in his time was spreading westward from Phrygia. A few aspects of his view of the Spirit resemble theirs. First, the divine Spirit moved the Old Testament prophets "in the ecstasy of their thoughts" and blew through them like musical instruments (9.1). The prophetic Spirit spoke in the name of the Son and said, "The Lord made me the beginning of his ways for his works" (Prov. 8:22). To be sure, the passage in Proverbs concerns Sophia,[40] not the Son, but Justin had already taken it as a reference to the Logos[41] and Athenagoras follows him. "This same holy Spirit, which is active in those who speak prophetically, we regard as an emanation of God like a ray of the sun" (10.4) or "like fire from fire" (24.2). Here "emanation" echoes what Wisdom 7:25 says about Sophia, but Athenagoras adds the comparisons. Philo had already used such language of *pneuma,* while the comparison with both fire and light occurs in Justin—in regard to the Logos, not the Spirit.[42] The Montanists also used the comparison, at least in the time of Tertullian,[43] but its appearance in Athenagoras does not make him a Montanist sympathizer.

Beyond that, the Spirit is also the source of the unity between Father and Son. "The Son is in the Father and the Father in the Son by a powerful unity [or, by the unity and power] of spirit [or, of the Spirit]" (10.2). The language is certainly Johannine (John 10:38), and Athenagoras may also be thinking of the Paraclete sayings in John, in which the Father will send the Holy Spirit in Jesus' name (14:26) or Jesus himself will send him from the Father (15:26). One might also remember 2 Corinthians 13:14, with its reference to "the grace of the Lord Jesus Christ and the love of God and the fellowship *(koinōnia)* of the Holy Spirit." But Athenagoras never mentions Jesus Christ.

The Trinity

The explicit doctrine of the Trinity in Athenagoras is probably the oldest we possess. He speaks of "God the Father, God the Son, and the Holy Spirit," indicating that Christians "proclaim both their power in their unity and their diversity in rank" (6.1). There is unity between Son and Father and communion between Father and Son, while God, his Logos, and the Holy Spirit are "united in power yet distinguished in rank" (10.5 = 24.2; 12.3). The relation of Spirit to Father and Son is still imprecise, as would be expected in this early period.

Angels and Demons

Athenagoras' theological doctrine also contains "a host of angels and ministers whom God, the maker and fashioner of the world, set in their places through the Logos coming from him, commanding them to be concerned with the planets, the heavens, and the world with what is in it, and with the good order of all" (10.5). Unfortunately, these angelic administrators included a spirit who was opposed to God because untrustworthy, and he led others to "violate both their own nature and their office." As "prince of matter" he operated wickedly when governing the material world, while subordinates, "stationed at the first firmament," lusted after virgins and succumbed to the flesh (24.5). They fell from the heavens and cannot ascend again. Their offspring were the giants, whose souls are "the demons who wander about the world" (25.1). In turn the demons, eager to delude mankind, invade the thoughts of "the many" and persuade them to offer meat and blood to themselves (27.2). Polytheism and idolatry alike are delusions.

Athenagoras on the Resurrection

At the end of the *Embassy* Athenagoras explains that many philosophers teach that bodies will rise (again) and that nothing in Pythagoras or Plato opposes such a notion; he proposes to discuss the subject later. It is no surprise, then, that the manuscripts of the *Embassy* also contain an apologetic treatise *On the Resurrection of Corpses,* whether by Athenagoras or not. Though the argument seems to follow Peripatetic lines, not Platonic, this first attempt to "prove" the resurrection of corpses is fairly superficial, whoever wrote it. My arguments that it was not Athenagoras[44] are not fully conclusive, as several scholars have insisted.[45]

The author's encounter with medical literature possesses some interest. Critics of a doctrine of physical resurrection were urging that if fish consumed a dead Christian sailor and in turn were eaten by fishermen, the particles of the corpses would be blended. Whose body would rise? Our author replies that the human body does not digest, i.e., assimilate, unnatural food but eliminates it in one of the three stages of the digestive process. Only natural food can be digested. People cannot digest people.

Galen had already explained, notably in his treatise *On the Natural Faculties*, just how "the threefold purification and secretion" works. Only "natural" food is digested. The Christian writer follows Galen or someone like him. Unfortunately the argument requires the claim that since cannibalism is unnatural animals cannot digest the flesh of their own kind. Galen, like more skeptical philosophers, rejected the claim as untrue.[46] If Galen ever saw this pamphlet he must have considered it distasteful.

Achievements of the Apologists of 176

By their petitions to the emperor in the year 176 the Christian apologists accomplished very little in the political sphere. Marcus Aurelius found their claims unimpressive and ordered the execution of Roman citizens from Lyons and Vienne. Around this time, moreover, the court physician Galen criticized Christians for their traditionalism and their lack of rational proof for doctrines. He thus stood close to Marcus Aurelius.

On the other hand, unlike the emperor, he praised them for their contempt of death and the way in which both men and women pursued self-discipline, self-control, and justice.[47] Walzer notes that Galen is "the first pagan author who implicitly places Greek philosophy and the Christian religion on the same footing" and obviously commends their virtues.[48] Here if anywhere the influence of the apologists is plain, for they often described Christianity as a philosophy and defended its moral teaching.[49]

Their influence within the churches was stronger still, for Christian teachers could make use of their approaches to politics, morality, and culture and, above all, their structures for philosophical theology. There were variations among them, and there would be more in the future, but in the century before the rise of the Christian school at Alexandria the major apologists gave Christianity a theology related to philosophy. Some of their leading ideas, including those of Theophilus, were corrected by Irenaeus of Lyons and thus became part of the mainstream of Christian thought (see chapter 21).

We cannot close with mere encomium. The apologists of 176 were propagandists, not entirely given to telling the truth. Apollinaris began by relating fiction about a Christian Twelfth Legion. Melito continued with a highly imaginative sketch of the church in the Roman empire. Athenagoras asserted that the slaves of Christians had never testified to their godless banquets and promiscuity, whereas Justin had already admitted that under torture slaves had given such testimony. These apologists were enthusiastically following rhetorical conventions, and in the circumstances they were aiming at justice, not historical truth. Indeed, it is highly probable that the books written by Apollinaris and Melito *On Truth* dealt with philosophical, not historical, aspects of the topic. Certainly that is what Athenagoras meant by "truth" and "true" in his *Embassy*.

13
The Gallican Martyrs and Tatian

There is a great gulf fixed between the conciliatory petitions to Marcus Aurelius from Christians in 176 and the bitterly antagonistic essay of Tatian addressed to "the Greeks" within the next year or so. Apollinaris, Melito, and Athenagoras offered adulation, while Tatian denounced almost every aspect of Greco-Roman culture and religion in his *Oration Against the Greeks*. A particular event, and perhaps the accompanying propaganda tract by Celsus, brought his hostility to fever pitch.

Imperial Approval of the Martyrdoms in Gaul

Urban violence at Vienne and Lyons in Gaul kept Christians off the streets but there was further violence before a military tribune took them into protective custody until the imperial legate arrived. A general search followed, contrary to the rule of Trajan, and under torture some household slaves stated that their Christian masters were given to cannibalism and incest. Their testimony brought even the more moderate citizens of Lyons to hatred of the Christians. Eventually a series of trials began. No specific charges were involved, for Christians were members of a group despised by society. When the legate wrote Marcus Aurelius for instructions, he was told that Roman citizens were to be released if they recanted, executed if they did not. The noncitizens were killed by wild animals, strangled, or burned. This was the other side of Trajan's regulation.

The massacre gained significance because of the martyr-acts soon sent to other churches, perhaps by Irenaeus of Lyons. Their date is not as certain as it looks, given its origin in the researches of Eusebius. A reasonable guess still gives a year close to 177. The mob hysteria directed against Christians could have arisen as Marcus' interminable frontier wars began again after the PAX AETERNA AUGUSTI claimed on some coins of 176. The emperor confirmed the death sentence for convinced Christians in spite of the clemency of which Dio made so much. The list of martyrs includes forty-eight names, and while some may be made up from the double or even triple names of individuals, there are still too many for an emperor with Marcus' philosophical pretensions and claims to be clement. His response, if any, to the three conciliatory apologists had been negative, like his comment on Christian martyrs in the *Meditations* (see chapter 9). Perhaps one reason why the account of the martyrs was sent to the churches of Asia and Phrygia was that the bishops of Sardis and Hierapolis had failed in their appeals for imperial justice.[1]

When Tatian Wrote

The martyrdoms in Gaul show that by 177 or 178 relations with Christians had worsened. These years probably saw Tatian's *Oration* appear, if we can take a date from a passage in chapter 19 where the author criticizes philosophers who "receive 600 aurei annually from the Roman emperor" just for "letting their beards grow long." Presumably he had in mind the publicity at Athens in the autumn of 176 that accompanied the emperor's donation of four distinguished professorships of philosophy and one of rhetoric, each with a stipend of 10,000 drachmae (= 400 aurei). The event

A coin of Marcus Aurelius from 176: PAX AETERNA AVG, with Peace setting fire to stacked weapons (photo: Special Collections, University of Chicago Library)

was so memorable that Lucian soon devoted his *Eunuch* to ridicule of the struggles for appointment, and like Tatian he mentioned not only the claims of some philosophers to despise wealth but also their long beards that supposedly inspired the confidence of prospective pupils. The historian Dio Cassius briefly noticed the episode, and Philostratus told how the emperor chose the "sophist" Theodotus to be the first regius professor of rhetoric, leaving the choice of philosophers to the rhetorician Herodes Atticus.[2] The event was important, especially for the "Greeks" whom Tatian was addressing and for rhetoricians like himself.[3] He therefore probably wrote not long after the end of 176, at a time when even the emperor was becoming aware of the philosophers' greed.[4] The exaggerated figure 600 for the aurei must be due to envy.[5]

Tatian also criticized poor men who sold themselves to be murdered and rich men who bought the prospective victims (ch. 23). A bronze tablet from Italica in Spain preserves part of a speech made in the Roman Senate between 176 and 178 in relation to an imperial address and a decree limiting the prices to be paid for gladiators.[6] A fragment of the imperial speech itself was found at Sardis in Asia[7] and proves that the topic was widely discussed. Like Tatian, the senatorial orator treats gladiatorial combat as a dread disease and the taking of human life as forbidden by divine and human law.[8]

Beyond that, Tatian seems to have written after the corpses of the Gallican martyrs had been "burned and reduced to ashes" and "swept down into the river Rhone . . . so that not even a trace of them might remain upon earth." The pagans acted thus "so they may not have even a hope of a resurrection." Other Christians were torn by wild beasts.[9] Tatian therefore replies that "even if fire makes my flesh vanish, the cosmos contains its vaporized matter; and if I am consumed in rivers and in seas or torn apart by wild beasts, I am laid up in the treasuries of a rich master" (ch. 6). Such a challenge and response suggests that Tatian wrote fairly soon after the martyrdoms in Gaul, imprecise though such a date may be.

We may add that the emperor agreed with his principal argument. "What dies does not fall outside the cosmos. If it remains here and changes here, it is also resolved here into the eternal constituents, which are elements of the cosmos."[10] But Marcus did not believe in the power of the "rich master."

Apparently Tatian also replied to Celsus when he wrote that "you say that we talk rubbish at meetings of women and girls and aged crones and you jeer at us" (ch. 33), for Celsus had bitingly described the success of Christian missions among stupid children and women.[11] On the other hand, Celsus almost sounds as if he were responding to Tatian when he urges Christians to "help the emperor" and "cooperate with him in what is right and fight for him" and "accept public office in our country, if necessary, to preserve the laws and piety."[12] Like other Christians Tatian insisted that he paid taxes and gave due honor to the emperor (ch. 4). More particularly, he argued that he did not desire wealth or military command (ch. 11). Was he answering Celsus or not? It is hard to tell.

In addition, he remembered the Cynic "philosopher" Crescens, who a decade earlier at Rome had claimed to despise death and apparently accused both Justin and Tatian as Christians in order to get them executed. Tatian escaped, but he insisted that one should despise death. Marcus Aurelius thought that Christians did not seek death "after reflection and with dignity."[13] Tatian disagreed with him.

Literary Form of the *Oration*

Various ideas have been expressed about the literary form of Tatian's work. Was it simply a "diatribe" against Hellenism? Could it be the inaugural address, a *logos eisitērios* delivered at Antioch in Tatian's semi-Gnostic school?[14] Is it a work of propaganda, with echoes of the *protreptikos* form? Or does it belong to the *genos epideiktikon* and devote itself to vituperation?[15] The title does not give much help. The work was known to Clement and Origen as *Pros Hellēnas,* but the word *pros* does not necessarily imply hostility. In Greek one can speak of love or friendship toward *(pros)* someone. It is the work itself that shows that here *pros* means "against."

It is not an inaugural address, for Tatian is not making an entrance but an exit and offering not a greeting but a farewell, and certainly not praise but blame. At least in part the *Oratio* is a *logos syntaktikos* or "farewell discourse" to the culture of Greece and Rome. He says "good-bye to all that" near the beginning and near the end. "Though highly distinguished in your wisdom, we said farewell to it" (ch. 1). He has witnessed performances by actors and boxers and rejects them (chs. 22–23). Indeed, he has seen all the culture of Greece and Rome and has even taken part in mystery rites (ch. 29).

> By much traveling I became expert in your studies and encountered many devices and notions; at the end I lived in the city of the Romans and learned the varieties of statues which they took home with them from you. For I do not try to strengthen my case with the opinions of others as is the custom of most people. I want to compose an account of what I personally know. Therefore when I said good-bye to the arrogance of the Romans and the nonsense of the Athenians with their incoherent doctrines, I sought for the philosophy that you consider barbarian. (ch. 35)

He was leaving Rome and Greece and returning home, where he would be "a philosopher among the barbarians, born in the land of the Assyrians" (ch. 42). Presumably he refers to Syria. Lucian too called himself an Assyrian in his Herodotean treatise *On the Syrian Goddess* and knew Herodotus' statement that the Greeks call Syrians those who are called Assyrians "by the barbarians."[16] Hence Tatian's choice of terms.

The rhetorician Menander discusses such "leave-taking" addresses. "The orator should acknowledge his gratitude to the city from which he is return- ing, and praise it on whatever grounds the occasion permits."[17] Obviously this orator is delivering an encomium.[18] Tatian, on the other hand, is saying good-bye in no friendly manner. He does not expect to come back to Rome or Athens, and he is producing an exercise in vituperation *(psogos)*, not an encomium. Rhetoricians regularly discussed vituperation in their introduc- tory manuals but treated it simply as the opposite of encomium. Apparently Aphthonius provides the only example, a summary of a speech against Philip of Macedon, a "Philippic."

Menander tells us that the author of a friendly "leave-taking" address will praise the city "on whatever grounds the occasion permits," including

> the beauty of its appearance—colonnades, harbors, acropolis, lavish temples, and statues. He should then praise the festivals and holidays, shrines of the Muses, theaters, and competitions. . . . He should also praise the inhabitants— priests, torchbearers, hierophants, and also the character of the people, their civilized manners and hospitality. (Pp. 194–197)

Obviously Tatian offers the reverse of this picture. He certainly could not follow Menander's further counsel to "take leave of his friends and show grief and tears at the parting"! Elsewhere Menander explains how to lay emphasis on a city's achievements in politics and in such branches of knowledge as astrology, geometry, music, grammar, and philosophy, in such arts as sculpture and painting, and in such skills as rhetoric, athletics, and the like (pp. 32–75). Tatian deals with strikingly similar topics, but only in order to denounce his hearers.

Menander provides the opposite of Tatian's ideas largely because his basic model was the Panathenaic speech by Aelius Aristides, written about 165–167. Aristides doted on Athens as the bastion of Hellenes against barbarians (see illustrations on pages 40 and 94). Tatian hated it for the same reason, presumably loathing Aristides' statement that Athens alone "purely represents the Hellenes and remains most alien to the barbarians,"[19] as well as his claim that "as a linguistic model for the whole Hellenic world she has introduced an unadulterated, pure, and flawless idiom"(14).

Tatian also rejected rhapsodic statements about Attic Greek, such as Aristides' assertion that "over the whole earth by some divine fortune there comes a yearning for your wisdom and your way of life, and all have ordained this one idiom to be the common language of the human race . . . ; through you the whole civilized world has become united by a common tongue" (226; cf. 227). Aristides spoke for himself and others when he claimed that "there is no Hellene who would not give much to have been born an Athenian rather than a citizen of his original city" (233). Presuma- bly he had his own birth in Mysia in mind. Tatian would not have given anything, but he was no Hellene. He had no desire for Athenian birth, for he came from the Assyrian world, old when Athens began—as Aristides had noted (234).

Tatian and Athens

Tatian must have been appalled by Aristides' obsequiousness, not to mention the emperor's concern for "protecting the reputation of Athens," expressed on an inscription from about 175.[20] He rejected Attic Greek as normative and at the beginning of his *Oration* insisted not only on the creativity of barbarians but also on the striking diversity among Greek dialects such as Doric, Attic, Aeolic, and Ionic (cf. ch. 26 beginning).[21] "If you [like Aristides] speak Attic Greek when you are not an Athenian, tell me the reason for not speaking Doric.[22] How can one seem more barbaric to you and the other more attractive?" (ch. 26 end). In his opinion Attic speech went with foolish intellectualism. "What's the use of Attic diction and the 'heap' argument by philosophers and their plausible arguments, and geographical measurements and the locations of stars and the courses of the sun?" (ch. 27). Tatian also observed that Greeks could not understand one another's dialects and hinted that their plight went back to the Old Testament story of Babel (ch. 30). Most of his denunciations are not original, in any event, but find parallels in Sextus Empiricus' attacks on grammarians.[23]

Tatian on Himself

At one point Tatian dramatically claims to be a herald of truth crying out as if from a high podium (ch. 17), but his most striking self-portrait is based on what he claims people are saying about him. "Tatian is innovating *(kainotomei)* with his barbarian doctrines, beyond the Greeks and the countless throng of philosophers" (ch. 35). Apparently he presents himself as a new Socrates.[24] But Lucian held a similar view of himself and could imagine his audience as saying, "What novelty, what marvelous paradoxes! How inventive he is! Nothing could be fresher than his thought."[25] The Attic response to these Syrians must have been that of Herodes Atticus to a young Stoic visitor who claimed he alone could deal with philosophical problems, and that compared with himself "all Greek-speaking authorities, all who wore the toga, and Latins in general were ignorant boors." Herodes ordered a passage of Epictetus read aloud to indicate the difference between a real Stoic and a conceited babbler.[26] Presumably if he had encountered Tatian's pamphlet he would have reacted unfavorably again.

Tatian at Athens

Where was Tatian when he turned his back on Greco-Roman culture and used Greek rhetoric to say good-bye? Though the culture he denounced could be found throughout the Greco-Roman world, its center was Athens (ch. 27), where "the philosophers among you" received salaries from "the emperor of the Romans." At Rome he had seen the statues stolen "from you" (ch. 35), that is, primarily from Athens. Toward the end of his address he coordinates a list of Argive kings with Greek mythology and the founding of Athens as well as with the life of Moses (ch. 39). Last of all he speaks of wise legislators such as Minos, Lycurgus, Draco, Solon, and Pythagoras, dating Minos by the Argive king-list and the others in relation to Olympiads (ch. 41). All this reflects special interest in Athenian traditions. Under Hadrian, as we have seen, the Athenians asked to return to their ancient laws (see chapter 4). This evidence suggests that he prepared the *Oration* for delivery at Athens, whether he gave it there or not.

Grammar and Rhetoric

Because of his training and occupation, Tatian was deeply concerned with grammar and grammarians and often criticized both. Indeed, at one point he declared that "teachers of grammar were at the beginning of Greek nonsense," and "set the letters of the alphabet at war" (ch. 26). The war of the letters alludes to Lucian's *Consonants in Court,* which describes a suit brought by Sigma against the Atticizing use of Tau. Tatian writes in the atmosphere of Greek satire and insists that the letters are not "natural" but conventional (ch. 17).[27] Again, his theme is not only philosophical but also grammatical when he attacks the usual division of time into past, present, and future and asks, "How can the future become past if the present exists?" (ch. 26). The Stoic Chrysippus had tried to respond with the claim that "part of present time is future and part is past."[28] Tatian, who is not dealing with philosophy and does not mention Chrysippus' proposal, relies on similar discussions among grammarians.[29]

When he learned grammar and rhetoric he must have studied with an Atticist and learned to use Attic words and forms. Thus he felt he could explain how pointless the various dialects of Greek are, criticize the use of foreign terms, and attack Attic style and diction (chs. 1, 26, 27). Heiler shows, however, that he employed neologisms and, like Lucian, was glad to coin new words.[30] Both authors reflect the literary manner of the late second century, for example in the Hermetic literature.[31]

Proverbial and Conventional Expressions

Pagan and Christian authors regularly make use of proverbs and maxims, but they are especially common in Tatian and Lucian. The only earlier Christian who is really fond of them is Ignatius of Antioch, himself perhaps a Syrian; he used many of them in order to instruct his younger colleague Polycarp of Smyrna.[32]

As a rhetorician Tatian also loved such language and like Lucian enjoyed piling one proverbial example on another, notably in chapters 26 and 27 of the *Oration*.[33] In those chapters he refers to the proverbial jackdaw with borrowed plumes[34] and compares Greek books to labyrinths,[35] their readers to the leaky wine jar of the Danaids.[36] He also speaks of those who (like Thales) looked into the sky but fell into wells.[37] Another allusion sounds sententious: he refers to "those who sail in a ship and because of inexperience think the mountains are running past." Their notion is an *adynaton,* "impossibility," of the kind well known in Greek literature.[38] Similarly the reference to "a blind man speaking to a deaf" is proverbial, as a citation in Athenaeus shows.[39]

Even Tatian's farewell to Greco-Roman culture contains conventional wording. He says good-bye to "the arrogance of the Romans and the nonsense of the Athenians" (ch. 35). Lucian too used stereotypes, though more favorable ones, when speaking of Athens. Such expressions were common; Diogenes Laertius spoke of the "arrogance" of Athens.[40] But Lucian is our best witness to the milieu in which Tatian lived, or wanted to live.

A Little Learning from Grammarians and Poets

Inventors

In the grammarians' schools lists were readily available, for example, of those who discovered or invented various arts. Tatian uses such a list to show that barbarians, not Greeks, were inventors.[41] He begins with divination and traces various kinds—prediction from dreams, stars, birds, and sacrifices—to non-Greek peoples. Then he turns to literature and science, assigning the alphabet to the Phoenicians, epistles to a Persian woman, and poetry, song, and religious initiations to Orpheus (a Thracian). The Egyptians created geometry, the calendar, and history-writing. Sculpture came from the Etruscans, various kinds of music and magic from others. Tatian says nothing about the sources he obviously used, but when Clement later rewrote his statements he may have used the sources themselves, mentioning eight writers "on discoveries," including Aristotle and the Peripatetics Theophrastus and Strato.[42] Evidently the basic source was Greek, for it named a wide range of barbarian inventors.

Philosophers

After praising barbarian inventors Tatian turns to revile the lives and doctrines of the Greek philosophers, beginning and ending with cases among the Cynics. He is simply repeating scandalous stories like those favored by such contemporaries as Lucian, Athenaeus, and (especially) Diogenes Laertius. The Cynic Diogenes, he tells us, pretended to be an ascetic but died after eating raw octopus (Diogenes Laertius 6.76). Aristippus was a famous profligate who wore scarlet (2.78). Plato was sold into slavery by Dionysius of Syracuse; he was famous for his gluttony (3.19; 6.25). Aristotle was an adulator of Alexander the Great, who put Callisthenes (not an adulator) into a cage (5.5). Heraclitus investigated himself, hid his poem in a temple where Euripides found it, and died after covering himself with dung (2.22).[43]

Tatian tells no tales about Zeno the Stoic, perhaps because he was using a source close to Stoicism, but he attacks his doctrines of cosmic return and conflagration and parodies the Stoic god who permeates matter and therefore is present in sewers, vermin, and sexual activities.[44]

Returning to the scandals, Tatian next claims that Empedocles' suicide proves he was merely mortal, while both Pythagoras and Plato followed Pherecydes, who taught "old wives' tales."[45] His list ends, as we should expect, with "the dog-marriage" of the Cynic Crates, supposedly consummated in public with Hipparchia. This memorable event received considerable attention in the literature of the time.[46]

This is certainly not a sketch of the history of philosophy, for Tatian is not writing history but denigrating Greek philosophers. He also knows a good deal about the treatise On Sympathies and Antipathies falsely ascribed to Democritus, and associates it with the Persian sage Ostanes. Here he is attacking medicine as the product of demons (chs. 16–17).[47]

Geography

Tatian even denounces "those who worked out geographies" because they "claimed there were seas, one leek-green, another muddy; and regions, one burning hot, another cold and frozen" (ch. 20). The beginning of what is now the first of Plutarch's Lives, that of Theseus, offers something of a parallel. Like Tatian, Plutarch describes how geographers "crowd to the outer edges of their maps the parts of the earth that escape their knowledge." They mark the edges as "waterless sands" or "obscure mud" or "Scythian cold" or "frozen sea." Conceivably Theseus stood first in Tatian's time, and he read no more after finding a model for attacking geographers.

Differences remain, and we shall not try to explain what Plutarch had in mind. For Tatian himself a clue is given by the unusual term "leek-green," used, according to the lexicon, of part of the Indian Ocean. This means that he is following "the probable Greek concept of the oikumene,"[48] in which the corners were occupied clockwise by Indians (leek-green sea), Ethiopians (burning hot), Celts (muddy; shoals and marshes), and Scythians (cold and frozen).

Mythology and Astrology

A rather jumbled section (chs. 8–10) attacks mythology as inconsistent and the planets and constellations as demonic. The demons (pagan gods) under their leader Zeus arranged for "honors in the sky" to be paid to reptiles, fish, and quadrupeds "so that they themselves might be thought to dwell in heaven"—and might control life on earth through the movements of the stars (ch. 9)! Tatian mentions the planet Saturn but takes much more interest in the constellations. His list of them begins and ends with signs of the zodiac, "Demeter" (Virgo),[49] and "the Dioscuri" (Gemini). In between he names three other signs: Scorpio, Aries, and Taurus. Beyond that, he mentions nine other constellations, three from the southern sky, six from the northern.

Tatian is distressed by sexual immorality and finds it on display in the sky. He suggests that Antinous was set on the moon after death because he was a "beautiful youth." Apparently he is borrowing Justin's language against deification so that he can describe what happened to Antinous.[50] But why place Antinous on the moon? Ptolemy and Dio knew nothing of this location but mentioned a star named for him in the constellation Aquila.[51] Perhaps Tatian placed him on the moon because he was about to mention the similar case of Helen.

Before coming to Helen, however, he referred to the adultery of Cygnus, the swan, with Leda, Helen's mother; then to her brothers the Dioscuri, who spend alternate days in the sky and beneath the earth,[52] and who abducted the daughters of Leucippus.[53]

Tatian places their "fornicating" sister Helen in the Elysian plain because this postmortem location was foretold in Homer *Odyssey* 4.563,[54] and Plutarch explains that the Elysian plain was "the side of the moon toward heaven."[55] Euripides, on the other hand, said that Apollo made her "the sailors' savior"—i.e., a star—in the sky near her brothers.[56] Tatian neglects Helen as star and claims that "Euripides wisely brought in her killing by Orestes." Since in Euripides' play Apollo keeps her from being killed, the comment is stupid.

Tatian's discussion is intemperate, incomplete, and poorly arranged. It may reflect unintelligent use of something like Pseudo-Eratosthenes' *Catasterisms.*

Later in his work Tatian dealt with the relative dates of Homer and Moses, but we shall discuss this kind of study in relation to his use of the Bible. On his way to it he waxed enthusiastic about a theme not closely related to chronology, perhaps inserted to revive the reader's lagging interest.

Tatian's Hostility to Women and Art

Tatian devotes two lengthy chapters (33–34) to an attack on Greek statues of women, especially the poetesses, whom he considered immoral.[57] Rhetoricians had already discussed statues like these. Plutarch says that "when [the Cynic] Crates saw a golden statue of the prostitute Phryne standing at Delphi, he shouted that it stood as a monument to Greek licentiousness."[58] Again, when writing on education Plutarch himself insisted that "some painters depict immoral actions" and compares them with poets who "often give imitative descriptions of evil deeds."[59] The theme was thus fairly common, and it gave impetus to Tatian's restless and morbid mind. There is literary evidence for statues of Sappho, Telesilla, and Corinna.[60]

Tatian provides a misogynistic discussion of Sappho and other women lyric poets, clearly relying on a contemporary list. In the *Greek Anthology* (9.26), for example, nine are named and praised. Our apologist names eight of these plus six others and praises none. He considers Sappho a prostitute, "a wanton girl, maddened by love," who "sang of her own lewdness." The poetesses were "good for nothing." As we should expect, the grammarian Didymus reflected a similar interest when he inquired whether Sappho was a prostitute or not, and Aelian differentiated two Sapphos, one the poetess praised by Plato, the other a prostitute in Lesbos.[61] Tatian's onslaught was thus not unique.

Not everyone shared his opinion, however. After Plato, Strabo referred to Sappho as "wonderful," and the first-century treatise *On the Sublime* cites her brilliant depiction of "erotic madness"[62]—though "erotic madness" was not always highly regarded.[63] Similarly the more orthodox Christian Clement of Alexandria presented a picture that contrasts sharply with Tatian's; and since he knew Tatian's work we assume he was correcting it. He had learned from Plato's *Phaedrus* that Sappho was good and/or beautiful. He praised innovative women poets and used a brief list with the names of Corinna, Telesilla, Muia, and Sappho.[64] To be sure, he made little use of their works and cited only two lines from Sappho to illustrate the use of roses for wreaths,[65] but he did praise the poetesses he knew. A little later neither Origen nor—as we should expect—Tertullian took any interest in these women, but Eusebius gave dates for five of them in his *Chronicle.*

Tatian attacked not only Sappho but other women whom he viewed as morally inadequate though portrayed by sculptors. He referred to Phryne,[66] Glycera, Neaera, and Lais as prostitutes like her. Some of his examples treat women as unduly sexual beings. He notes that Glaucippe bore an elephant boy,[67] while there was a statue by Periclymenus of a woman who bore thirty children.[68] Other statues portrayed a woman pregnant after rape, a queen of the Paeonians who bore a black child,[69] and Praxiteles' Aphrodite at Cnidus, stained by an admirer who tried to have intercourse with it.[70]

Bryaxis made a statue of Pasiphae, mother of the Minotaur after intercourse with a bull. Kalkmann suggests that this collection of peculiar subjects may owe much to authors on marvels. It owes even more to Tatian's ascetic motives and his sophistic feeling for the grotesque.

He may also have been motivated by such a treatise as Suetonius' Greek work *On Famous Prostitutes*. This work, extant only in fragments, was later used with enthusiasm by such Christian apologists as Tertullian and Lactantius.[71]

Tatian on Erotic Literature

At the very end of these chapters in the *Oration* he drags in "the unspeakable ideas of Philaenis and Elephantis" and claims that pagans malign Christian morals while favoring these two women (ch. 34). His teacher Justin had already denounced Philaenis; very little is known about Elephantis.[72] It is not clear what Tatian knew about either of these writers. The Christian polymath Clement had heard of the "postures of Philaenis," which he ironically compared with the labors of Hercules. Elsewhere, apparently following the Stoic Musonius, Clement says that such topics should not be mentioned even to one's wife. He includes "hetaeric" kisses among them—a theme probably discussed by Philaenis.[73]

14

Tatian
on the Bible and Theology

The leave-taking aspect of Tatian's work does not exhaust its content or meaning, for as he departed from the Greco-Roman world he was still trying to win converts. A Christian message is interspersed among the farewell elements. In chapters 4–7 Tatian treats of God, the Logos, the resurrection, the creation of men and angels and their fall; in chapters 12–15 he discusses soul and spirits and demons, returning to the subject in chapter 20. Farther on he describes his own conversion in chapters 29–30 and analyzes the priority of Moses to Greek culture in chapters 31 and 36–41. Such materials deal with subjects different from those found in the "farewell address" and are properly "protreptic," inviting readers to follow Tatian into Christianity. Rich and poor alike may come. "We admit all who wish to hear, even if they are old women or children. Every age without distinction enjoys respect with us," and he adds (warming to his usual theme) "from whom everything indecent is excluded" (ch. 32).

He himself became a convert when he was by himself at Rome, "seeking how to discover the truth" and "carefully considering what was worthwhile," perhaps looking at ancient oriental theologies. At that point he "happened to read some barbarian writings, older compared with the Greeks' doctrines, more divine compared with their errors." (His future teacher Justin could have told him how old the Old Testament writers were.) He found them persuasive first because of rhetorical considerations: "the lack of affectation in the wording, the artlessness of the speakers"; second because of the subject matter: "the easily intelligible account of the creation of the world" (he had not yet noticed the ambiguity in Genesis 1:3; see below), the foreknowledge of the future, the remarkable quality of the precepts, and the doctrine of a single universal ruler." His soul was "taught by God" (ch. 29).

Like his teacher Justin and his contemporary Theophilus, Tatian ascribes his conversion to reading the Old Testament. Obviously he could have understood much of it, though we suspect that for Christological exegesis he would have had a Christian teacher. Certainly Luke (24:25–27) and Acts make this point. In Acts 8:30 the Ethiopian eunuch asks Philip how he can understand the prophet Isaiah without someone's guidance. It is possible that Tatian's guide was Justin, but it could have been someone else. Either before or after entering Justin's school, Tatian undertook further Bible study and used the resources of his grammatical education for exegesis.

The Date of Homer and the Date of Moses

Tatian already knew about grammarians' discussions of the nationality and the date of Homer, but now he could use them to prove that the Old Testament revelation was older than the oldest extant Greek literature (ch. 31). Naturally he took his authorities on the subject from schoolbooks, following them from Theagenes of Rhegium in the time of Cambyses through Stesimbrotus of Thasos, the poet Antimachus of Colophon, the historian Herodotus, and the unknown Dionysius of Olynthos. After them, he says—thus possibly referring to his own source or sources—came Ephorus the Athenian and two Peripatetics.

Then there were the Alexandrian grammarians: Zenodotus, Aristophanes, Callimachus (Wilamowitz, cited by Schwartz, more sensibly suggested "Callistratus," a pupil of Aristophanes), Crates, Eratosthenes, Aristarchus, and Apollodorus. Tatian is evidently close to what Allen printed as the sixth *Life of Homer,* listing the views of Heraclides, Pyrandros and Hypsicrates, Crates, Eratosthenes, and Apollodorus, thus including three of Tatian's seven names. The opinions about the date are also similar, though not identical with his.[1]

Tatian	Vita Homeri
Crates, 80 years after Troy	60 years after Troy
Eratosthenes, 100 years after Troy	100 years after Ionic migration
Aristarchus, at Ionic migration, 140 years after Troy	
Apollodorus, 100 years after Ionic migration, 240 after Troy	80 years after Ionic migration

As is sometimes the case, Clement of Alexandria provides a clearer picture. Tatian cited his authorities anonymously, but Clement names authors and titles to prove his own erudition and reliability. Probably they come from the single handbook Tatian had used.[2]

Clement starts with Philochorus and a date eighty years after the Ionic migration and continues with Aristarchus, who dated Homer and the migration 140 years after Troy in his *Notes on Archilochus.* After mentioning the chronicler Euthymenes he goes on to the dates of Crates (80 years after Troy), Eratosthenes (100 years), and others. Apparently both Tatian and Clement were more accurate than the *Life of Homer,* at least in its present form.[3]

Tatian obviously took no interest in history as such. His training in grammar and rhetoric led him to grammatical prolegomena for his proof of Moses' priority to Homer and though he used historical works when discussing various dates he took them from the studies of grammarians.

Once Tatian had set a date for Homer he was ready to use oriental historians to set a date for Moses. He was the first Christian apologist to use these authors more or less directly. Perhaps he looked them up because of his own oriental origins, though among Hellenistic Jews Josephus (an oriental) had already appealed to them in his apology *Against Apion* to "prove" the antiquity of Moses and the Jewish people. The idea of citing Egyptian, Chaldean, and Phoenician authorities comes from Josephus,[4] not from the authorities Tatian names. He undertook a measure of original research into apologists for ancient oriental nations, however, and his erudition impressed Clement of Alexandria and Eusebius, largely because he used sources not shared with the other Greek apologists.

His relatively original discussion of the date of Moses comes toward the end of his work (chs. 35–40), where several passages reveal how he conducted his research. A discussion of the Babylonian priest Berosus ends with the statement that "Juba writing on the Assyrians says that he learned the account from Berosus; he has two books *On the Assyrians.*" Evidently he knew Berosus through Juba II, king of Mauretania in the first century B.C. Felix Jacoby notes that Berosus' work on the Chaldeans was handed down in two ways:

> (1) via Alexander Polyhistor (a) to Africanus, (b) to Josephus, thence to Theophilus and Eusebius, and (c) with interpolations, to Eusebius; and (2) via Juba (a) to Tatian, thence to Clement and Eusebius, and (b) to the grammarian Didymus of Alexandria, thence to Clement.[5]

This complex pattern makes it hard to tell just what an early Christian author is using at each point, but Tatian's place in the stemma seems assured.

In similar fashion Tatian notes the existence of the historians Theodotus, Hypsicrates, and Mochus among the Phoenicians and states that "Laetus . . . edited their books in Greek." He adds that "Menander of Pergamum produced an account of the same events." Presumably this means that Menander was his source for Laetus.

Finally he speaks of the Egyptian chronicler Ptolemy, priest of Mendes, but cites the "very famous" grammarian Apion (against whom Josephus wrote) as quoting from him. Perhaps Tatian was drawn to Apion and his

Egyptian Studies because of his negative comments on the gods of Egypt, or even because of his anti-Jewish sentiments; we shall see that Tatian later came to consider the Creator an inferior god.

Tatian's sources for oriental history thus probably consisted of Juba, Menander of Pergamum, and Apion but not their sources, even though he mentions them. It is barely possible that reading of Josephus guided him to these materials, a few of which Josephus mentioned but did not use. Josephus was not likely to use the anti-Jewish writer Apion in any case.

Tatian's Rewriting of Genesis

The most striking examples of his use of grammar in exegesis occur in writings later than the *Oration*. First, Tatian thought that by philology he could find his new theology in Genesis 1:3, "Let there be light." The Greek verb *genēthētō* is the third-person imperative, but Tatian argued that it was optative in force. God was requesting, not commanding, the creation of light "because God was in the dark."[6] Grammarians had noted that the imperative was often used for the optative; Origen himself gave examples of this usage from the Greek Bible[7] but insisted that in fact the mood was imperative, not optative.[8] Second, Tatian in his dualistic theological mood presumably appealed to a Pauline dualistic reference to "the God who said, 'Light will shine out of darkness' " (2 Cor. 4:6). The expression could be understood as implying that there was at least one other god and that the god in question was in darkness, for in the same context Paul referred to "the god of this age" (2 Cor. 4:4). Was this god the same as the one who spoke about light? Irenaeus tried to explain away the expression "the god of this age" as due to *hyperbaton,* "transposition," claiming that Paul really spoke of "the unbelievers of this age" instead.[9] Once more philology is pressed into service as the handmaid of theology.

Tatian's Rewriting of Paul

In his later period Tatian certainly could not accept everything he found in the Gospels or the epistles; he had to "twist" some of the basic texts.[10] Eusebius says he "ventured to paraphrase some of the apostle's words, as if correcting his grammar,"[11] and this is what happens in a fragment of his later, *On Perfection According to the Savior.*[12] The fragment expresses his attitude toward wives and sex as he gives exegesis of 1 Corinthians 7:2–5, where Paul justified Christian marriage "because of fornication" and told couples not to "defraud" each other of marital intercourse, except by mutual agreement and then only "for a season" so as to provide opportunity for prayer. They were then to reunite so that Satan would not tempt them because of their lack of self-control. This, Paul says, is a concession, not a command.

By this time Tatian was an avowed Encratite and could not accept such doctrine. The apostle evidently meant that "agreement" led to "prayer," though partnership in corruption (i.e., sex) destroys intercessory prayer. Paul's "concession" must be intended to shame the couple and restrain them. Since their reunion would be "for the sake of Satan and incontinence," and their "agreement" to abstain was for the service of God, they otherwise served "incontinence, fornication, and the devil." God had told them they could not "serve two masters" (Matt. 6:24). The Savior himself demanded perfection (Matt. 5:48; 19:21) not compromise, and Paul cannot have meant what he seemed to say. The exegesis arises out of Paul's ambiguous reference to "concession."

Tatian's Interpretation of John and Hebrews

Tatian certainly used the Gospel of John. At the beginning of chapter 4 he says that "God is Spirit" (John 4:24) and adds that "God is the beginning of all." In chapter 5 he returns to the opening verse, citing it as "God was in the beginning." John 1:1 says that the Logos was in the beginning but immediately adds that the Logos was God. In chapter 19 he cites verse 3 as "everything was made *by* him," not "through him," since he is emphasizing the deity of the Logos. In chapter 13 he refers to "what was said," i.e., in scripture: "The darkness does not overcome the light." He uses the present tense in John 1:5 because he takes the verse in a timeless sense as referring to the Logos (the light) and the human soul (the darkness). Even though he can also say that "the soul did not save the spirit but was saved by it" and "the light overcame the darkness," he is not looking back to the creation of the world.

Similarly when he cites the "saying" of Hebrews 2:7 or 2:9 as "they were [plural] made inferior to the angels for a time," he is referring the verse to humanity in general, not (as in Hebrews) to Jesus, the Son of Man (ch. 15).

Secret Christian Exegesis

A mysterious passage in the *Oration* is addressed directly to "our own people" (ch. 30). Tatian has described his conversion through reading in the Old Testament, when his soul was taught by God and he realized he was now freed from "many rulers and countless tyrants" (the demons) and had been given "not something we had never received but what we had received but had been prevented from keeping by our error." This, we should assume, was the divine Spirit. Now, he says,

> I wish to strip myself like infant children. For we know that the constitution of wickedness is like that of the smallest seeds, since it grows strong from a tiny origin (Matt. 13:32) but will be dissolved[13] again if we obey God's word

and do not "scatter" (Matt. 12:30) ourselves. It held power over what was ours like a kind of hidden treasure (Matt. 13:44); in digging it up we were filled with dust, but provided the occasion for it to exist. For everyone who recovers his own property has obtained possession of the most precious wealth (Matt. 13:46).

Translation and exegesis alike are difficult. Irenaeus insists that Christ is the "hidden treasure,"[14] but Tatian obviously treats the seed and the treasure as bad. His contemporary Clement is aware that treasure and wealth can be either good or bad,[15] and Tatian's exegesis of Matthew 12–13 (if that is what it is) oscillates between these two poles. He seems to be discussing the recovery of the divine spirit in man (chs. 13, 15). But who are "our own people" whom he addresses? It is hard to believe that ordinary Christians would have understood his allusions, and while he may not yet have reached Valentinian Gnosticism, he was soon to be viewed as a heretic, a member of a sectarian group.[16]

Tatian's Theology

The Perfect God

For Tatian "the perfect God" is ineffable and superior to the spirit that pervades matter (ch. 4). Men long for knowledge of him (ch. 12) who is incorporeal (ch. 25) and without flesh (ch. 15) and is not the source of evil (ch. 17). He is the Creator, the invisible and intangible "Father of things perceptible and visible" (ch. 4). The Word is his "firstborn work" and "proceeded from the Father's power" (ch. 5). Christians follow "the law of the imperishable Father" (ch. 32).

A few years earlier the Valentinian Gnostic Ptolemaeus had spoken in his *Letter to Flora* of "the perfect God and Father,"[17] who did not ordain any part of the Mosaic law but is essentially good as the Father of our Savior; he is ungenerated and imperishable. He made the world through another God, the Logos, who is just and hates evil but is inferior to the perfect God. The commandments of the creator are imperfect and needed to be "completed" or repealed by the Savior when he came. This is certainly not the early theology of Tatian, who at this time identified Father with Creator.

The Word

Tatian explains the generation of the Word by comparing it with the light kindled from a torch or the word spoken by a speaker. "I speak and you hear: yet surely when I address you I am not myself deprived of speech through transmission of speech, but by projecting my voice my purpose is to set in order the disorderly matter in you" (ch. 5). Since a theologian like Irenaeus explicitly rejects this comparison between the generation of the Logos and speech and says, "You scrutinize the generation of the Word by the Father and apply the expression of a human word by the tongue to the Word of God,"[18] it seems possible that other notions expressed by Tatian have to do with grammar rather than philosophy, even though there is a verbal parallel in Justin (*Dialogue* 61.2).

Thus when he says that the Word "came into being by partition, not by section," he may perhaps be thinking of one of the many meanings of *merismos* as a grammatical term, for example, the "distinction" of topics under different headings,[19] or "distinctness" as compared with "confusion" *(synchysis)*.[20] The word for "section" *(apokopē)* is used by grammarians of cutting off letters at the end of one word to make another, as *dōma, dō*.[21] A little farther on Schwartz's emendation makes Tatian speak of "division" again,[22] but this would be tautological and cannot be accepted.[23] When Tatian refers to bringing to order or amending "confusion," he may once more have good grammar or good rhetoric in view as his model. In the light of Elze's discussion one cannot deny his background in Middle Platonism (not least through the Platonist Justin), but he still stands closer to literary studies than to philosophy.

The Word of the Father, generated at the beginning (or even "as the beginning," in turn "generated our creation by fabricating *(dēmiourgēsas)* matter for himself" and then shaped it into an orderly cosmos (ch. 5), later making angels and human beings (ch. 7). Did the Word become incarnate? Presumably Tatian thought he did, for Christians "declare that God has been born in the form of a man" (ch. 21) and he himself refers to "the God who suffered" (ch. 13 end). Paul uses an expression close to "the form of a man" in Philippians 2:6–7, while the Synoptic Gospels stress the suffering of Christ, Ignatius the suffering of God.[24] Elze suggests that Tatian may have been something of a docetist;[25] but like Ignatius he may well have been willing to allow paradox in theology. The God born in the form of a man and suffering is in any case not the perfect God but, presumably, the Word. Tatian does not name Christ in relation to the last judgment, but he is not presenting his full theology in this treatise.

Spirit, Spirits, Demons

Tatian insists that there are two spirits, one pervading matter and equivalent to the Greek world-soul, the other divine as the image and likeness of God. God himself is a spirit and constructed material spirits or souls. The first human beings had both soul and spirit, but the spirit left them when the soul refused to follow it. The soul is not immortal and, if in ignorance, it dies (though rising later for eternal punishment). If united with the divine spirit it ascends into heaven. The spirit can also be regarded as "the Minister of the God who suffered" (ch. 13 end), perhaps because he infused it into his disciples (John 20:22).

The Spirit appears as Minister in Gnostic exegesis as set forth in the *Excerpts from Theodotus* (ch. 16) with various explanations of the dove at Jesus' baptism. Christians call it the Holy Spirit, while followers of Basilides call it "the Minister," presumably of the Father of Christ.[26] The expression does not prove that Tatian was a Gnostic, however.

The Word made angels before men, he says, but the firstborn of these angels, cleverer than the rest (Gen. 3:1), was proclaimed as God by both men and angels. His transgression led to rebellion and he was banished from life with the Word; he and his followers became demons. They lived with the animals, deified them, and paid them celestial honors in the sense that many stars are named after them. Demons do not die easily, but they do die and will suffer forever. (Only spiritual men can easily see the bodies of the demons, though sometimes psychics see them too.)

Tatian's demonology is simply early Christian, and it can be claimed that his language about some men as "psychic" is merely Pauline (cf. 1 Cor. 3). It is at least unguarded, however, for Valentinian Gnostics were using the term of ordinary Christians in his day.

Tatian on Animals

Tatian sharply differentiated mankind from animals and referred readers to his earlier work on the subject. There he rejected what "the croakers [i.e., the Stoics] dogmatize about man" as "a rational animal capable of intelligence and knowledge" because these philosophers themselves believed that "irrational animals" were intelligent (ch. 15).[27] Therefore to define man as a rational animal is meaningless.

Man—that is, true man who does not behave like an animal but has advanced beyond humanity toward God himself—is really "the image and likeness of God" (Gen. 1:26).

Healing by medicines means slavery to demons. Human beings cannot be like the animals, which cure themselves by instinct. The dog eats grass when distressed by unwholesome humors, while the deer eats a snake, the hog eats river crabs, and a lion eats monkeys. These examples (ch. 18) come from contemporary animal lore[28] and are used in discussions of the rationality of animals. Thus a speaker in Plutarch's essay on the use of reason by beasts uses their cures to prove they are rational,[29] but of course the examples could be used on either side. Celsus too insisted that "irrational animals" were rational, but Origen rejected the notion, specifically claiming that their use of antidotes was due not to reason but to nature, that is, "instinct."[30] Here Origen agrees with Tatian.

Eschatology

"There will be a resurrection of bodies after the completion of everything," when God "will restore to its original state the substance that is visible only to him." After the last judgment, made by the Creator God, those who have obeyed him will "share in eternal life" and receive "immortality with delight" and, united with the divine spirit, will ascend to "the abodes above." They have already "overcome death by death through faith," but those who have not obeyed, also immortal, will be punished everlastingly in eternal fire (chs. 6, 13–15). No doubt this point comes from Justin.

15
Celsus
Against the Christians

All we know about Celsus' *Logos alēthēs* or "True Account," a polemical treatise against Christianity, comes from Origen, who provided lengthy quotations from the work when he refuted it about 248, perhaps about seventy years later. The exact date of Celsus could be important for determining the targets of the Christian apologists who wrote late in the reign of Marcus Aurelius. Conceivably several important apologists were responding not only to the general situation but also to Celsus' criticisms of Christianity. In fact, however, their relation to him remains highly uncertain.[1]

Apologetic Answers to Celsus?

Many discussions of Celsus' relations with other authors do not affect the question of his date. For example, if it could be proved that he knew the apology of Aristides nothing would be changed in Celsus' situation,[2] any more than if he replied to Justin's work.[3] If "Diognetus" replies to Celsus, we find ourselves simply dealing with two unknown dates rather than one,[4] while the possible use of Celsus by Tertullian or Minucius Felix[5] or Clement, as discussed by Vermander, does not fix Celsus in time.[6] Early dates for the *Ridicule* of "Hermias," Pseudo-Justin's *The Sole Rule of God,* and the Syriac apology ascribed to Melito or Ambrose do not inspire confidence in Vermander's system, though presumably he is right when he dates the *Exhortation* in the third century.[7]

The Case of Theophilus

Vermander has argued that the third book of Theophilus, unlike the first two, replies to Celsus' work.[8] The point could provide a more adequate date, since this third book was not written before the second or third year of Commodus' reign.

The thesis is not altogether convincing, however, since along similar lines one could argue that there are attacks on Celsus in book 2, and the difference between book 3 and the others would be diminished. For example, Celsus says that

> the Jews, being bowed down in some corner of Palestine, were totally uneducated and had not heard of these things [creation narratives] which were sung in poetry long before by Hesiod and thousands of other inspired men. They composed a most improbable and crude story that a man was formed by the hands of God and given breath, that a woman was formed out of his side, that God gave commands, and that a serpent opposed them and even proved superior to the ordinances of God.[9]

This is part of a fairly long and hostile account of the Jewish people and the Old Testament, largely based on earlier anti-Jewish literature, which Vermander sees Theophilus answering in his third book.[10] The reason he appears to be answering Celsus, however, is that he is relying on the Old Testament and Josephus while defending Judaism.

Book 2 provides a better parallel. There Theophilus attacks the supposed inspiration of Hesiod and other poets, explains that many inspired Hebrew prophets agreed with "the Sibyl among the Greeks," insists that Adam was made by God's hands (his Logos and Sophia), interprets the point of the creation of Eve, and identifies the serpent as Satan. He is quite willing to speak of the prophets as illiterate and thus could be making his own use of Celsus' criticism.[11] Possible use of Celsus thus occurs in book 2 as well as book 3.

Vermander argues that in book 2 (ch. 30) Theophilus identifies Noah with Deucalion, then discovers Celsus' claim that Moses stole the story of Noah from the one about Deucalion,[12] and therefore rejects the identification in book 3 (ch. 19). This description is not correct. Like Philo and Justin as well as Celsus, Theophilus consistently identifies Noah with Deucalion. In book 3 he adds that the name Deucalion comes from a Greek verse, presumably spoken by Noah: "Come, God calls" *(deute, kalei)* and adds that Noah's name also means "rest" in Hebrew.[13] In addition, he calls Noah a eunuch.[14]

It is true that Theophilus quotes from the *Sibylline Oracles* in book 2 (3, 31, 36) but not in book 3 and that Celsus criticized Christian use of them.[15] The fact does not prove that he knew Celsus' work, for he does not quote the oracles in book 1 and had no special need of them in book 3 either.

Does Theophilus Answer Celsus' Accusations?

Vermander also believes that in book 3 Theophilus is replying to anti-Christian accusations mentioned by Celsus. He is answering what "godless mouths" have said against "the godly who are called Christians" and lists five accusations. The first three of them are moral in nature. First, "our wives are the common property of all and practice promiscuous intercourse"; second, "we have intercourse with our own sisters"; and third, "most godless and savage of all . . . we partake of human flesh." Such charges are not new. They are already implicit in what Tacitus, Pliny, and Fronto say of the Christians,[16] and are made explicit in the writings of the apologists. According to Justin and the letter of the Gallican martyrs some crimes were attested by household slaves, though Athenagoras denies that this happened.

Celsus does not mention any of these charges, however. He says only that the biblical story of Lot and his daughters is "more iniquitous than Thyestean sins."[17] The point is not especially important to him. It arises out of criticism of the Bible in response to which Philo vigorously allegorizes the story.[18] In any case, either Celsus or his critic Origen meant to refer to Oedipus' relations with his mother, not to Thyestes' eating his children.

Two further charges mentioned by Theophilus are more closely related to philosophy and theology. First, "our message has been made public only recently." But Celsus thinks it is secondhand, not novel.[19] Second, "we have nothing to say to prove the truth of our teaching, but our message is foolishness" (1 Cor. 1:18). This is indeed the view set forth by Celsus,[20] but it is surely not novel; it is implicit in the almost universal accusation of "superstition."

Theophilus militantly attacks the pagans who bring the moral accusations, for they are the ones who practice or advocate cannibalism, recommend promiscuity, incest, homosexual acts, and atheism, or describe the gods as wicked (3.5–8). This is not to say, however, that he is attacking Celsus, any more than when he writes, "I do not mention the temples of Antinous and those of the other so-called gods, for descriptions of them produce laughter among the intelligent" (3.8). Both Justin and Tatian had sharply criticized the cult of Antinous, and so did Celsus himself.[21] It is therefore hard to imagine that Theophilus was replying only, or especially, to him.

He criticizes Greek behavior once more when he tells how Christians refuse complicity in murder at gladiatorial shows and avoid defilement by plays mentioning the cannibalized children of Thyestes and Tereus or the adulteries of gods and men, set forth in tragedies by authors who "euphoniously proclaim the gods for honors and prizes" (3.15). The statement probably reflects Greek charges again, but not those made by Celsus.

Celsus and Other Apologists

Finally, Vermander criticized Schoedel's suggestion and mine that the treatise of "Athenagoras" on the resurrection had Origen's discussions in view. He held that the real target was Celsus.[22] Whether this is so or not, the date of *Resurrection* is as uncertain as that of Celsus himself. We are therefore left with none but the traditional methods for dating the *True Account.*

Inconclusive Evidence for the Date of Celsus

Treatises like that of Celsus can often be dated by references to Roman emperors. Unfortunately, in his eighth book Celsus speaks both of one emperor and of several.[23] His opponent Origen similarly oscillated between singular and plural, even in a single chapter (8.73). Chadwick notes that Justin likewise referred to Antoninus Pius and his sons as "emperors," though there was only one emperor at the time.[24] Such references therefore are not reliable guides to the date of the treatise.

More Conclusive Evidence for the Date?

More solid evidence appears when Celsus insists that Christians are subject not only to the death penalty but to search. "If anyone does still wander about in secret, yet he is sought out and condemned to death."[25] Trajan had forbidden such search, and Hadrian had implied disapproval. Marcus Aurelius, however, officially authorized search for them, as we have learned from Melito and the account of the Gallican martyrs. As for the death penalty—"Christians perform their rites and teach their doctrines in secret, and they do this with good reason because of the penalty of death that hangs over them"[26]—this had existed under Trajan and, though rarely employed by Hadrian and Antoninus Pius, was reiterated by Marcus Aurelius, precisely in the case of the Gallicans. These martyrs can be dated at any time between 175 and 180,[27] but 177 remains quite possible. The same kind of reference, as we have seen, helps date the apology by Melito of Sardis.

Outline of the *True Account*

The best outline of Celsus' work is provided by Carl Andresen.[28] He divides it into a preface (book 1.1–27), with special emphasis on the true ancient religious doctrines which Jews and Christians have falsified, and four main parts. First comes a Jewish speech against Christ and Christians (book 1.28–2 end). Second there is a discussion of the revolt of Christians against Jews (book 3), pointless because no god or son of gods comes down to earth (book 4). Third, Celsus states that angels (demonic beings) do come down, but have given no preference to the Jews (book 5.2–41), still less to Christians, who have no origin independent from them (book 5.33–65); their teaching is almost entirely secondhand (book 6.2–7.58). Fourth, Celsus attacks the principal Christian doctrines, which lead them to reject the worship of the gods as paid to daemonic beings (book 7.62–8 end).

Celsus and Politics

Celsus insisted "that the gods ruled the world under a supreme god more or less as the satraps governed the Persian empire under a king of kings," and he therefore regarded rebellion as morally wrong. Momigliano cites an important parallel in a speech that Dio Cassius ascribes to Augustus' adviser Maecenas. In regard to revolt the most important words are these: "You should abhor and punish those who attempt to distort our religion with strange rites . . . because such men, by bringing in new divinities in place of the old, persuade many to adopt foreign practices, from which spring up conspiracies, factions, and partisan groups, none of them beneficial to a monarchy." He adds that no one should be allowed to be either an atheist or a sorcerer. Since sorcerers sometimes speak the truth, they encourage many to attempt revolutions.[29] This is traditional Roman wisdom, though it was especially significant just after the revolt of Avidius Cassius.

Celsus describes the Jews as rebels against whom the Christians in turn rebelled.

> The Jews were Egyptian by race, and left Egypt after revolting against the Egyptian community and despising the religious customs of Egypt. What they did to the Egyptians they suffered in turn through those who followed Jesus and believed him to be the Christ. In both instances a revolt against the community led to innovations.[30]

In Celsus' view Christianity was revolutionary by origin and nature. Its so-called unity was simply "unity in revolt *(stasis)*."[31] To be sure, he used the term "great church" *(megalē ekklēsia),* when he compared the majority with the sects, but the term may have originated in liturgy and come from Judaism, since it occurs in Psalms 21:26 and 39:10.[32]

Practically, Celsus argues that if everyone were to maintain neutrality as the Christians do, the emperor would be left alone, while "earthly affairs would come into the power of the most lawless and savage barbarians." In addition, if the Romans were to call upon the god of the Christians, he would not come down and fight on their side.[33] Perhaps he has not heard either Apollinaris' claim for the Twelfth Legion or Melito's sketch of imperial history; or perhaps he heard them and rejected them.

Celsus is especially critical of the Christian attitudes and actions that he discusses toward the end of his treatise. For example, Christians "deliberately rush forward to arouse the wrath of an emperor or governor which brings on blows and tortures and even death." He is referring to volunteer martyrs,[34] especially prominent after 172 with the rise of Montanism.

Again, he tells them that "if someone orders you to take an oath by an emperor among men, that is nothing dreadful." Epictetus had accepted the fact of the oath when he said that "you ought to take an oath to the god within (your *daimōn*) as the soldiers do to Caesar," though he also used irony in regard to it when pointing out that the men of Nicopolis, supposedly free, were accustomed to shout, "By the fortune of Caesar, we are free men!"[35]

Christians held varying views, though all opposed oaths. Justin stated that they did not take oaths at all.[36] Some refused to take an oath by the Genius or Fortune of the emperor,[37] sometimes specifically because they "did not acknowledge the empire of this age."[38] The apologists Tatian, Athenagoras, and Theophilus do not discuss the subject, however, and apparently consider it less crucial than other matters.

Celsus says Christians should take the oath because "earthly things have been given to him (the emperor), and whatever you receive in this life you receive from him." Christians did not agree. Origen says that this statement is "certainly not true."[39] The giver is "God and his providence."

Toward the end Celsus urges Christians to "help the emperor with all their power and cooperate with him in what is right and fight for him and be fellow soldiers if he presses for this, and fellow generals with him; to accept public office if necessary, for preserving law and religion."[40] Origen agrees on cooperation but rejects the specific proposals.

We conclude that while Celsus certainly knew a good deal about the Christianity of his time, his work reflects no special effort to reply to the apologists, who in turn paid little if any attention to his arguments. The only clear exception is made by Tatian, who seems to decry what Celsus said about Christian converts among women and children (see chapter 13).

Sources of Religious Authority

Celsus' main religious authorities were the sages of Greek and oriental antiquity who with others relied on an ancient original wisdom. Pherecydes and Heraclitus stood closer to this tradition than later philosophers did, but Celsus was devoted to Plato and his successors.[41] He may even have had some contact with Hellenistic Judaism, for he represents a Jew as holding that "the Logos is Son of God."[42] Chadwick compares two significant passages in Philo.[43] On the other hand, Celsus may simply have been relying on statements by Justin with which he agreed.[44] We recall Andresen's hypothesis that Celsus had read Justin's *Apology* and intended to answer it.[45] It is hard to imagine him as conducting research in Philo's works.

Celsus Not Significant for the Apologists

The significance of Celsus' work lies in the fact that he has investigated second-century Christianity and knows a good deal about it, perhaps more than Origen admits. He attacks it not on the basis of slander and scandal but from the standpoint of an enlightened, philosophically minded, pro-

Roman Greek of the late second century, intolerant of innovation especially in religious affairs. The work is not directly relevant to the second-century apologists, however. Both Christians and pagans failed to communicate before Origen replied to Celsus about seventy years later.

16
Theophilus
of Antioch

Commodus, the son of Marcus Aurelius, inherited the throne on March 17, 180. Eusebius wrongly supposed that a new era dawned for the church, claiming that "during the reign of Commodus our affairs took an easier turn and, thanks to the divine grace, peace embraced the churches throughout the whole world. . . . Already large numbers even of those at Rome, highly distinguished for wealth and birth, were advancing toward their own salvation with all their households and kindred." The only martyr-acts Eusebius possessed were those of the illustrious Roman Apollonius, whose judge Perennius invited him to offer a defense before the Senate.[1]

The Scillitan Martyrs (180)

In fact, Commodus' reign began with the persecution of Christians. Four months after his accession, on July 17, 180—a definite date given by the consuls of the year and the day "XVI kalendas Augustas"—some Christians of Scillium near Carthage were brought before the proconsul of Africa, Vigellius Saturninus, the first governor to have Christians put to death in Africa. He was offended by their criticism of Roman religion and its rites and told them to follow his example by taking an oath by the Genius of the emperor and offering prayers for his health *(salus)*. To this demand their leader replied, "I do not recognize the empire of this world, but I serve the God whom no man has seen or can see with these eyes."[2] He added, "I have not committed theft, and I pay the sales tax on whatever I buy, for I recognize my Lord as the emperor of kings and all nations." When the proconsul advised him to recant, he claimed that to commit murder or bear false witness is worse than lack of devotion to the state. The basic outlook of the martyrs, or at least of their leader, is related to a moral stand resembling the teaching of the Decalogue and of Theophilus of Antioch— essentially an ethical monotheism close to Hellenistic Judaism.

The Acts of Apollonius (184 or Earlier)

The continuance of martyrdom, as well as some of Theophilus' ideas, are reflected in the Acts of Apollonius, which depict the trial of a martyr, this time set at either Ephesus or Rome, under Commodus.[3] Apparent echoes of Theophilus doubtless owe much to the literary construction of the document but something also to historical tradition.[4] J. Schwartz suggests that because of affinities with the *Martyrdom of Ignatius* and Theophilus, the *Acts* come from Antioch.[5] Certainly the document is closer to the apologists than to political reality, but it could have been produced at Rome (for example) as well as Antioch.

Like Theophilus, Apollonius begins by proclaiming himself a Christian and refers to his worship of the creator God "who made heaven and earth and sea and everything in them." This God gave "just and good and marvelous commandments" against "all injustice and lawlessness and idolatry and evil thoughts." He opposes even "the beginnings of sins," and the Logos of God has taught us to avoid such sins. For this reason Christians cannot take oaths, even though they are quite willing to honor the emperor and pray for his power. Apollonius is thus prepared to discuss moral topics such as "repentance and oaths" and "sacrifice," already treated by Theophilus.

He refuses to sacrifice to idols, made of gold or silver or bronze or iron or wood or stone. These are not gods, for they "neither hear nor see but are works of carpenters and goldsmiths and carvers." The true God breathed a "living soul" into all men and daily pours life into all. There follows a carefully structured analysis of what idols are or imitate, going beyond Theophilus into Stoic philosophy.

Men sin when they worship beings held together by cohesion (stone, bits of wood) or growth (plants) or sense perception (animals) or reason (man). This classification, derived from the Stoic Chrysippus, was known to both Philo and Clement of Alexandria.[6] Apollonius adds invidious comments expressed by various apologists, especially Theophilus: Egyptians worship a foot basin, while at Athens Socrates derisively took an oath by a plane tree. For the worship of human beings he cites Dionysus, torn to pieces, Heracles, burned alive, and Zeus, buried on Crete. Mythological stories about the offspring of the gods are equally impious.[7]

Apollonius now turns back to Christian morality, insisting that it involves "continence," in glances as well as deeds. This is so because "the Lord's word is for the heart that can see, just as eyes can see the light," even though "nothing is accomplished by the light that shines on the blind." (This is part of Theophilus' argument for the vision of God.)

The Roman official, like an interlocutor in an apology, agrees with this part of the discussion. "We too are aware that the word of God is the generator of the soul and body of the just, speaking and teaching how dear it is to God." He shares the martyr's strong emphasis on morality.

Unlike Theophilus or the Scillitan martyrs, however, Apollonius goes on to speak explicitly about "our Savior Jesus Christ," who "became a man in Judea" and was essentially a teacher. He taught about the God of all things, virtue and how to achieve it, the immortality of the soul, judgment after death, and "a reward given by God after the resurrection for the labors for virtue undertaken by those who have lived piously." His coming was foretold by the prophets, who said that he would be "just and virtuous in every respect." "By doing good to all men he would persuade them to worship the God of all for the sake of virtue." This is the kind of doctrine we should expect from Theophilus had he discussed Jesus at all. It is what Laeuchli calls "monotheistic nomism."[8]

Under Commodus, then, Christians were put to death at least in Africa and Italy or Asia. At the end of Theophilus' third book he claims that Greeks

> slander the glory of the imperishable and only God (Rom. 1:23); they have persecuted and daily persecute those who worship him. Moreover, they have appointed prizes and honors for those who euphoniously insult God,[9] while they have stoned some and killed others who are zealous for virtue and practice a holy life; and to this day they afflict them with cruel tortures. (3.30)

Conceivably he is referring to the cruel and unusual tortures of the Gallican martyrs. He may have eastern Christians in mind.

A faint indication of moderation in Asia is mentioned by Tertullian in reference to Arrius Antoninus, proconsul of Asia in 183/184. He was conducting a vigorous persecution when all the Christians of a certain city presented themselves together before his tribunal. He had a few of them executed but addressed the others thus: "You wretches, if you desire to die you have cliffs and nooses."[10] He thus expressed the attitude of the earlier authorities Marcus Aurelius and Celsus (see chapter 9): Christians are suicidal.

Persecution does seem to diminish around this time, and Irenaeus gives a different picture, perhaps related to the situation in the Roman church. Christian influence on the court increased toward the end of Commodus' reign, as we shall see. In any event, Irenaeus enthusiastically praised the Romans for the *pax Romana*. "The world has peace through them, and we walk the roads without fear and sail wherever we wish."[11] Irenaeus' exegesis of Romans 13:1–7 is more subtle than what we find in the apologists. Political authority, he says, has been developed in opposition to savagery and crime. It is generally beneficial and keeps men from consuming one another like fish, although only one out of three kinds is really good, presumably monarchy, which leads to the correction and assistance of those ruled. Another kind, probably aristocracy, is good but under worse circumstances ultimately produces fear, retribution, and rebuke (cf. Rom. 13:3–4). A third kind, however, is bad. This is either tyranny or mob rule, and results in mockery, insult, and arrogance for the citizens. Irenaeus insists that magistrates under this form of government who govern unjustly, illegally, or tyrannically will be punished at the last judgment.[12] Presumably he has in mind magistrates like those who persecuted the Christians in Gaul, or the earlier governor who put Polycarp to death.

In a more apocalyptic mood, he notes an interpretation of the mysterious "666" of Revelation 13 as the Greek word LATEINOS and adds that the Latins are ruling now; "but we will not boast about that." He does not want to identify the Antichrist with an emperor and prefers the guess that the Antichrist will bear the mythological name TEITAN.[13] It appears that he had not read the third book of Theophilus' treatise with its clear reference to persecution.

The Date of Theophilus

The third book by Theophilus seems to have been unknown to Eusebius, who dated his episcopate in the years from 169 to 177.[14] Book 3 was certainly written after the death of Marcus Aurelius and the accession of Commodus. In it Theophilus provides a list of Roman emperors, without reference to any co-regents, that ends with the death of Marcus Aurelius (3.27) in March 180.

Eusebius' notion that Theophilus was bishop in 169–177 may well come from what he says about the emperor in book 1. Like God, the one emperor "has subordinates whom he does not allow to be called emperors, for 'emperor' is his name and it is not right for another to be given this title." The statement was not correct for most of Marcus Aurelius' reign, since he ruled jointly with Lucius Verus from 161 to 169 and with Commodus from 177 to 180. The only period of real monarchy was thus 169–177, the time of his episcopate according to Eusebius.

He could have written, indeed did write, under the monarch Commodus, but Eusebius did not consider this possibility. While it is possible that books 1 and 2 were written under Commodus, and book 3 was certainly composed under him, the use of the first two books by Irenaeus suggests that they may have been written earlier.

Theophilus and Rhetoric

Eusebius substitutes rhetoric for exact information when he claims that Theophilus was not concerned with apologetic or theology but with heresy. "The shepherds of the churches everywhere," he wrote, "as though driving off wild beasts from the sheep of Christ, excluded [heretics] at one time by rebukes and exhortations to the brothers, . . . at another by correcting their opinions with most accurate refutations in written treatises."[15] These remarks have little to do with Theophilus' extant work. Book 1, for example, belongs to deliberative oratory and ends with Theophilus' statement that "this is my God; I advise (*symbouleuō*) you to fear him and believe him." The verb "advise" refers to the *symbouleutikon genos* of oratory. He begins the book with a denunciation of false rhetorical language, and each of the three books begins with a *proekthesis,* "introduction" or preface, setting forth the main points of the contents as commended by rhetoricians.[16]

Book 2 refers back to the first book, or at least its contents, as a *homilia,* an "instruction" or "lesson," as in Justin.[17] The second book itself is a "composition" or "treatise" *(syngramma),* that is to say a work rather carefully composed.[18] The first two books are catechetical in nature, like the other books, or the same books, mentioned by Eusebius.

Book 3 contains a *hypomnēma* or collection of notes or materials but presents itself as a letter. This book is independent of the others and does not presuppose their contents. It was written after 180, but the first two books could have been written some years, perhaps many years, earlier. There are echoes of book 2, not book 3, in Irenaeus.

The style of Theophilus is resolutely "plain," as one would expect from his denunciation of "fluent speech and euphonious diction" at the beginning of book 1. In the first sentence he says that these characteristics of rhetorical elegance produce "delight and praise," but then adds, "for wretched men who have a depraved mind," thus echoing 2 Timothy 3:8. Demetrius notes that the plain style aims at lucidity and is by no means either elevated or elegant.[19] Eusebius described the books as "elementary," a term he also applied to the *Shepherd* of Hermas to indicate its lack of style and sophisticated theology. He also told how Origen gave the task of "elementary" instruction to another teacher and kept the advanced students for himself.[20] The term seemed appropriate for Theophilus' work and, no doubt, his doctrine.

Beyond such considerations, Theophilus follows the advice of rhetors like Quintilian, who commends those who "pretend to conceal their eloquence."[21] His concern for history also encouraged him to begin with an attack on rhetoric as contrasted with truth. Herodian similarly insists on his own virtue as a historian when he contrasts "most writers engaged in compiling history" who "have shown a contempt for the truth and a preoccupation with vocabulary and style" and denounces their "sweetness" and inaccuracy.[22]

Political Apologetic

Theophilus' major political point is the distinction between worship of the emperor and honor paid him. Christians worship only the real and true God, the Creator. The emperor, on the other hand, is a creature of God and deserves not worship but legitimate honor as a man appointed by God to judge justly (1.11). The distinction between legitimate and illegitimate honor was an old one, expressed for example by Tiberius in a letter of the year 15 in order to refuse honors suitable for the gods while accepting those that were "more moderate and human." Only Augustus, deified after death, could receive honors as divine.[23] Since Christians did not accept the deification of emperors Theophilus drew the line differently, but the line was there to draw.

He went on to insist on loyalty to the emperor. "Honor the emperor (1 Peter 2:17) by wishing him well, by praying for him (cf. 1 Tim. 2:2), for by so doing you perform the will of God (1 Peter 2:15). The law of God says, 'My son, honor God and the king and disobey neither one; for they will suddenly punish their enemies' (Prov. 24:21–22)." The statement recalls Romans 13, a passage to be quoted in *To Autolycus* 3.14. "The divine word gives us orders about subordination to principalities and powers (Rom. 13:1–3) and prayer for them, so that we may lead a quiet and tranquil life (1 Tim. 2:1–2); and it teaches us to render all things to all, honor to whom honor is due, fear to whom fear, tribute to whom tribute; to owe no one anything except to love all" (Rom. 13:7–8). Why was honor due? Because the authority came from God. Theophilus is even willing to say that in the reign of the last Tarquin "the Romans were already becoming powerful because God was making them strong" (3.27). Perhaps he took this over directly from his pagan source for Roman chronology, where he could have found either "god" or "gods." It is unlikely that he was as loyal as the Asian apologists were.

Bishops had long advocated loyalty in moderation. Toward the beginning of the second century Polycarp had urged the Philippians to "pray for emperors and powers and principalities."[24] Theophilus simply repeats the exhortation. Until he reaches the very end of his work he says nothing about any persecution of Christians.

Commodus, Theophilus, and Antioch

Because of the revolt of Avidius Cassius, Marcus Aurelius was "deeply angered at the citizens of Antioch and took away their games and many of the distinctions of the city."[25] Later, however, he bestowed benefits on them, according to the chronicler Malalas. He built a large public bath, called the *Commodium,* and a covered running track next to it with seats and porticoes between the bath and a restored temple of Athena. Below the track was a temple to Zeus Olympios.

The upper classes of the city petitioned the emperor for permission to hold Olympic games and other spectacles, presumably to be restored after Marcus Aurelius' interdict, and Commodus therefore allowed them in honor of Zeus Olympios. They were to be held every fourth year for 45 consecutive days in July and August. The citizens themselves bought the rights to the games from the Pisans (people of Olympia) of Greece for a period of 90 Olympiads. Unfortunately Malalas gives the date of the original temple of Zeus Olympios, in the Antiochene year 260, or 40 B.C., not the date of the new games.[26] The *Paschal Chronicle,* however, sets the games in 181.[27]

Theophilus seems to have Antiochene events in mind at several points. In his first book he lists various Zeuses who were in fact worshiped at Antioch. He names the Olympian first and, among others, Zeus Kassios and Zeus Keraunios.[28] His chronography is partly based on Olympiads, and he explains that "the foundation of the Olympiads, they say, received religious observance from the time of Iphitus, though according to some it was from Haimon, also called 'of Elis.' " When (after Justin) he refers to "prizes and honors" awarded for insulting God he may have Olympic contests in mind (3.27, 29–30).

What Is Christianity?

The term "Christian" appears in these books only five times. Autolycus attacks the name but does not recognize either the utility of oil or the fact that "Christian" comes from being chrismated with the oil of God (1.1, 12). Theophilus' singular explanation is close to the Jewish-Christian notion that both Adam and Christ were thus anointed.[29] "Only Christians have held the truth," he says, for they have been "taught by the Holy Spirit who spoke in the holy prophets" (2.33). This notion too is Jewish-Christian and points to the Spirit as the source of revelation from Adam onward.[30] Admittedly the picture of unction may be no more than what we find in Hippolytus, who explains that kings and priests were called the Christs of God because they were anointed with the holy oil that Moses once prepared.[31] But this too explains a term originally Jewish.

Like other apologists Theophilus attacks the false accusations levied against Christians, who in fact practice the highest virtue. We shall later see that he ventured into realms of Christian theology not frequented by others and taught a Jewish-Christian doctrine not unlike what can be found in the Pseudo-Clementine *Homilies* and *Recognitions,* though considerably closer to the "orthodoxy" of his time and later. His "mainstream" position is confirmed, at least in part, when both Irenaeus and Novatian occasionally use his work and excerpts appear in John of Damascus.

The Last Days of Commodus and Marcia

We should imagine that Theophilus was dead before the latter years of Commodus, when the emperor was devoted to a concubine named Marcia, "whom he loved to have portrayed as an Amazon, and for whose sake he even wanted to enter the arena at Rome dressed as an Amazon." Whether or not this notice from the Augustan History is reliable, Marcia's influence over Commodus was such that after Victor, bishop of Rome after 189, asked her to obtain the release of Christians from the mines in Sardinia, the emperor immediately agreed.[32] Toward the end of 192, however, he was planning to murder her along with the consuls for the new year, but with the leading courtiers she struck first and murdered him on the night of December 31. She did not survive him long but was executed by the emperor Didius Julianus.[33]

It is doubtful that Theophilus' apologetic theology could have survived the political and moral complexity of this court situation. A few years later Tertullian did his best, insisting that Christians had not joined the factions of Avidius Cassius against Marcus or Niger and Albinus against Septimius Severus. In addition, he implied that none had attacked Commodus when in retreat at Laurentum or as a gymnast had strangled him.[34] He made no reference to the Christian sympathizer Marcia, who once supplied valuable information to Commodus at Laurentum but later conspired to kill him.

17
Theophilus
and Literature

Like other apologists, Theophilus appeals to his reader's "love of learn-ing." The term, with the related "learn-loving," occurs in Christian authors first in Melito, then in Tatian and Athenagoras,[1] and fairly often in Clement and Origen. Theophilus is fond of the expression.[2] Perhaps he is looking back to Isocrates: "If you are a lover of learning, you will learn much."[3]

Theophilus was acquainted, often through anthologies, with some of the better known works of Greek literature, though he derided the futility of all and also attacked Greek authors for their lack of historical sense.

> What good did it do Homer that he wrote the *Trojan War*—and led many astray? or Hesiod, the catalogue of the *Theogony*—of those whom he called gods? or Orpheus, the 365 gods—whom he himself rejected at the end of his life when he said in his *Testaments* that there is one god? What use to Aratus was his description of the sphere of the cosmic circle, or to those who made statements like his—except for the human fame that they wrongly acquired? What truth did they speak? Or of what use were their tragedies for Euripides and Sophocles and the other tragic poets, or their comedies for Menander and Aristophanes and the other comic poets, or their histories for Herodotus and Thucydides? or the shrines and the pillars of Hercules for Pythagoras? or the Cynic philosophy for Diogenes? or the dogmatic denial of providence for Epicurus? or the teaching of atheism for Empedocles? or the oath by dog and goose and plane-tree for Socrates, not to mention his oath by [the lightning-struck] Asclepius and his invocation of demons? For what purpose was he willing to die? What kind of reward did he hope to receive after death? And what use was Plato's famous "education" for him? (*To Autolycus* 3.2)

In this passage Theophilus follows Tatian in deriding the foundations of Greek literary education *(paideia)*, beginning with the ancient epic poets and passing onward to the most famous tragic and comic poets before turning to historians and philosophers. He reserves his main attacks for

Plato, Socrates, and the pre-Socratics, though he also denounces the Cynic Diogenes and the atheist Epicurus.

In his apology he frequently refers to such authors, though his citations from almost all come from anthologies of poetry and philosophical opinions. He is no student of literature, though he tries to give the impression that he is one. We shall examine some of his references to Greek literature and art.

Art and Philosophy

Musaeus

Like Justin, Theophilus was especially concerned with the immoral aspects of Greek philosophy, literature, and art. He criticizes Zeus severely and knows how on Mount Ida in Crete he was "nourished by a goat which he slew and skinned to make himself a garment" (1.9). The *Theogony* of the old epic poet Musaeus contained the story about the goat as nurse and shield; from Lactantius, early in the fourth century, we learn that Zeus used the shield when fighting the Titans; but though he knew Theophilus in Greek he obviously did not get this point about Musaeus from our apologist. Ogilvie traces Lactantius' source to a commentary on Germanicus' *Aratea,* a Latin translation of Aratus.[4]

Did Theophilus Use a Commentary on Aratus?

Presumably Theophilus himself did not use Latin sources but may have gleaned the item from some Greek commentary on Aratus, where we find some other fragments of Hyginus.[5] His description of Aratus' work as the "description of the sphere of the cosmic circle" (3.2) is not a book title,[6] and perhaps Theophilus took it too from a Greek commentary on Aratus (there were at least 27 of them) and found Musaeus quoted there. The first nine lines of Aratus' poem came from the anthology he was following in *To Autolycus* 2.8 and elsewhere, but he may have looked at commentaries as well.

From Chrysippus?

More simply, however, Theophilus may have derived his story of Zeus and the goat from the Stoic Chrysippus. According to the Epicurean critic Philodemus, Chrysippus made use of Musaeus in his treatise *On the Gods* and tried to make him a Stoic.[7] Perhaps this was one of the stories Chrysippus allegorized. Theophilus takes it literally.

Later in his treatises Theophilus says that Zeus once lived on Mount Ida but now is unknown there and therefore has left it—not to ascend into the heavens but to go to Crete and be buried there (2.3). Theophilus seems unaware that Ida is on Crete. His comments oppose the view of Callimachus, who in his *Hymn to Zeus* referred to those who call him "born on the Idaean hills" and say he has a tomb built by Cretans. While Callimachus insisted that Zeus was everlasting, Theophilus claimed that he was mortal, and in his third book treated him as a sometime king of Crete (3.23). Evidently he is taking stories about him literally (see chapter 2).

Theophilus on Hera and Zeus

Rather surprisingly, Theophilus twice mentions the immoral kisses of Hera and Zeus in the course of an extended attack on Zeus himself, but there is no reason to accuse him of originality. As in the case of Justin, either Chrysippus or a critic of Chrysippus must be responsible for the discussion.

The apologist begins by attacking Zeus for initiating "unspeakable unions and unlawful meals." He not only consumed his daughter Metis but also prepared "disgusting banquets for the gods." Theophilus takes such stories literally and insists that according to Greek poets "Hera, Zeus' own sister, not only married but had intercourse with him *(arrētopoiein)* with impure mouth." A few chapters later he repeats the complaint and names Chrysippus, "who uttered so much nonsense," as the source of it (3.3, 8).

Von Arnim's collection of Stoic fragments contains four texts on this topic, three of them Christian, and all refer to Chrysippus. Theophilus provides the oldest reference.[8] Next comes Origen.[9] Another fragment states that Chrysippus mentioned an image at Argos in his *Erotic Epistles.*[10] Such a bibliographical reference does not inspire confidence, for these erotic epistles led to violent controversy. Some Stoics claimed that Epicurus, not Chrysippus, wrote fifty "licentious epistles," which they called "the epistles commonly attributed to Chrysippus,"[11] while the Epicurean Zeno was said to have killed a Stoic for ascribing them to Epicurus.[12] In any event, the passage confirms Chrysippus' discussion of Hera and Zeus.

The fourth text, from Diogenes Laertius, shows how controversial the subject was. He knows "people who run down Chrysippus for having written much in a tone that is gross and indecent."[13]

> In his book *On the Ancient Natural Philosophers* at line 600 or thereabouts he interprets the story of Hera and Zeus coarsely, with details no one would soil his lips by repeating. He may be commending physical doctrine, but the language used is more appropriate to prostitutes than to deities. Moreover, it is not even mentioned by bibliographers who wrote on the titles of books. What Chrysippus makes of it is not to be found in Polemo or Hypsicrates or even in Antigonus. It is his own invention.

Diogenes and his source obviously regarded the three last-named pornographers as the acme or nadir of immoral literature. Since he views Chrysippus' allegorizations as even worse, he may well be following not Chrysippus himself but a source with strong philosophical objections to the allegorization as well as moral objections to the myth. This kind of criticism flourished in the Academy after Plato. Bidez and Cumont modernized it when they denounced Chrysippus' "scabrous speculations, worthy of a Freudian."[14]

Conceivably Theophilus too read some militant critic of both Epicurus and the Stoics. We know he was acquainted with Clitomachus, the pupil and scribe of Carneades (3.7), and he may have relied on Carneades and the New Academy for his criticism. Certainly he felt that both Epicurus and Chrysippus wrote pointlessly, and this was a stock Academic-Skeptical complaint.[15] Indeed, Carneades said that "if Epicurus wrote something, Chrysippus out of rivalry also produced a work of the same volume."[16]

As Carneades criticized both Epicurus and Chrysippus he inevitably became involved in the quarrels between the two, especially with Epicurus' defense of his hedonism against "some who do not understand our teachings, disagree with them, or give them an evil interpretation"[17] and with Chrysippus' defense of allegorized mythology. Out of this concatenation of charges and arguments an apologist like Theophilus could and did find grist for his mill.

Carneades and the Skeptics

Theophilus also seems to have used some of Carneades' analogies for the need of "faith."

> Faith leads the way in all activities. What farmer can harvest unless he first entrusts the seed to the earth? Who can cross the sea unless he first entrusts himself to the ship and the pilot? What sick man can be cured unless he first entrusts himself to the doctor? What art or science can anyone learn unless he first delivers and entrusts himself to the teacher? (*To Autolycus* 1.8)

Carneades insisted that one follows "probability" in voyaging, sowing a crop, marrying, begetting children, and in many other activities "in which you will be following nothing but what is probable."[18] Similarly (but without "probability") Xenophon had pointed out that in every activity people are willing to obey those whom they consider the best—in sickness the doctor, on ship the pilot, on a farm the farmer.[19] Origen too uses Carneades' analogies for faith: sailing, sowing seeds, marrying, and begetting children.[20]

Theophilus may also owe much of his "skeptical" manner of argument about Greek inconsistency to Carneades. He tries to show that Greek ideas about revelation, the gods, and the nature of the world are inconsistent.[21] For a framework he seems to rely on what had become the "tenth mode" of Skeptical argumentation as set forth by Aenesidemus and reported by Sextus Empiricus and Diogenes Laertius. This mode was used for criticizing ethics and was based on "rules of conduct, habits, laws, legendary beliefs, and dogmatic conceptions."[22] Sextus recommends opposing each category to itself as well as to the others.[23] Just so, in Theophilus' third book he plays materials in such categories against one another.

Poets and philosophers disagree with themselves and one another over the existence of the gods and providence. "Undertaking to write about purity, they advocate lascivious acts and fornication and adultery and even introduce abominable obscenities." The Stoics "advocate cannibalism and the cooking and eating of fathers by their own children." Plato treats wives as common property, while Epicurus and the Stoics advocate atheism, incest, and homosexual acts. Beyond such disagreements like the contradictions of philosophers in theological matters such as God and the soul.[24]

Skeptical ideas are related to the collections of conflicting philosophical opinions *(doxai)* which, like Athenagoras, Theophilus used (2.4; 3.7). In one passage he ascribes the godless theology of Epicurus to the Stoa. His error can be explained by recalling that in a similar doxography used by Epiphanius such views are assigned to the Middle Stoic Panaetius.[25] Presumably he is following a source critical of both Epicureans and Stoics—in other words, someone like Carneades.

He then turns to those who ascribe automatic operation to the universe, call the world uncreated and nature eternal, and say there is no divine providence but that each person's conscience is God. Here he first relies on some doxographical collection like the one used by Hippolytus, in which Epicurus "acknowledges God as eternal and imperishable but says he cares for no one but himself, and in general says neither providence nor fate exists but everything takes place of its own accord."[26] Theophilus has substituted "nature" for "God"—perhaps following an anti-Epicurean source. For other information he seems to rely on the *Monostichoi* ("one-liners") ascribed to Menander. The idea that each person's conscience is God appears in the *Monostichoi.*[27]

History

Theophilus was aware that the histories of Herodotus and Thucydides formed part of the Greek school curriculum (3.2). He pointed out that these historians, and Xenophon as well, began their histories late, around the reigns of Cyrus and Darius (3.26). Herodotus referred to eating children or parents (3.5),[28] and both historians gave meaningless details. For example, Herodotus mentioned Zopyrus, a deserter from the Persians to Athens, while Thucydides named Hippias as a Greek tyrant; both told of the wars of the Athenians and Spartans. They discussed the deeds of Xerxes and of a certain Pausanias "who almost died of hunger in the enclosure of

Athena," not to mention events related to Themistocles and the Peloponne-sian War and to Alcibiades and Thrasybulus.[29]

For oriental-Hebrew chronology Theophilus relied on nothing but Jose-phus' apologetic treatise *Against Apion* and used what Josephus was quoting to show the antiquity of the exodus and the building of the temple in Jerusalem. The authors Josephus cited were the Hellenistic Egyptian Mane-tho, Menander of Ephesus, and Berossus (3.20–23, 29). In addition Theoph-ilus appealed to a certain Thallus for the correlation of Greek and Assyrian history (see below). He found Roman chronology in the records of Chryse-ros the Nomenclator, who wrote soon after 180 (3.27).

What makes Theophilus unusual among the Greek apologists is his cita-tion of two Greek works having to do with Egyptian religion, and a third on the demes of Alexandria related to the god Dionysus there. It is not the interest in Egypt that is unusual, for we find it in Athenagoras too. What makes the difference is Theophilus' use of specialized treatises. He refers to the book entitled *Semenouthi* by "Apollonides surnamed Horapius" as mentioning Egyptian "demons." In some instances these were really men, Theophilus avers. Apollonides also wrote "histories" about Egyptian reli-gion and kings (2.6).[30]

A papyrus in *Papiri Greci e Latini,* published by the Società italiana per la ricerca dei papiri greci e latini in Egitto (x.1149), contains excerpts from decisions made by Roman prefects of Egypt (up to A.D. 12) and says that "the priestly law 'Semnouthi' [*sic*] has a content like that of the decrees." The topic under discussion is Egyptian religion, with the functions of the priests and the *pastophori* being kept separate.[31] The papyrus thus confirms the reliability of Theophilus' reference.

A different Egyptian author, Apollonius, appears in Theophilus' work (3.16, 26), though Jacoby[32] suggested that he might be the same person as Apollonides. This man said that the world had been created 153,075 years earlier. As a Greek chronologer in Egypt he must have paid attention to the "Sothic years" of the Egyptians. These consisted of periods of 1,460 Julian years (1,461 Egyptian) in which the months "rotated through all seasons of the solar year." When they returned to their starting point, the rising of Sirius fell on the first day of the month Thoth, as was the case in A.D. 139.[33]

Two explanations of Apollonides' figure seem possible. First, Theophilus' figure may need to be emended. Lydus says that some Egyptians could calculate the time from one "new creation" to another in reference to a solar cycle of 1,461 years and reach a total of 1,753,200 years.[34] Lydus' figure amounts to 1,200 Sothic years. Theophilus gives the number "myriads of years/ five and ten/ and three thousand/ seventy five." Lydus has "myriads of years/ a hundred/ seventy five/ and three thousand." Possibly the two figures could have been confused. Second, Theophilus' figure may be cor-rect. If the Sothic year was calculated at 1,460 solar years, 104 of them would be equal to 151,840, and this number would be correlated with 1321 B.C. In this case, 153,075 years would take us to 86 B.C. On the other hand, if the year was calculated at 1,461 solar years, the product would be 151, 944, in 1322 B.C., and the final date would be 191 B.C. Either date would be appropriate for a Greco-Egyptian author, but—after all this—Apollonides' date remains unknown.

The third writer on matters in Egypt, though in this case at Alexandria, was a certain Satyrus, who wrote *On the Demes of the Alexandrians* (2.7). Satyrus traced the ancestry of the Ptolemies back to Dionysus and Althaea in order to explain how the Dionysiac tribe had demes named after Dionysus' wife and daughter. Other tribes also took their names from Dionysus' relatives and descendants. A papyrus fragment partly overlaps what Theophilus quoted; this is Oxyrhynchus Papyrus xxvii.2465 of the second century A.D.[35]

Though Theophilus could not display the kind of erudition demonstrated by Clement of Alexandria, he was showing that he had access to literature on Egyptian matters and could make use of collections of abstruse materials. One can only compare it with the kind of pedantry ridiculed by Epictetus. "How do you know this?—Hellanicus says so in his *Egyptian History.*"[36]

In addition, he knew something about the chronologist Thallus, citing him for the rule of Bel over the Assyrians when Kronos ruled the Titans. Bel lived 322 years before the Trojan War (3.29).[37] The fragments of Thallus survive only among Christian authors, and Theophilus is the earliest of them.

Poetry

Naturally Theophilus was acquainted with Homer, probably also with Hesiod and some forged Orphic poems. The criticisms he levies against Homer and Hesiod are conventional, especially prevalent among skeptics, Academic or otherwise. Like Hesiod and Orpheus, Homer falsely claims to be inspired. All of them really "spoke out of imagination and error" (3.2, 17; 2.8).

Homer's theology is erroneous. When he mentioned "Ocean, origin of the gods" he was obviously referring to water, which is not God (2.5).[38] Homer said that Zeus lived on Mount Ida, and also that Helios, the Sun, looked on all things and heard all. From Ida Zeus could not do what God must do (2.3). He rejects the notion, found in an anthology, that "Zeus increases or diminishes virtue in men" (2.8). Like other critics, he points to Apollo as afraid of Achilles, in love with Daphne, ignorant of the fate of Hyacinthus. In Homer Aphrodite is wounded and her brother Ares is called the "bane of men," while "ichor" flows from the gods (2.9). Finally Theophilus notes, perhaps following an anthology once more, that Homer contradicts himself on the fate of the soul. In the *Odyssey* the soul takes flight "like a dream," while in the *Iliad* it goes down to Hades (2.38).

Hesiod too is thoroughly unreliable. He should have known that Zeus was king of Crete and therefore that his father Kronos, against whom he waged war, lived later than the creation of the world. His daughters, the Muses, were later still. They cannot have known what Hesiod asked them to tell him (2.5). The poet was not inspired and did not provide a true account of the origin of the world. Indeed, as Davids suggests, Theophilus noted that Hesiod himself depicted the Muses as telling him that they "know how to speak many false things as though they were true."[39] Sometimes the poets became sober in soul and agreed with the prophets, and therefore Hesiod could come close to Genesis when he spoke of the world as created and of chaos at the beginning of things (*Theogony* 116). The chaos was clearly prior to the gods, however; and if so, who set it in order?[40] Hesiod's whole discussion of the origin of the gods, not to mention the Titans, Cyclopes, and Giants, is ridiculous (2.6). (After further discussion of authors on the gods and providence, Theophilus turns to the true account in the first chapters of Genesis.)

Much of what Theophilus quotes from Greek tragedy and comedy comes to him from anthologies, notably from one used by Johannes Stobaeus in the fourth century. It includes his two quotations from Aeschylus, three from Sophocles, and eight from Euripides, but very few from other tragic poets. As for the comic poets, there are only one quotation apiece from Aristophanes and Menander but six from others. Most of these also come from anthologies, as do the first nine lines of Aratus' *Phenomena*.

Proverbs and the Like

Like his contemporaries, Theophilus does not shrink from using hackneyed expressions and commonplaces. He joins other rhetoricians in suggesting that ten thousand mouths or tongues would not suffice to describe the wonders of his topic (2.12). Homer was content to mention ten, but the number grew and the image became popular in Greek and Latin literature of the Empire.[41]

A proverbial expression suggests that if a master behaves well his slaves necessarily live properly (2.17). This is close to the proverb cited by Clement and others: "As is the mistress, so is the dog."[42]

Biblical Chronology

The achievement of which Theophilus was probably proudest comes at the end of book III, which thus received the title Lactantius knew: "On times." He prays for divine aid in accuracy as he begins to follow the biblical genealogies, relying first on Genesis from creation to the death of Jacob, a total of 3,468 years. Then he follows other biblical books (chiefly Judges and 1–2 Kings) and traditions (chiefly from Josephus, whose *Antiquities* he knew) to the end of the Babylonian exile. This gives a new total of 4,954 years, to which he adds six months and ten days because of the notices in 2 Chronicles 36:2 and 9. Adding twenty-eight years and reaching the date of the death of Cyrus in the 62nd Olympiad, he crosses over to the beginning of the 25-year reign of the last Roman king. He then summarizes his source which gave him 463 years for the Roman republic. Finally the Empire began, viewed as starting when Julius Caesar defeated Pompey at Pharsalus on August 9, 48 B.C. After many inaccuracies due to copyists or Theophilus or his source (Chryseros the Nomenclator), we finally reach "the period of the Caesars to the death of the emperor Verus" (Marcus Aurelius) in March 180, and since the period from the death of Cyrus and the reign of Tarquin to the death of Verus was 741 years, the total time from creation was 5,695 years and the odd six months and ten days.

Daniélou could not believe that this chronology had no eschatological meaning. He claimed that Theophilus was setting the birth of Christ in the world-year 5500.[43] Unfortunately the interval between the death of Marcus Aurelius in 180 and the birth of Christ (anywhere from 4 B.C. to A.D. 6) takes us back roughly to the world-years 5510 to 5520, dates without special significance. The key points in the historical scheme must be the ones Theophilus himself emphasizes when he gives subtotals: the deluge (2,242 years); the birth of Isaac, son of Abraham "our patriarch" (3,278 years); the death of Moses and the reign of "Jesus" (3,938 years); the death of David "our ancestor" and the reign of Solomon, who built the temple "in accordance with the will of God" (4,436 years); the destruction of the temple and the sojourning in Babylon ending under Cyrus (4,954 years); and the death of Marcus Aurelius, presumably recent (5,695 years). One can see that these events had historical-typological meaning for Christians, especially Jewish Christians. Theophilus' chronology remains within such limits. It has no eschatological referent at all, and this is why all his successors except Lactantius neglected it. (See chapter 22.)

Apparently Theophilus wrote other treatises on biblical history and theology. He probably alludes to such a work on the origin of Satan (2.28) or another (?) entitled *Genesis of the Cosmos* (2.29, cf. 30). It traced events at least as far as the deluge (2.30; 3.19). In addition, Eusebius tells us that he wrote catechetical works as well as against the heretics Hermogenes and Marcion.[44]

18
Theophilus
and the Bible

In Theophilus' view the prophets like the evangelists were inspired by God (2.9, 22). Contemporary pagans could easily accept such a presentation. The rhetor Aelius Aristides, for example, raises the question whether the poets were the only "friends of God" and concludes that "the prophets of the gods" were their friends *(theophileis)* as well.[1]

The Inspiration of Genesis

Following the prophets, Theophilus depicts the wonders of the creation in his first book, alluding to phrases from Job, Psalms, and Proverbs, and perhaps using the language of the Antiochene eucharistic anaphora (1.4, 6, 7). In the second book he says that no one can adequately express the wonders of the Genesis account—far superior to the "creation" in Hesiod's *Theogony*—but he tries to do so by providing elaborate exegesis, apparently both Jewish and Christian in nature, of the Genesis narratives about creation and the early history of humanity (2.10–32).

Jewish Exegesis of Genesis

Theophilus' exegesis of the Old Testament is primarily Jewish and even rabbinic. It does not have what R. P. C. Hanson described as "a clearly Alexandrian flavor"[2] except insofar as both Philo and his opponents were from Alexandria.[3]

One can show that his exegesis of Genesis is essentially Jewish by making use of two collections of Jewish materials: *Bereshith Rabbah* (abbreviated *BR*)[4] and Philo's *Questions on Genesis* (abbreviated *QG*).[5] There are discussions of these materials by Marmorstein[6] and me,[7] and one should not neglect the pioneering work of L. Ginzberg on Genesis.[8] Later we shall discuss Theophilus' antiheretical exegesis, often directed against Marcionites and thus favoring Jewish interpretation.

In *To Autolycus* 2.13, Theophilus notes that the creation began from above, and *BR* 1.15 is similar: "parallel to the case of a king who first made his throne and then his footstool" (Isa. 66:1).

Again in 2.13, the waters are described as half on the firmament, half on earth; and *BR* 4.4 states that "the Holy One, blessed be he, took all the primeval water and poured half in the firmament and half into the ocean."

2.15. Things on earth do not come from the planets; compare Philo, *On the Creation* 45–46: the sun is not the source of physical life and growth.

2.22. God walks in paradise; compare *QG* 1.42: "Though no voice is given forth, through a certain power prophets hear a divine voice sounding what is said to them."

2.23. There are pangs in childbirth; so in *QG* 1.49: "This experience comes to every woman who lives together with a man."

2.23. The serpent was condemned to creep on its belly and eat dirt, and the story is proved by the serpent's movements; so in *QG* 1.48: "The text is plain, since we have as testimony what we see. . . . He crawls upon his breast and belly, stuffed with food and drink, and has the insatiable desire of a cormorant."

2.24. The plants in paradise were most beautiful, as in *QG* 1.9: "It would be natural that plants should be ever flourishing and ever green, as belonging to the divine paradise." The tree of knowledge was unique; compare *BR* 15.7: "The Holy One, blessed be he, did not and will not reveal to man what that tree was."

2.24. Theophilus treats the rivers of paradise as real. Since this view is rejected by Philo (*QG* 1.12–13) it was accepted by other Jews.

2.24, 27. Adam was created neither mortal nor immortal but with an "opportunity for progress." Compare Nemesius of Emesa (*The Nature of Man* 5): "The Jews say that man was created at first neither avowedly mortal nor yet immortal, but rather in a state poised between the two . . . capable of becoming immortal when brought to perfection by moral progress." This is not Philo's allegorical doctrine, set forth in *On the Creation* 135: "Man is on the borderline between mortal and immortal nature, . . . mortal in body, immortal in mind."

2.24. Adam could have won immortality; compare *QG* 1.51, 55: "If he had been desirous of virtue, which makes the soul immortal, he would certainly have obtained heaven as his lot," [but] "after he began to turn to wickedness and to hurl himself down thereto, desiring mortal life, he failed to obtain immortality."

2.24. "To work" is "to keep the commandment of God"; so in *QG* 1.14: Paradise did not need to be worked, but Adam was "a law to husbandmen in all things which it is fitting to labor in." Compare *BR* 16.5: Man's duty was to study and keep the law.

2.26. God was beneficent in allowing Adam's future return to paradise, as in *BR* 21.7: R. Nehemiah: "He was sent forth from the garden of Eden in this world, but not in the next." R. Joshua b. Levi: "When he created him, he created him by his attributes of justice and mercy, and when he banished him, he likewise banished him in accordance with his attributes of justice and mercy."

Theophilus may be opposing Tatian, who when a Gnostic denied that Adam would be saved (Irenaeus *Heresies* 1.28.1). Hippolytus *(Refutation)* adds that Adam was the instigator of disobedience, whereas Theophilus 2.28 calls Eve the instigator of sin (cf. Micah 1:13 for the expression, Sir. 25:24 for the idea).

> 2.26. By calling Adam, God gave him an opportunity for repentance and confession, as in *QG* 1.45: "not a question but a kind of threat and reproach" (also anti-Marcionite).
> 2.28. Error through the serpent was going to refer to a multitude of nonexistent gods, just as in *QG* 1.36: "There was to be among mankind a belief in a multitude of gods . . . (introduced) through the most noxious and vile of beasts and reptiles."
> 2.28. Eve was created from Adam to show that God is one; compare *Mishnah Sanhedrin* 4.5: "[But a single man was created] so that the heretics should not say, 'There are many ruling powers in heaven.' "
> 2.28. Literal interpretation of the union of Adam and Eve; so also in *QG* 1.29: "When scripture says that the two are one flesh, it indicates something very tangible and perceptible to the senses."

In addition, Theophilus presents a high view of marriage and points out that husbands have sacrificed their lives for their wives. This Jewish attitude may well be aimed at the extreme statements of Tatian (see chapter 14).

> 2.29. God gave Cain an opportunity for repentance and confession (as with Adam, 2.26); compare *QG* 1.68: "He wishes that man himself of his own will shall confess."
> 2.29. After the murder of Abel the earth no longer "yawns" to accept blood, somewhat as in *QG* 1.67: "The ground was not to be the same after being forced to drink human blood unnaturally."

These passages prove that Theophilus' exegesis is essentially Jewish in origin.

Christian Exegesis of Genesis

At several important points, however, it is definitely Christian. In 2.14 Theophilus compares some of the islands in the sea to "assemblies *(synagōgai)* called holy churches," where lovers of the truth who desire to be saved can take refuge and escape the wrath and judgment of God. Other islands are more dangerous; they are "the doctrines of error, I mean of the heresies." Pirates "disable"[9] ships and run them on to rocky islands to destroy them.[10] The pirates are obviously heresiarchs. It seems likely that Theophilus or a predecessor is building on the reference in 1 Timothy 1:19 to heretics as having "made shipwreck of the faith."

In 2.15 we learn that "the three days prior to [the creation of] the luminaries are prefigurations of the triad, God and his Logos and his

Sophia. For a fourth prefiguration there is man, who needs light, so that there might be God, Logos, Sophia, Man." This exercise in numerology resembles the fantasies of Valentinian Gnostics on the opening words of Genesis and John. Ptolemaeus taught that two tetrads were revealed in Gen. 1:1–2: God, Beginning, Heaven, Earth, and Abyss, Darkness, Waters, Spirit, as well as in John 1:14: Father, Grace, Onlybegotten, Truth, and in John 1:3–4: Logos, Life, Man, Church.[11] Theophilus' triad and tetrad are different but contain very similar elements.

In 2.16 the blessing given marine animals (through whom was manifest "the manifold Sophia of God," Eph. 3:10) points toward "men's future reception of repentance and remission of sins (Luke 24:47 Codex Bezae, etc.) through water (John 3:3) and a washing of regeneration (Titus 3:5) for all who approach the truth and are reborn (John 3:3) and receive a blessing from God." The echoes of New Testament baptism are obvious.

Some of Theophilus' exegesis is also specifically antiheretical, as we should expect from an author who wrote against Hermogenes and Marcion.[12] In 2.25 he states against the Marcionite Apelles that the tree of knowledge did not contain death.[13]

His claim in the same chapter that Adam was an infant may be Jewish, but rabbinic views on Adam's age varied. Irenaeus repeated the claim that Adam was an infant, even though heretics might ask, "Could not God have shown forth the man mature from the beginning?"[14] Similarly Clement urged that Adam and Eve in paradise were "still children."[15] But heretics themselves sometimes held the same view. Saturninus of Antioch insisted that the infant Adam "wriggled like a worm,"[16] that is, like an infant, and Apelles said that man was not created perfect but was essentially a *baby*.[17] Theophilus replies to Apelles' criticism by holding that even a child is rightly punished for disobedience.[18] He cannot deny that Adam was an infant, for both his theology of growth and his scheme of chronology require the point.

Again in this chapter he replies to Apelles by insisting that God was not jealous of Adam in regard to the trees of knowledge and life.[19] Finally, he states against Marcion that God's question to Adam, "Where are you?" does not point to his ignorance.[20]

Moral Teaching in Creation

Theophilus (2.16–19) is aware that "marine animals and birds are of one nature, and some remain in their natural state, not harming those weaker than themselves but keeping the law of God and eating seeds from the earth," though others "transgress the law of God, eating meat and harming those weaker than themselves." Why should this be so? The wild animals "were not originally created evil or poisonous, for nothing was originally created evil by God." (This remark is directed against Marcionite criticism of the creation and the Creator.)[21] When man their master sinned, they sinned with him. "When man returns to his original state and so no longer does evil, they too will be restored to their original tameness" (2.16–17; cf. Isa. 11:6–9).

God's primeval command was that "man should have a diet of the fruits of the earth and seeds and herbs and fruit trees." In addition, "animals were to have the same diet as man." At that time "the earth brought forth everything spontaneously in accordance with the commandment of God" (2.18–19). Theophilus likes vegetarianism but treats it as optional, following the apostle Paul (Rom. 14:1–2) and joining several early patristic witnesses.[22] Presumably he was aware that colleagues like Irenaeus opposed the "so-called abstinence" of heretics from "so-called animate beings" and regarded them as "ungrateful to the God who made everything."[23] Irenaeus may have written the account of the Gallican Martyrs, which tells of a martyr who viewed such abstinence as normal.[24] In general, however, abstinence from meat was not compulsory, though it was a live option.[25]

The Law of God

The pinnacle of the moral law consists of "the ten chapters of the great and marvelous law which suffices for all righteousness" (3.12; cf. Matt. 3:15). This was the law of God, though given through Moses; it teaches the practice of "justice and piety and beneficence." Piety is enjoined in Exodus 20:3–5: "Thou shalt have none other gods but me. Thou shalt not make an idol for thyself . . . for I am the Lord thy God." Beneficence is enjoined in "Honor thy father and thy mother" (Ex. 20:12), and justice requires abstaining from adultery, murder, theft, false witness, and covetousness (Ex. 20:13–17) and, positively, demands honest judgments by judges (Ex. 23:6–8).[26] This much, then, is the great and marvelous law, though a chapter later another verse from Exodus (23:9) on sojourners or proselytes appears as part of God's "teaching through the law."

Two commandments are missing from Theophilus' decalogue, those on taking God's name in vain and on keeping the Sabbath, while the last two or three injunctions come from another section of Exodus, the "judgments" (chs. 21–23), which according to the *Didascalia apostolorum* belong to the Law along with the Decalogue.[27] Theophilus thus comes close to the *Didascalia*. Irenaeus limits the basic law to the traditional Decalogue, however.[28] as does the compiler of the *Apostolic Constitutions,* who cites Exodus 23:7–8 as expressed by "the divine voice of the Lord."[29]

Theophilus must be omitting two commandments from the Decalogue because according to the Gospels Jesus himself set them aside. On the one hand, Jesus ratified the commandments which Theophilus includes (Matt. 19:18), and forbade fraud as well (Mark 10:19). On the other hand, Jesus himself was accused of violating two of them—notably in the Gospel according to John, the one evangelist whom Theophilus calls inspired (2.22). John says that Jesus was accused of blasphemy (John 10:33, 36; cf. Mark 14:64) and did not observe the Sabbath (John 5:18; 9:16; cf. Matt. 12:1–4, etc.). The principle Theophilus follows is the one set forth in the Jewish-Christian *Clementine Homilies:* the teaching of Jesus shows which passages in the scriptures are true, which false.[30] The example of Jesus, then, explains the deletions from the Decalogue. It does not explain why Theophilus rewrote it thus. After all, he was still aware that, as the Second Command-ment says, "it is not right to take God's name idly and in vain," and his statement about the Sabbath seems to show that he knew that command-ment too. "Sabbath," he says, is "hebdomad" in Greek, but men "do not understand why they give it this name" (2.10, 12).

Elsewhere he echoes the Decalogue when he says that "the divine law" forbids idolatry and the worship of nature, alluding to Deuteronomy 4:19 and citing "the holy law" against adultery, murder, theft, false witness, and coveting a neighbor's wife. He goes on to note agreements among the law, the prophets, the *Sibylline Oracles,* and the poets (2.35–38),[31] and also discusses prophetic teaching about repentance and the agreement among law, prophets, and Gospels concerning justice,[32] chastity, and benevolence. He ends with a Gospel saying on not boasting and citations from the divine word (Romans and 1 Timothy) on obedience to the state (3.11–14).

Theophilus does not refer to the ceremonial law at all. He knows it exists, however, for he says that Solomon "built the temple in Jerusalem in accord-ance with the will of God," and later it was rebuilt "for God" (3.25–26). He also says that the Hebrew priests "devoted themselves to the temple by God's command and at that time cured every disease so that they healed lepers and every blemish" (3.21; cf. Matt. 4:23). The only parallel seems to appear in a fragment of Clement: "The priests healed lepers on fixed days by God's power."[33]

His picture of the law has verbal parallels with what the Gnostic Ptole-maeus said about the Decalogue, the "pure law of God," which forbids what must be avoided and enjoins what must be done.[34] Ptolemaeus, how-ever, insisted that this law "was given not by the perfect God and Father" but by the Demiurge and Maker of this world.[35] Theophilus argues that the holy law comes from the God who really exists (3.9). For him the perfect God is the Demiurge.

Exegesis of the Prophets

For Theophilus the basic classification for Old Testament writers is "prophet." Adam himself predicted the nature of human marriage: hus-bands would leave parents and unite with wives, a prophecy now fulfilled (2.28). Moses, author of the Pentateuch, was a prophet inspired by the Holy Spirit, as were many others among the Hebrews, including Solomon, who was prophet, king, and author of Proverbs.[36] Since Solomon was a prophet we may suppose that Theophilus could use not only the book of Proverbs but also the apocryphal Wisdom of Solomon. Perhaps he had doubts about its authorship and therefore did not cite it explicitly. After the people abandoned God's law he sent prophets to "teach and remind" them (John 14:26) of its content and bring them to repentance.[37] In addition, the Sibyl was a prophetess among the Greeks.[38]

Their teaching, therefore, was essentially the same as that of the law, especially the essential law of the Decalogue. The first two commandments deal with monotheistic piety, on which the prophets made pronouncements (3.9; 2.35). The Fifth Commandment was concerned with beneficence, just as Isaiah and the gospel were concerned with goodwill (3.9, 14). The last five dealt with justice and chastity, as did the prophets (2.34–35; 3.12–13).

Exegesis of the New Testament

Theophilus knows of "Gospels" as well as "the gospel" and "the Gospel voice." Echoes indicate that he knew Matthew, Luke, and John, if not Mark. These works were among "the holy scriptures" containing the words of "those inspired by the Spirit" (3.11–14; 2.22). The whole discussion ends with a hymn-like sequence on virtues among Christians (3.15), where

> chastity is present, continence practiced, monogamy kept, purity preserved; injustice is driven out, sin uprooted, justice practiced, law lived, piety performed, God confessed; truth controls, grace preserves, peace protects; holy Logos leads, Sophia teaches, Life triumphs,[39] God reigns. (*To Autolycus* 3.15)

The Acts of the Apostles

The book of Acts is probably Theophilus' source for the "negative Golden Rule" of Acts 15:20 and 29 (2.34).[40] There was no special reason for him to employ the book often in his apologetic work, since he never mentioned the apostles.

The Epistles

One might imagine that the epistles stand on a lower level because Theophilus does not name authors or titles; but he echoes all the Pauline epistles, with the Pastorals, except 2 Thessalonians. These writings are inspired. In book 3 he refers to the "prophet" Solomon and the Gospel voice (of Matthew) as expressing "the holy Word" and ascribes to "the divine Word" commands taken from Romans 13 and 1 Timothy 2. The Word commands us to obey principalities and authorities and pray for them "so that we may lead a peaceable and quiet life" (1 Tim. 2:2). When he adds that "it teaches the rendering of everything to everyone, honor to whom honor is due, fear to whom fear, tax to whom tax, and to owe no one anything except to love all," he is clearly echoing Romans 13:7–8 (3.13–14). The Pauline epistles, including the Pastorals, are part of his Bible.

On the other hand, he provides only one possible allusion to Hebrews, if that, using the phrase "attaining to the resurrection" (Heb. 11:35) (2.27). He is not likely to have used a letter that treated Christ as the one priest "after the order of Melchizedek" when in his own view Melchizedek was "the first priest of all the priests of God Most High," from whose time "priests are found in existence over the whole earth" (2.31). He thus shares the reticence of Irenaeus.

There are several allusions to 1 Peter and one to the *Preaching of Peter,* but none to 2 Peter, James, Jude, or the Johannine epistles. It seems odd that when he differentiates honor for the emperor from worship for God (1.11) he cites Proverbs 24:21–22, "Honor God and the king," not 1 Peter 2:17, "Fear God, honor the king." The Petrine passage provides just the distinction he is making. Perhaps something has gone wrong with the text. The phrase "lawless idolatry" may be a cliché, but the statement that "eight souls in all were saved" in Noah's ark is likely to come from 1 Peter 3:20.[41]

The Apocalypse of John

Theophilus certainly utilizes the Apocalypse of John at one point in book 2 (2.28). He explains that "the maleficent demon, also called Satan, who then spoke to Eve through the serpent and is still at work in those men who are possessed by him, . . . is called 'demon' and 'dragon.' " These points are derived from Revelation 12:9—a verse not evidently cited by other Christians before Origen.[42] Presumably, as Bolgiani suggests, Theophilus ascribed the Apocalypse to the inspired evangelist.[43] Earlier Justin had said that the book was written by "John, one of the apostles of Christ."[44] In addition, Eusebius reports that in Theophilus' treatise *Against the Heresy of Hermogenes* he used "testimonies from the Apocalypse of John."[45] Bolgiani rightly insists on the importance of Theophilus as the main source of Tertullian's treatise against Hermogenes (see chapter 22).

Theophilus' New Testament thus closely resembles that of his contemporary Irenaeus,[46] and the way in which he correlates the two "libraries" is rather similar. Both bishops have a high regard for the Old Testament as history, prefiguration, and prophecy. Both are concerned with the details of biblical exegesis, though Irenaeus cares more about the whole sweep of biblical history than Theophilus does.[47] His "reserve" in regard to New Testament teaching may be partly due to the peculiarities of his theology, which we shall discuss in the next chapter. His Christology, we shall see, is based on exegesis of Genesis in the light of the Gospel of Luke, not on Paul or indeed John.

19
The Theology
of Theophilus

The most surprising feature of Theophilus' theology is his remarkable silence in regard to Jesus, Christ, the incarnation, and the atonement. Indeed, the books to Autolycus present "the first grave problem of Christian apologetic language," for a pagan reader could easily have been "converted to Diaspora Judaism" rather than Christianity.[1] Among the other early apologists, Athenagoras and Tatian also refrain from mentioning Jesus, while a little later Minucius Felix offers even more mysterious silences.[2] What Theophilus does supply is teaching on scripture, on God, his Word and his Wisdom, on creation and resurrection, about some apostles, baptism, churches, and heresies. Perhaps the silence about Jesus is due to apologetic convention, perhaps to Theophilus' peculiar doctrine about Christ.

Clearly Theophilus is a Christian, as the many parallels with Justin show. He is also a Hellenistic Jewish theologian. Book 1 provides a useful starting point. There Theophilus clearly states that he is a Christian but explains the name as based on being "anointed with the oil of God," without any reference to Christ (1.12).[3] References to the Gospels and the epistles confirm his Christianity, but his teaching is essentially Jewish in tone and is based on the Old Testament as understood by Hellenistic Jews—not allegorizers like Philo but the more literal-minded exegetes in view in his *Questions on Genesis* (see chapter 18).

The atmosphere of the first book to Autolycus, primarily on the doctrine of God, is in part that of the Jewish-Christian prayers found in the *Apostolic Constitutions.*[4] The parallels, some of which I noted earlier,[5] are between *To Autolycus* 1.6–7 and the prayers, originally Jewish, of *Apostolic Constitutions* 7.34–35 as well as the faintly Christianized version in 8.12.[6] Theophilus' eucharistic prayer must have differed from that of Justin, farther from Judaism, who describes his own in the *Dialogue with Trypho* (41.1) and specifically refers to the bread of the Eucharist, which Jesus Christ our Lord commanded us to offer for the remembrance of the passion which he suffered for those whose souls are cleansed from all wickedness; so that we might give thanks to God not only for his creation of the world with everything in it for the sake of humanity but also for having freed us from the wickedness in which we had lived and for having completely destroyed the principalities and powers through him who became passible in accordance with his will.

Theophilus' whole work is concerned with creation but not redemption. Because of his ambiguous theology one cannot be sure that he reflects Christianity rather than Judaism or if, indeed, there was a clear line between the two in his mind.

In part book 1 is also (and obviously) apologetic in intent. It finds a good parallel in the recently discovered *Letter of Annas* [*the high priest*] *to Seneca on Pride and Idols,*[7] which is not a letter but an address, probably made to proselytes whether to Judaism or to Jewish Christianity. In lines 21 and 45 of the 93-line fragment the hearers are addressed as "brothers," but they are also rebuked for their adherence to pagan idolatry. The first section (lines 1–12) deals with God as creator and life-giver. He is loving and merciful, "just to the just," and known in the power of the winds and of fire, air, winds, clouds, thunder, lightning, movements of heaven and the whole earth, etc. "We live when he wills it and we are preserved by his judgment; as he breathes, we draw breath; what we are and what we say is from him." Almost exactly the same ideas are expressed in *To Autolycus* 1.6–7.

The second section (13–26) is concerned with the errors of philosophers who fail to understand the workings of providence; the third (27–44), with errors and contradictions concerning the immortality of the soul. Theophilus too attacks philosophers (though in a different way) and criticizes their lack of belief in both providence and the soul. The fourth section (45–71) attacks the images made by men as powerless and the worship of them as irrational and useless. The fifth (72–83) returns to the true and invisible God as known from the creation. Much of the content, for which Bischoff cites lines from the first Sibylline fragment, preserved in *To Autolycus* 2.36, is repeated from the first section. Almost everything also appears in Theophilus.

The final section (84–93) breaks off in a discussion of images and their cult as due to error and sin, and it resembles both Tatian and Theophilus. It remains within the limits of Jewish apologetic with its frequent attacks on the immorality of the gods.

The "borderline" nature of the document is especially clear in its echoes of the Wisdom of Solomon, a work originally Jewish but influential upon Christians from the author of Hebrews to the Alexandrians. Though Theophilus does not cite it, he clearly follows its doctrine on the envy of the devil (2.29).[8] Book 1 of Theophilus is thus related to Jewish-Christian liturgical prayer (in Greek) and to Hellenistic Jewish apologetic. The *Letter of Annas* provides a good witness to the apologetic.

The central section of the second book to Autolycus consists of exegesis of the story of creation in Genesis. This exegesis is remarkably unlike what we find in Justin, Irenaeus, or Tertullian,[9] and its focus is not exactly centered on Christ. Indeed, the work of either Logos or Sophia in creation is mentioned only in order to explain what the "beginning" of Genesis 1:1 was and how God is said to "walk" in paradise (2.10, 22). There are certainly Christian items in the exegesis, such as "churches" and "heresies," an allusion to baptism, and opposition to heresy along the way, but they are not central (see chapter 18). Underneath what Theophilus says about what Adam could have done (2.24–27) lies a uniquely Jewish-Christian picture of what Jesus actually did, based on the Gospel of Luke, but this reflects and expresses his unique Christology.

Doctrine of God

Like Philo of Alexandria, Theophilus sets forth a doctrine of God essentially Jewish in nature even though expressed in the language of Middle Platonism. He says that "we acknowledge (1) a God, (2) but only one, (3) the Founder and Maker and Demiurge (4) of this whole cosmos, (5) and we know that everything is governed by providence, by him alone (3.9)." These five points are exactly the same as those listed by Philo in a "creed" placed toward the end of his treatise *On the Creation* and noted by Erwin Goodenough.[10] Theophilus is an heir of Hellenistic Judaism and presumably reflects some of its major developments in the second century.

His doctrine of God uses biblical texts for philosophical conclusions. Following the *Preaching of Peter* he makes use of the traditional "negative attributes." Indeed, he insists that one can speak only of functions or attributes of God, never of God in himself. For example, one cannot say that God is Logos or Mind or Spirit or Wisdom. These terms express modes of God's working, not God (1.3).[11] Because of Theophilus' concern for scripture we might expect a more detailed and varied picture of how God works but he does not provide one. Instead, he treats God's Logos as equivalent to his Mind, Spirit, Wisdom, and Forethought (1.7; 2.22). Like Irenaeus, he refuses to differentiate mental activities within God, since Gnostics could then slip in their theories about sequential emanations. Unfortunately he makes use of Greek mythology and Stoic technicalities when he makes his own differentiations.

"If I call him 'fire' I speak of his wrath," says Theophilus (1.3). Autolycus questions his statement. "Will you tell me that God is angry?" Against most philosophers, not to mention his Marcionite opponents, Theophilus replies, "Certainly: he is angry with those who commit evil deeds but good and merciful toward those who love and fear him.[12] For he is the instructor of

the pious and father of the just, but judge and punisher of the impious."
Here he is on firm ground both biblical and Stoic: Plutarch notes that in
the Stoic view God punishes evil and acts to punish wicked men.[13] Even
Origen takes a similar line.[14]

What Theophilus says of God's wrath is important because it contradicts
a Platonic attitude common in second-century Christianity though not in
the New Testament. The second Hermetic treatise speaks of "the incorporeal" as impassible,[15] while Neoplatonic usage is illustrated by the Neo-
platonist Proclus.[16] The apologists Justin and Athenagoras regard God as
impassible and expect Christians to imitate him both after the resurrection
and now.[17] Theophilus follows a different tradition, which is related to
thinking about Christ and can be traced back to Paul, "He loved me and
gave himself for me," Gal. 2:20; Ignatius, "The passion of my God,"
Romans 6.3; and Tatian, "the God who suffered," *Oration* 13. Others
rejected negative thinking. Aulus Gellius tells how the rhetor Herodes
Atticus denounced the Stoic doctrine of impassibility as subhuman.[18]

Theophilus then returns to philosophy and continues with school definitions and etymologies (1.4). The etymologies come from Herodotus and
Plato.

> God has no beginning because he did not come into existence; he is immutable
> because he is immortal. He is called "God" *(theos)* because he has set *(te-
> theikenai)* everything on his own stability (Ps. 103:5 [104:5 Eng.]), and because
> of *theein,* which means to run, to move, to energize, to nourish, to exercise
> forethought, to govern, and to give life to everything. He is Lord because he
> lords over everything, Father because he is before everything, Demiurge and
> Maker because he is the founder and maker of everything, Most High because
> he is above everything, All-controlling because he controls and surrounds
> everything.

The section concludes with Old Testament passages, but Greek ideas are
also present. The derivation of *theos* from *tithēmi* is as old as Herodotus
2.52, while that from *theein* comes from the *Cratylus* (397D) of Plato,
where it refers to star-gods. It hardly fits a Jewish or Christian context, but
Theophilus manfully distorts the meaning of *theein* and adds other verbs
that change its meaning entirely.[19] Given Christian insistence on divine
transcendence, presumably shared with a pagan reader, an apologist could
then denounce the all too human stories about the gods to be found in
mythology, while neglecting the human suffering of Christ—and so Theophilus does (1.9–10; 2.3, etc.).

In addition, he makes use of a bizarre analogy when he compares the
created universe to a pomegranate, held in the hand of God. Apparently he
is thinking of the many pomegranate seeds that illustrate multiplicity in
unity (1.8).[20]

Doctrine of Sophia and Logos

It is hard to tell why Theophilus' language is as loose as it is when sometimes he treats Logos as different from Wisdom, *Sophia* (1.7; 2.10, 16, 18)—and in the manner of Philo calls Logos and Sophia God's hands but is willing to speak of God's one hand even when discussing the creation (2.18 versus 1.4–5)—and like Philo identifies God's Wisdom with his Logos (2.10, 22).[21]

God created the universe through his Sophia (1.7; 2.10, 22). She named the stars, inspired the prophets, and created fish and birds (1.6; 2.9, 12, 16). Theophilus also refers to her as God's "offspring" *(gennēma)* and thus points toward the traditionally quoted Proverbs 8:25 as the source of all this. Probably Theophilus reflects both the earlier doctrine, according to which God's agent and aide was Sophia, and the later doctrine, which replaced Sophia with Logos. By retaining both figures and not working primarily with the terms Father, Son, and Spirit, Theophilus allowed a considerable measure of confusion to remain.

He strives to be precise in describing the Logos, and insists that like Sophia the Logos was originally *in* God (2.10, 22). On this point he agrees with Valentinian Gnostics and almost every early Christian theologian. Indeed, Irenaeus and Clement state with Theophilus that the evangelist John meant that the Logos was in God when he said that "the Logos was *pros ton theon."*[22] Tertullian finally renounced the idea, but followers of Paul of Samosata picked it up again, as did Marcellus of Ancyra.[23] Presumably it won favor for a time because of the Johannine emphasis on the coinherence of the Father with the Son. When Marcellus insisted that the Logos was in the Father he naturally referred to John 1:1 ("in the beginning") and 10:38 ("the Father in me and I in the Father").[24]

The Generation of Logos and Sophia

Theophilus goes into considerable detail when describing the generation of the Logos and Sophia. He tells us that the Logos was originally within God's "bowels" *(splanchna)* but before the creation God "disgorged" him along with Sophia (2.10). He justified this notion with a naively literal allusion to Psalm 44:2 LXX (45:1 Eng.), "My heart overflows with a good *logos."* (Justin had cited a similar text from Psalm 109:3 [110:3 Eng.], "Before sun and moon I generated you from my belly *(gastēr),"* so such notions were not shocking.)[25]

The inelegant metaphor did not appeal to Irenaeus, who ridiculed the Gnostic notion that the aeons were within the Father's viscera and insisted that nobody knew the mode of the Son's prolation.[26] Origen expressly denied that Psalm 44:2 (LXX) refers to the Son.[27] Unfortunately Tertullian liked the notion.[28]

A strikingly similar expression occurs in a version of Hesiod's *Theogony,* or of some other theogony, quoted by Chrysippus. (I owe this observation to Carl Curry, whose note is forthcoming in *Vigiliae Christianae.*) When Zeus swallowed Metis he "put her in his belly"[29] and she "remained hidden beneath his bowels" after she had conceived Athena, to whom Zeus gave birth through his head.[30] Perhaps Theophilus followed Chrysippus, or even a source critical of Chrysippus, for this point as for other allegorizations. Certainly he knew the story of Metis in a context related to the Stoic philosopher (3.3, 8).

No doubt he was influenced by the common allegorical interpretation of the birth of Athena as Forethought *(phronēsis)* from the head of Zeus,[31] but his regrettable language about the prolation of the Logos seems to come from the story of Metis, whom some Stoics also identified as Forethought.[32] It is uncertain why he used it. Certainly Theophilus was acquainted with theogonies ascribed to both Orpheus and Hesiod (2.5, 7; 3.2, 17), but the fact explains nothing. It is more significant that in the *Clementine Homilies,* which in some respects stand close to his doctrines, there are fragments of Orphic rhapsodies. There we find mention of Zeus's "drawing out almost subtle divine spirit, called Metis, from the subsisting moisture."[33] Another fragment calls her the "will" of Zeus, while two fragments possibly later refer to her (or him) as the "first genetrix" or "first generator" lying "within the great body of Zeus."[34] It appears that there were Hellenistic Jewish Christians who found Orphic language meaningful, and Theophilus may have been one of them.

A different way of describing the generation uses language borrowed from rhetoricians and philosophers (including Chrysippus again). Philo had already differentiated human thought, the *Logos endiathetos,* from expression in speech, the *Logos prophorikos.*[35] Theophilus applied the terms to the divine Logos, but Irenaeus vigorously opposed such anthropomorphism; Origen followed Philo by applying the distinction only in human psychology.[36]

However the Logos came forth, it was the agent of creation and later appeared in Eden, as both Philo and Justin had said. In Genesis 3:10 Adam said he heard the voice of God who was walking in paradise, and since God cannot be present in a particular place, this Voice must have been his Logos, his Power and Sophia (1 Cor. 1:24). The Logos was "assuming the role" *(analambanōn to prosōpon)* of God. Probably Theophilus has not considered the implications for Christology but simply offers exegesis of Genesis 3:8: Adam and Eve hid from the *prosōpon* or "face" of God. Exegetes like Philo could have taught him that He who Is has no face and contains all, is not contained by anything.[37]

For Theophilus as for his predecessors the Logos (or Sophia, or Spirit) inspired the prophets. God sent them "from among their brothers" (Deut. 18:15) to "teach and remind" the people of the Mosaic law (3.11). According to John 14:26 the Paraclete, the Holy Spirit, will "teach and remind" Christians of everything Jesus said to his disciples. These allusions suggest that Jesus reiterated the law of Moses. This is what we should expect from a reader of the *Preaching of Peter.* Like the *Preaching* Theophilus lays strong emphasis on the Old Testament law and its complete agreement with the prophets and the Gospels (3.9–14). Similarly his contemporary Hegesippus spoke of the authority of "the law and the prophets and the Lord."[38]

Christology

Two basic questions arise over Theophilus' Christology. First, did the Logos become incarnate? In Theophilus' view there was no necessity for such an action. He could write that "whenever the Father of the universe wills to do so, he sends the Logos into some place where he is present and is heard and seen, sent by God and [unlike the Father] present in a place." The phrasing reminds us of John's insistence on Jesus as the "one sent" by the Father. In the same chapter when Theophilus denies the existence of "sons of gods born of sexual union" he speaks of the Logos as "always innate in the heart of God" (2.22). Does this mean that the Logos was not born? not incarnate? Later theology at Antioch offers such a possibility, and we note Theophilus' resolute silence concerning Jesus. On the other hand, he does allude to the "Power of the Most High" in Jesus' conception (2.10). He seems to have concealed his basic view on this subject.

Second, what did Theophilus think about the life and work of Christ? He says nothing directly, but gives an account of Adam in *To Autolycus* 2.24–25 that seems to refer to Christ. God gave Adam an opportunity for "progress" (Luke 2:52). Had he taken it he would have grown (Luke 2:52; 1:80) and become "mature" or "perfect" (Eph. 4:13), would have been "declared a god" (as Jesus was in John 20:28) and would have ascended into heaven, as Jesus did ascend in Luke-Acts. Jesus seems to be a second Adam, or rather, Adam seems to be regarded as a first Christ.[39]

The treatment of obeying parents cannot be based on the biblical Adam, who had none. It was natural enough for Origen to speak of such obedience in his 20th homily on Luke, where the subject came up, not natural for Theophilus.

Theophilus says it is a holy duty not only "before God but also before men" (Luke 2:52 again) to obey one's parents (Luke 2:43). If children must obey their parents (Luke 2:43, 51), how much more must one obey the God and Father of all (Luke 2:49)? As one grows in age in orderly fashion, so also in thinking (2.25, with allusions to Luke 1:80; 2:40, 52). Interestingly enough, Theophilus seems to have grasped the main points of this section of Luke as understood by a modern exegete.[40]

Another general statement apparently based on Luke occurs even in Theophilus' defense of resurrection (1.13). "You may say, 'Show me even one person raised from the dead, so that I may see and believe.' " (The discussion of belief is itself based on John 20:27–29, important for Theophilus because of 20:28.) Next Theophilus says that "if I were to show you a dead man raised and alive you might perhaps disbelieve this." His words seem to echo Luke 16:30–31, where Lazarus asks Abraham to send someone from the dead to his brothers, and Abraham replies that if they do not believe Moses and the prophets they will not believe if someone rises from the dead. The Gospel words have lost their specificity in the context of apologetic theology.

We conclude that Theophilus has applied to Adam, generic man, what Luke said about Jesus' childhood, even though for the apologist Adam in Eden was an infant, not a boy of twelve.

He also takes Paul's comparison of Adam with Christ and rewrites it so that it contrasts man then with man now.

To Autolycus 2.27	Romans 5:15–21
What man acquired for himself through his neglect and disobedience, God now freely [for]gives him through love and mercy.	Many died through one man's trespass. The grace of God and the free gift abounded for many.
For as by disobedience man gained death for himself, so by obedience to the will of God	As by one man's disobedience many were made sinners, so by one man's obedience
whoever will can obtain eternal life for himself.	many will be made righteous to eternal life.
For God gave us a law and holy commandments; everyone who does them can be saved and attaining to the resurrection can inherit imperishability.	Rom. 7:12, the law is holy and the commandment is holy and just and good; cf. Gal. 3:12. 1 Cor. 15:50, inherit imperishability.

God is a just judge who appointed the Roman emperor to judge justly, as he himself will judge when he rewards those who seek imperishability through good works.[41] The prophets, instructed by God, became holy and just and the Greek poets at their best derived their teaching from them. The holy law of God proclaims justice too.[42] Theophilus' Jewish-Christian emphasis on obedience to the law of justice leads him to regard the work of both Adam and Christ as exemplary, not efficacious. The saving work of Christ disappears.[43] For Theophilus, Adam, Moses, Solomon, and perhaps Jesus himself were prophets.[44] In the fourth century Marcellus of Ancyra espoused a theology like his and also called these men prophets; Eusebius ridiculed him for doing so.

To sum up: for Theophilus God possesses various faculties through which he acts and reveals himself. He thereby shows man what is good and expects him to do it. If Jesus differed from others it was in the obedience for which God finally gave him the name above every name and made him Lord and Christ, probably indeed God (Phil. 2:8–9). Theophilus does refer to the Logos of God as "also his Son," but he is speaking only of the generation of the Logos before creation (2.22). And while he does allude to a Lucan verse about the conception of Jesus (2.10), he never mentions the angel's prediction that the son of Mary would be called Son of God. There is a sharp break between the incarnational Christology of Ignatius and the reticent monotheism of Theophilus. Who was to say that one was orthodox and the other not? These problems, arising in very early times, were to plague the church at Antioch for centuries. Paul of Samosata, bishop of Antioch about eighty years later, shared Theophilus' ideas and was deposed by a synod of Origenist bishops from outside. He was so influential in Antioch itself, however, that the emperor Aurelian had to intervene in the case.[45]

Ultimately something not unlike Theophilus' doctrine of man, akin to Origen's emphasis on free will, was maintained by Pelagius against the innovations of Augustine, but without much success.[46]

Demons and Angels

We should say something about demons and angels, although unlike other apologists, Theophilus says little about them. He merely notes after Psalm 95:5 (96:5 Eng.) that pagan gods are "unclean demons" to whom pagans offer sacrifice. They inspired pagan poets to write about them. Satan, now a demon, was once an angel, but Theophilus refers readers to another book for details about his fall (1.10; 2.8, 28, 36). His idea of apologetic had room for neither angels nor demons, and in his lengthy interpretation of Genesis he does not discuss "the angels of God" who took human wives for themselves and generated giants (Gen. 6:3–4). In his view Logos, Sophia, and Spirit are the essential intermediaries between God and the world.

Resurrection

We have already seen that he refuses to argue for resurrection by citing examples. Instead, he relies on the traditional analogies taken from nature but, as is his wont, uses the more bizarre instances. In place of the day-night sequence found in Clement of Rome, he turns to the phases of the moon which wanes and "practically dies," then waxes again. He also speaks of the loss of weight in sickness and gain in recovery. A patient may ascribe the gain merely to food and drink, but the recovery is really divine since God caused it. The parallel with resurrection is highly forced. Finally, in place of Clement's rather incredible analogy of the phoenix[47] Theophilus mentions the seed which a bird picks up and swallows, then excretes in a rocky place or on a tomb; after passing through so much heat it still becomes a plant (1.13; 2.15). It is hard to believe that Autolycus found such analogies convincing. They exemplify the pitfalls of apologetic theology. Theophilus might have done better had he remained within a scriptural framework at this point.

20
Early Alexandrian Christianity

During Commodus' last years he encountered much opposition. The fictitious *Acts of the Pagan Martyrs* represent an Alexandrian senator as denouncing him because he manipulated the grain market and was in every way inferior to Marcus Aurelius. "The divine Antoninus was fit to be emperor. First, he was a philosopher; second, he was not avaricious; third, he was good." Commodus is entirely different. He is "tyrannical, dishonest, uncultured."[1] Historians shared this estimate of him. Herodian claimed that he had "debased all his talent by corrupt living," while Dio insisted that from his accession "our history descends from a kingdom of gold to one of iron and rust."[2]

Christians After Commodus

The Christian chronographer Julius Africanus says that "Clement the author of *Stromata* was well known at Alexandria" in Commodus' time,[3] although Clement himself ends his discussion of Roman emperors in the first book of the *Stromata* with the death of Commodus. In the *Church History* Eusebius used this fact to give Clement a date under Severus.[4] (He could also have written under Pertinax.)

Further, while it is still often held that Clement wrote first the *Exhortation,* then the *Tutor,* and finally the *Stromata,* a fresh examination by J. van Pottelberge has suggested that the *Exhortation* was not composed before the first book of the *Stromata.*[5] This means that Clement, writing the *Exhortation* under Pertinax or Severus, felt free to criticize severely the Eleusinian mysteries into which both Marcus Aurelius and Commodus had been initiated.[6] It also means that Clement must be viewed not as an apologist but as an independent literary figure. The age of the second-century apologists had come to an end. It began to terminate with Theophilus, whose treatises *To Autolycus* contain highly diverse materials originally composed for occasions within the life of the church.

If we look back before Clement in search of Alexandrian apologists we find almost nothing Christian. He owes much to his Hellenistic Jewish predecessor Philo, and this debt may explain why Eusebius wrongly supposed Philo was describing early Christians when he wrote about the Therapeutae, ascetic allegorizers who lived near Alexandria.[7] He was wrong, but Alexandrian Christians obviously owed much to Philo.

The epistle to the Hebrews and the *Epistle of Barnabas* seem to be among the earliest monuments of Alexandrian Christianity. Both deal with allegorical exegesis of the Old Testament, which they insist has a purely Christian meaning. Hebrews allows for a diversified revelation in the past but a final revelation now given in Jesus Christ, but Barnabas denies that the Old Testament has any meaning in relation to the Jews. The second interpretation points toward the Gnostic attitude which dominated Christian life and thought at Alexandria for half a century—the period during which apologetic flourished elsewhere.

Clement himself taught at Alexandria but was probably first trained at Athens. Like other authors of his time, including the apologist Justin, he undertook a spiritual pilgrimage before settling down, and this fact makes it difficult to isolate his Alexandrian sources from others. He speaks of his Christian teachers who kept "the true tradition of the blessed teaching straight from the holy apostles." One was an Ionian from Asia who was in Greece, while others had come to southern Italy from Coele-Syria and Egypt. These cannot be identified, unless the Ionian could be Athenagoras. Two more taught in "the East." Of these, one came from the land of the Assyrians; presumably this was Tatian, since he called himself an Assyrian in the oration *To the Greeks,* which Clement knew. The other was a Hebrew from Palestine, otherwise unknown.

Last of all, says Clement, he hunted down the best, possibly a Sicilian (for he calls him a "Sicilian bee") who was concealed, or at least lived quietly, in Egypt.[8] Eusebius rightly supposed that he meant Pantaenus, Clement's teacher according to his *Outlines.*[9] Obviously Pantaenus was earlier than Clement, but not necessarily much earlier. Eusebius describes him as once a Stoic but later "a herald of the gospel of Christ to the nations of the East." Supposedly he went to India, where he found the Gospel of Matthew in Hebrew, left by the apostle Bartholomew.[10] The story of the visit does not inspire confidence, though it is not incredible.

None of Clement's teachers was really an apologist. Tatian was not an apologist in the ordinary sense of the term, and Pantaenus seems to have been no apologist at all. Instead, he seems to have taught in whatever kind of Christian school existed at Alexandria in the latter years of the second century. Clement says that such earlier Christian teachers did not record their teaching in writing,[11] and the so-called fragments from Pantaenus could be based on oral tradition, even though some topics are shared with apologetic writers.

The first fragment deals with the tenses of verbs in prophecy. "Generally speaking, prophecy uses expressions without making distinctions. It uses the present tense sometimes for the future and sometimes for the past."[12] This kind of question had already been raised and given a similar answer in Justin's school at Rome. Justin said that the prophetic Spirit predicts future events as already past by describing them as past.[13] Pantaenus thus fits the context of a teaching both catechetical and apologetic.

The second fragment comes from the writings of Maximus Confessor in the seventh century. Presumably Maximus took the passage from Clement's treatise *On Providence,* which he used several times.[14] Learned philosophers are described as asking how God knows things that exist. Pantaenus replied,

> Neither objects of sense by sense nor intelligibles by intellect; for it is impossible for him who is beyond things that exist to apprehend things that exist in relation to [other] things that exist. We [Christians] say that he knows things that exist as his own acts of will and we claim that the proof is rational. If God made everything by his will—and no argument is opposed to this—and it is always pious and right to say that he knows his own will, and by willing he made each of the things that came to be, then God knows things that exist as his own acts of will, since by his will he made things that exist.[15]

This is certainly close to the teaching of Clement himself, who differentiates sense from intellect[16] and speaks of God as "beyond the One and the Monad itself" and "beyond the intelligible cosmos."[17] He lays strong emphasis on the creative act of God as consisting of his "willing to create," and indeed can speak of the cosmos as "the will of God."[18] To be sure, we cannot find a passage where he says that God knows by willing, but since for the Christian Gnostic the reverse is true ("the will of God is the knowledge of God," Clement *Stromata* 4.27.2), he may well have accepted Pantaenus' statement.[19] But the topic is not one that apologists were likely to discuss. It belongs to the more technical theology being developed at Alexandria.

It is significant that the subjects of these two fragments agree well with three important meanings of "gnosis" for Clement. These are the understanding of scripture and philosophy; the knowledge of time, creation, intelligibles and spirits; and the knowledge of God and his Son. In addition, the fragments deal with matters not only anticipated in the *Stromata* but also included in the *Outlines,* which involved "a brief exposition of the scriptures" and of the creation of the world.[20] Clement was thus the continuator of Pantaenus' philosophical theology.

The Epistle to Diognetus

It is possible though not certain that the so-called *Epistle to Diognetus*—essentially an apology—should be ascribed to Pantaenus.[21] This little work is usually printed with the apostolic fathers, but it belongs with the apologists instead. The introduction makes clear, in any event, that it is not an epistle but an address. In addition, it is a composite document. The last two chapters come from a homily on the Epiphany of the Logos and are written in cola strikingly similar to those employed in Asian rhetoric, notably by Melito of Sardis and Hippolytus. The description of church life in the last chapter resembles what Theophilus says on the same subject.[22] Both the apology and the homily probably come from the late second century or the early third.

The thirteenth-century manuscript of the *Epistle* was in the library at Strasbourg after 1795 but was destroyed by fire in 1870. Fortunately there are copies from the sixteenth century, and collators twice inspected the original for J. C. T. Otto.

The apologetic address begins with a list of apologetic subjects to be discussed: who the God of Christians is, how they worship him in disregard of the world and death, why they reject pagan idols as well as "the superstition of the Jews," how they love one another, and why "this new race or practice has entered into life now and not formerly." The question about the new race and its recent arrival may be related to the attack of Celsus on Christians,[23] but the topics are shared with the apologists generally.

Something can be said about the date in relation to the author's remarks about persecution. He describes Christians as "sought for by the Greeks" and "thrown to wild beasts so that they may deny the Lord."[24] The reference to wild beasts provides no definite clue, for such beasts appear at Rome and in Gaul from 64 to 177,[25] not to mention Ephesus in 1 Corinthians 15:32. The events at Lyons in 177 shocked the Christian world, however, and the "search" for Christians must reflect the new situation under Marcus Aurelius, discussed by Melito in his *Apology* (see chapter 11). The *Epistle* should therefore be dated after 176. Indeed, it shares a comment on idols with Melito. In the *Epistle* human beings, endowed with sensation and reason, are contrasted with stones which lack sensation (2.8–9). Melito insists that Christians "are not worshipers of stones which have no sensation."[26] The author may address Diognetus around the time when other apologists are approaching Marcus Aurelius.

Perhaps Diognetus is more than a stock figure. His title *kratistos,* a term of address Luke too employs at the beginning of his Gospel, does not necessarily have any official significance, though it is ordinarily used of an imperial procurator. As for the name Diognetus, it is barely possible that it refers to the sometime tutor of Marcus Aurelius, who taught him to avoid idle enthusiasms and disbelieve what sorcerers and charlatans said about

spells and exorcisms.[27] A phrase like "sorcerers and charlatans" may perhaps be picked up in the *Epistle* (8.4): "sorcery and the deceit of charlatans,"[28] and while the *Meditations* did not circulate at this early date, the
author may know the emperor's attitude, or his tutor's. Marcus' tutors
included two prominent officials who opposed Christianity: Rusticus, who
condemned Justin Martyr, and Fronto, who denounced Christian immorality. An apologist could have considered writing to a tutor, especially if there
was any reason to hope for more favorable treatment. As Meecham notes,
Diognetus is urged to "shed all prejudice and use his intelligence."[29]

The chief difficulty with this identification is that by 180 or so the old
tutors were dead, and if one supposes "Diognetus" to be a pseudonym the
whole case fails.

H.-I. Marrou followed E. Stein in proposing a different Diognetus, the
procurator Claudius Diogenes at Alexandria.[30] This official is known from
papyri dated between 197 and 203. In 197 he is called "procurator of
Augustus and interim high priest" (of Egypt), in charge of temple and
priestly finances.[31] In one document from 202/203 he is called simply "the
most excellent Diognetus."[32] Possibly, but by no means certainly, he is the
man we want.

Clement of Alexandria

Clement himself was undoubtedly the most significant Alexandrian
apologist, at least among Christians, for he wrote the important *Exhortation*. The Greek title was *protreptikos*, reflecting a special kind of literature.
At the beginning of the *Tutor* Clement looks back to "protreptic discourse"
and relates it to human habits, whereas preceptive discourse is connected
with actions and persuasive discourse with the passions.[33] Seneca took a
similar analysis from the Stoic philosopher Posidonius.[34] Many philosophers and scientists used the *protrepticus* form, and Clement was aware of
it. He even used an example derived from a predecessor, toward the beginning of his own *Protrepticus*, when he wrote that Satan punished humanity
"like those who are said to bind captives to corpses until they rot together"
(7.4); Aristotle had said this of the Etruscans in his *Protrepticus*.[35] In other
words, Clement knew what models he was following when he used the form
for attacking Greek religion, art, and philosophy.

The *Exhortation* begins with "the call of the Logos" in chapter 1 and
criticism of Greek religion (chs. 2–7), then sets forth God's call through the
Sibyl and the scriptures (chs. 8–9). It ends with an appeal to abandon
traditional pagan institutions and share in the universal mission of the
Logos (chs. 10–12).

The extended attack on Greek religion deals with oracles, mysteries
(especially those at Eleusis), and faults of the Olympian gods; with human
sacrifice and statues and images of gods like the newly invented Sarapis, not

to mention Hadrian's favorite Antinous; and with ideas of philosophers about God and his transcendence, as well as similar ideas in the poets.[36]

A brief conventional attack on oracles precedes an extended account of the mystery rites dedicated to Aphrodite, Demeter, Dionysus, and the Cabeiri, and recites the sacred formula of the Phrygians as well as that used at Eleusis. Clement also speaks scornfully of the symbols kept in the "mystic chests" and claims, without adducing evidence, that everything is ridiculous or savage or shameful. He is criticizing the mysteries into which the emperors Hadrian, Lucius Verus, Marcus Aurelius, and Commodus had been initiated. G. E. Mylonas has shown that he himself was not an initiate.[37]

Much of Clement's fifth chapter is based on doxographies, summaries of philosophers' views, but even Diels could not identify his source or sources.[38] These materials are combined with a learned discussion of oriental religion, obviously secondhand.

Like the earlier apologists, Clement sets the keynote for the section on monotheistic philosophy by a quotation from the third book of the *Sibylline Oracles*, followed by mention of Plato, Antisthenes, and Xenophon, and another Sibylline quotation, this time of four lines from a version also used by Theophilus.[39] The section ends with Cleanthes on the good and "the Pythagoreans" on the one god.[40]

Not all the resemblances adduced by G. Butterworth[41] are persuasive, but at the end of Clement's work his references to the Christian as truly rich, to God's sharing his possessions with his friends, and to "the attendants of Christ" are certainly based on expressions in the *Phaedrus*.[42] And if he echoes *Phaedrus* 252C, he may well rely on 252B as he speaks of Eros.[43]

From philosophy Clement turns to poetry. He begins with three lines from Aratus[44] and two from Hesiod[45] and continues with a fragment from Euripides and a forged monotheistic "fragment" from Sophocles.[46] Next he quotes ten lines from the monotheistic "palinode" of Orpheus[47] and erroneously adds two lines from the *Sibylline Oracles*.[48] These examples suffice to show that he is following nothing but anthologies in creating his display of literary learning.[49] Finally he turns to the prophetic scriptures, beginning with "the prophetess, the Sibyl," a fragment of the *Sibylline Oracles* once more cited by Theophilus (2.36), warming to his basic Christian theme as he moves to the end of his book.

Clement knew some of the earlier Christian apologists. In various works he used two of them: Melito's treatise *On the Passover*[50] and Tatian's *Oration*. At first he relied strongly on Tatian,[51] but later he criticized his bad exegesis of 1 Corinthians and Genesis[52] and called him a Valentinian.[53] One would expect Clement to read Justin after Tatian's praise of him, but there is little evidence that he did so.[54] It is barely possible, however, that the reason for his tacit use of the Stoic Musonius Rufus, beginning in the *Tutor*, is that Justin said he was inspired by the Logos.[55]

His most important source, usually employed without attribution, is

Philo, whom he begins to follow at the very beginning of the *Exhortation.* In the first chapter he borrows the term *symphōnia* in regard to the whole world,[56] and his description of the New Song comes from Philo too.[57] Later he makes more extensive use of his predecessor.[58] In the *Stromata* he would call him a Pythagorean who proved the antiquity of Jewish philosophy,[59] and would use his works even more intensively but, apart from the *Life of Moses,* without his name.

It is evident that Christian apologetic as such was not as important at Alexandria as elsewhere. In part this was the case because the Alexandrians had been involved in an intense struggle with Gnosticism, in part because they were on the verge of a theological development that went far beyond what the apologists had been able to achieve. In a certain sense apologies were irrelevant at Alexandria just because theology was to be apologetic even as it moved out beyond the apologetic movement.

21
Early Use
of the Apologists

During the reign of Commodus the bishops and teachers of the church gradually moved away from writing treatises like the earlier apologies. They stopped presenting petitions to the emperors and turned back to address the Christian communities themselves, though in a way much more sophisticated than was to be found among the old "apostolic fathers." Examples of the new approach occur in Theophilus, Irenaeus, and the teacher Clement, whose trilogy began with an *Exhortation* but passed on to a *Tutor* and *Stromata* for more advanced pupils. As these writers developed new forms, however, they did not disregard their predecessors but continued to use their works.

Irenaeus and Early Christian Literature Under Commodus

Fairly late in the reign of Commodus, Irenaeus wrote his treatises against heresy, in which he used the works of several apologists not as apologetic but as theological treatises. His five books *On the Detection and Refutation of Knowledge Falsely So-Called* contain a theology based on the earlier Christian tradition as he selectively understood it. He relied primarily on the nascent New Testament and like Theophilus insisted on the unity of the two Testaments, both inspired by the one God. In addition he made use of several of the "apostolic fathers" as well as oral teaching from a "presbyter" of Asia Minor and the writings of some major apologists.

When did he write? Harvey dated him after 181 because he wrongly accepted the statements of Epiphanius' *On Weights and Measures,* a work even more confused than his *Panarion.* In it we are told that Theodotion— whom Irenaeus mentions—wrote in the reign of "Commodus II," perhaps in the second year of Commodus (181).[1] The information is not worth much, but it helps create a general time frame. We also know more reliably that Irenaeus wrote during the episcopate of Eleutherus of Rome,[2] thus before about 189.

Irenaeus and the New Testament

Irenaeus relied on the theological authority of an extensive collection of New Testament books. Like Theophilus, he used several gospels but claimed that there were exactly four, equivalent to the four regions *(klimata)* of the earth, the four principal winds, the four cherubim, and the four covenants given mankind in the Bible.[3] In addition, he had a very high regard for the Pauline and pastoral epistles and quoted or alluded to all of them but Philemon.

Theophilus had begun his first book with an allusion to the antiheretical pastoral epistles, paraphrasing 2 Timothy 3:8 to attack "wretched men who have a depraved mind." Elsewhere he referred to baptism as the "washing of regeneration" (Titus 3:5) and ascribed to "the divine Word" the counsel of 1 Timothy 2:1–2 on subjection to rulers.[4] Just so, Irenaeus began his whole treatise, whose title is related to 1 Timothy 6:20, "the antitheses of knowledge falsely so-called," with an explicit reference to the words of the Apostle against heresy in 1 Timothy 1:4 and an allusion to 2 Timothy 3:6. Like Theophilus he alluded to the "washing of regeneration" but went farther than he did by speaking of Paul as the author of epistles (in the plural) to Timothy and by assigning a verse from Titus to him.[5] The intent of Theophilus and Irenaeus is much the same, but Irenaeus provides more precise citations.

While Irenaeus may have explicitly rejected Hebrews,[6] he made use of 1-2 John, 1 Peter (like Tatian and Theophilus), and perhaps James and Jude, as well as the Apocalypse of John (like Justin, Melito, and Theophilus). He collected information about the evangelists and the Apocalypse, presumably relying on Papias of Hierapolis for most of it, and somehow knew that the Apocalypse "was seen not long ago but nearly in our generation, at the end of the reign of Domitian."[7]

From him these books were inspired and consistent witnesses to the revelation of God. They had no historical context except in relation to the problems of orthodoxy and heresy or their authors' proximity to the time of Christ. The only exception to this rule could be the Apocalypse, but its author was viewed as exceptionally long-lived.

The "Apostolic Fathers"

Irenaeus was a collector of early Christian literature, not the apocryphal literature often used at Alexandria but the writings later used by Eusebius and Photius which constitute the "apostolic fathers." His usage is more catholic and, especially, more Roman than what we find in Alexandrian authors. Irenaeus refers to six early authorities: Clement, Ignatius, Polycarp, Papias, Hermas, and an anonymous presbyter of Asia. Two of these authorities were evidently related to his early years in the province of Asia; these were Polycarp of Smyrna, a vigorous opponent of heresy whom Irenaeus had known personally, and his friend Papias, another disciple of John, cited for his teaching about the earthly kingdom of God. Irenaeus knew that Clement had been a bishop of Rome and author of a letter to the Corinthian church with a theory of ministry like Irenaeus' own. He did not name Ignatius, though he quoted from his letter to the Romans, probably because he disagreed with basic elements of his theology. While he did not name Hermas, he cited his work as scripture when quoting what he agreed with; and he did not name the presbyter whose teaching he cited at length, perhaps because as an Asian he was following Asian traditions against Rome. For him the apostolic fathers were not timeless theological authorities but links in the chain of his tradition.

Use of the Greek Apologists for Theology

Just so, Irenaeus paid no attention to the apologists as authors directing petitions to Roman emperors or writing defenses of Christianity for various occasions. He was concerned not with their ideas of classical culture but with their theological teaching, especially as directed against heretics within the church.

The first apologist Irenaeus may have known was Quadratus, whose language and thought he parallels in a passage where he is criticizing Gnostics. He explains that Simonians and Carpocratians, said to work miracles, do not do so "by the power of God or in truth or as benefactors." They are incapable of making the blind see and the deaf hear (and so on). They are far from raising a dead man, as the Lord and the apostles did, whereas in "the brotherhood" raisings have frequently occurred. They simply mystify youthful witnesses, "producing appearances that cease at once and last only an instant."[8] This resembles Quadratus' argument so closely that the targets are likely to be identical, and probably Irenaeus knew Quadratus' work even though he did not mention it or its author.

Irenaeus cited Justin with approval twice, once with mention of a treatise against Marcion: "Justin well says in his work *Against Marcion* that he would not have believed the Lord himself if he had preached another God besides the Creator."[9] Justin had taught at Rome and fought heresy there.

Irenaeus did not know either Apollinaris or Athenagoras, though he may have been acquainted with nonapologetic treatises by Melito.[10] Perhaps he did not name Melito because he was a partisan on the Easter question (see chapter 11).

Irenaeus knew Tatian's *Oration* and was deeply concerned with his orthodoxy. Tatian remained orthodox as long as he attended Justin's lectures but left the church after his master's martyrdom. "Elated and inflated by his claim to be a teacher, as if he were better than the rest, he set up his own kind of doctrine."[11] In essence, Irenaeus is reproducing what Tatian said about himself in his *Oration.* Later he returns to the attack. "He invented [his teaching] on his own so that by introducing something new in comparison with others, but speaking inanities, he might acquire hearers devoid of faith while claiming to be a teacher."[12] Both descriptions are based on Tatian's own claims. He said he had not been taught by anyone else and supposed that people were talking about the way he "made innovations beyond the infinite multitude of philosophers."[13] Irenaeus may well have had Tatian in mind when he praised the Romans and then criticized anyone who (like a Cynic or Tatian) boasted of his knowledge, separated himself from pagan society, and had nothing that belonged to anyone else. If he lived naked, without shoes or abode, in the mountains like an animal that eats vegetation, perhaps he would deserve pardon because he was ignorant of the necessities of our life—otherwise not.[14]

The apologist Irenaeus knew best was Theophilus of Antioch.[15] Presumably he did not name him because he was correcting his doctrine while using some aspects of it.

When Irenaeus says that God contains everything, this seems to be an echo of *To Autolycus.*[16] More important is his treatment of the two "powers" of God, his Logos and his Sophia. Irenaeus states the basic idea in four passages: *Heresies* 3.24.2; 4.20.2, 4; *Demonstration* 10. These are obviously based on Theophilus *To Autolycus* 1.7 and 2.18 and explained in other passages where Irenaeus identifies Logos as Son and Sophia as Holy Spirit (*Heresies* 2.30.9; 4.7.4; 4.20.3). In another basic passage Irenaeus follows Theophilus in quoting biblical evidence from Proverbs 3:19–20 and 8:22–25, 27–31.[17] On creation by Logos and Pneuma Irenaeus also quotes Psalm 32:6 (33:6 Eng.) several times along with John 1:3.[18] The combination seems to come from Theophilus, *To Autolycus* 1.7 and 2.22.

Irenaeus' emphasis on God's hands in creation, notably in relation to Adam,[19] is based on Theophilus (*To Autolycus* 1.5; 2.18) but Irenaeus identifies the "hands" with Son and Holy Spirit in several of the texts cited in the note, once (4.7.4) with "Son and Holy Spirit, Logos and Sophia."[20]

Various items in Irenaeus' exegesis of Genesis owe something to Theophilus. Thus in *Heresies* 4.20.1 he explains that the creation was accomplished by God's hands, his Logos and Sophia (the latter being the Holy Spirit). He speaks of Adam as an infant, strongly emphasizes Adam's free will, and refers to deification and immortality as the result of obedience to God (4.37–39) just as Theophilus does.[21] Like Theophilus, Irenaeus rejects the view of "certain persons" that God begrudged Adam the tree of life and holds that God expelled him from paradise out of pity.[22] Irenaeus' statement that disobedience, not the law, results in punishment,[23] however, is based not on Theophilus[24] but, as Irenaeus says, on Justin—whose lost work must be Theophilus' source.

There are no borrowings from book 3 of Theophilus' work, which as has already been suggested was probably later than books 1–2. Like Theophilus, Irenaeus reinterpreted the Decalogue, but he made no use of Theophilus' revised version in book 3. Christians, he says in his *Demonstration,* have no need of the law as a tutor. The commandments about adultery, murder, covetousness, and Sabbath observance, for example, have no relevance for them, since they have put away all evil desires. He cites one of Theophilus' "chapters of the Decalogue" (Ex. 23:7), but from a different source, Susanna 53.[25] Obviously he is not following Theophilus' third book.

Loofs and others supposed that Irenaeus used not the treatise *To Autolycus* but Theophilus' lost work against Marcion. In view of all the parallels to the extant treatise, this hypothesis seems unnecessary.

Irenaeus thus stood at the end of the Greek apologetic movement of the second century and corrected the apologists' notions of philosophical theology in the light of his own system. He developed an anti-Gnostic theology out of his own Hellenistic education, not theirs, as well as from biblical insights.

From Commodus to Septimius Severus

Armed conflict followed the death of Commodus, and in 193 Septimius Severus, governor of Pannonia, was hailed as emperor, as was Niger, governor of Syria. The Christian editor of the eighth book of *Sibylline Oracles* welcomed Niger's seizure of power in Asia, believing that he would finally bring the Antonine house down and capture Rome 948 years after its foundation, thus in the year 195/196.[26] But Niger was killed in October 194, while in 195 Severus took steps to associate himself with the Antonines as "son of the divine Marcus Pius" and brother of the divine Commodus. By the end of that year another contestant, Albinus the governor of Britain, declared himself emperor and crossed the Channel to Gaul. Severus moved to Rome, where the Senate denounced Albinus and he himself insisted on legitimacy by making a dedication to his "ancestor" the deified Nerva.[27] He then took troops northward and decisively smashed the army of Albinus in a very bloody battle near Lyons on February 19, 197.

Tertullian's *To the Nations*

In this crisis the Christian rhetorician Tertullian at Carthage produced his two books *To the Nations.* He wrote not long after the battle, for he stated that "the Gauls still do not wash in the Rhone."[28] In the first book he defended Christians against the charges made against them, pointing to the role of ignorance in persecutions and arguing that the charges against them are entirely false. In the second he denounced pagan religion, especially Roman, and followed Varro in dividing it into philosophical, poetic, and national religion.[29]

Tertullian took important political points from the Greek apologists. He used Melito and took from him the claim that the name "Christian" arose under Augustus, perhaps also the claim that Tiberius favored the new religion. Though the acts of the persecutor Nero were invalidated, the *institutum Neronianum* which he began is still prevalent.[30] There is no direct mention of later emperors, though the titles Parthicus, Medicus, and Germanicus, which he mentions, are those awarded Marcus Aurelius in 166–169, just before Melito wrote.[31] Tertullian knew and described another work by Melito, criticizing his "skill in rhetorical elegance" but admitting that many ordinary Christians considered him a prophet.[32] He also may have used Miltiades, mentioned as a "sophist of the churches" in a late work.[33]

Barnes pointedly comments that "Tertullian revealed good judgment if he left the *Ad Nationes* unfinished."[34]

Tertullian's *Apology*

Not much later, when the "accomplices in guilty plots," the followers of Albinus and Niger, were still being hunted down, and "apparently when the Parthians were topical," Tertullian turned from the unfinished *To the Nations* to a new work, the *Apology*.[35] The year was 197 or 198 or even 199. He insisted that Christians took no part in plots against the emperors. They were not followers of [Avidius] Cassius or Niger or Albinus.[36] They had not plotted against an emperor (Commodus) at Laurentum "between two laurels."[37] It was not a Christian who practiced gymnastic exercises in order to strangle the emperor (Commodus again).[38] They did not "rush armed into the palace," like the murderers of Domitian.[39] Tertullian notes that "accomplices in guilty plots" are being revealed every day, and this remark recalls Severus' execution of twenty-nine senators.[40]

Such was the setting of the *Apology*, addressed not to the emperor or to the general reader but to the Roman provincial governors.[41] Perhaps it was Tertullian's research into the attitudes of provincial governors that led him to the Pliny-Trajan letters, unknown to the earlier apologists because written in Latin.

The *Apology* makes intensive use of the Greek apologists, plainly relying on Justin for the story of Simon Magus and Sanctus Deus.[42] Like Justin, Tertullian describes Christian life and worship. He also uses Apollinaris, Tatian, and Theophilus.[43] In a later work he expressed his admiration for Justin as philosopher and martyr, in a context of praise for Miltiades, Irenaeus, and the Montanist Proculus.[44]

Tertullian argues (probably after Melito) that Roman power was not due to Roman religion, for the one God ordains the rise and fall of empires. Christians preserve the empire by constant prayer to the one God, "always for all the emperors, long life to them, secure rule, a safe house, strong armies, a faithful Senate, an honest people, a peaceful world."[45] Persecutions are mere accidents due to the urban mob,[46] though Christians must resist the state if it tries to usurp God's place.

Tertullian also knew Tatian's *Oration* and occasionally used it in his *Apology*.[47] He relied on Tatian's gossip about Aristippus, Plato, and Aristotle in his *Apology* (46.15), and about Heraclitus and Empedocles in his *To the Martyrs* (4.5). Obviously, following Irenaeus, he regarded Tatian as unorthodox, for he named Justin and Irenaeus as authorities, not Tatian.

A section based on Theophilus stood in the Codex Fuldensis, now lost but with variant readings noted in 1584, which contained a different version of the 19th chapter.[48] This version of chapter 19 is not necessarily the original one, in spite of the arguments of C. Becker.[49]

Since Theophilus does not appear in the rest of the *Apology*, we may ask when Tertullian encountered his work. The text of Genesis Tertullian used in his treatise *Against Hermogenes* contains several readings shared only with Theophilus; he was therefore relying on Theophilus' lost work against the same heretic, perhaps composed in 204/205.[50] F. Bolgiani has gone much farther by demonstrating Tertullian's reliance on Theophilus for his own outline and many of his main points.[51] Presumably, then, Tertullian encountered Theophilus' apology only after, or when, he used the treatise against Hermogenes. "The *Fragmentum Fuldense* clearly constitutes an alternative and inferior version of a passage in the vulgate (19.1ff.)."[52]

Like the earlier apologies, Tertullian's work is a defense of Christians charged with the secret crimes of murder, cannibalism, and incest and the public crimes of refusing to worship the gods and offer sacrifice for the emperors. R. Heinze long ago related the work to forensic rhetoric and claimed that it thus advanced beyond the Greek apologists whose works Tertullian knew.[53] It is hard to differentiate forensic rhetoric, however, from the deliberative mode used by some of the earlier authors, or to be sure that their method was not forensic or even mixed. Like Tertullian himself in *To the Nations* they sometimes composed in the protreptic mode or presented extended petitions to the emperors. Theophilus clearly mixed his forms.

Theological Use of Various Apologists

By the end of the second century theology was on the move especially at Alexandria and the apologetic theology no longer seemed viable. Political circumstances also seemed to have changed and after Tertullian the writings of the earlier apologists were no longer valued for their political significance. In any case, Clement's *Exhortation* was so much better written than the earlier works (and Origen's *Against Celsus* would be so much more thorough and theologically astute) that there was no reason to quote the apologies except as witnesses against Greco-Roman culture or for their primitive orthodoxy.

An anonymous author against adoptionism in the late second century cites Melito and asks, "Who is ignorant of the books of Irenaeus and Melito and the others who proclaimed Christ as God and man?"[54] Scholars have sometimes thought that Hippolytus wrote this work, but Hippolytus (relying on Irenaeus) knew Tatian was a heretic[55] and therefore cannot have written a work citing Tatian, along with Justin, Miltiades, and Clement, as an authority for speaking of Christ as God.[56]

Clement of Alexandria probably refers to Tatian when he speaks of an "Assyrian" who taught him in the orient.[57] He certainly knew the *Oration* and used it later in the same book, where chapters 1, 4, 21, 28, 31, and 36–41 appear.[58] Clement omitted the misogynistic chapters 32–34 and (perhaps influenced by Irenaeus) the autobiographical conceits of chapters 35 and 42. In a later book, however, Clement criticized Tatian's unorthodox teaching about marriage in the treatise *On Perfection According to the Savior*.

Clement may not have known the treatise of Theophilus. Since it is virtually certain that he used the antiheretical treatise of Irenaeus, he probably took occasional points from Irenaeus rather than his source Theophilus. The idea of Adam as an infant is such a point. On the other hand, he stated that the prophets before Moses included "Adam prophesying on the woman and on the names of animals, and Noah preaching repentance,"[59] and this may echo Theophilus *To Autolycus* 2.28 (Adam's prophecy) and 3.19 (Noah and repentance). If Clement knew Theophilus, however, he did not regard his work highly. The simple style and thought must have repelled him, and what Photius says about Clement's Genesis exegesis in the lost *Outlines*[60] excludes Theophilus as a source.

Origen on Melito and Tatian

A generation later Origen criticized Melito because he merely stated that Absalom, son of David, was "a model of the devil who rebelled against the kingdom of Christ," and did not investigate the passage further.[61] Origen also admired the *Oration* and "great learning" of Tatian, but later in the treatise *Against Celsus* criticized his heresy without naming him. (See chapter 13.)

Theophilus in Novatian

The schismatic Christian author Novatian was certainly not a creative or original theologian, and we are not surprised to see him make use of a conventional discussion from Theophilus. A rhetorical passage on God in the second chapter of Novatian's *On the Trinity* is certainly based on Theophilus' earlier discussion. "If you call him Light you speak of his creature more than himself; you do not express him; if you call him Virtus you speak of his power more than himself; if you call him majesty you describe his honor more than himself. And why should I make a long story by passing through individual items?" Why indeed, since much of the surrounding context also comes from Theophilus' first book? Fausset intimates that Novatian's idea of the deification of man in consequence of obedience and immortality is also derived from Theophilus.[62]

22

The Apologists
in the Third Century
and After

The third-century use of the apologists is indirectly illustrated in the minor works mistakenly ascribed to Justin. These are attacks on Hellenistic culture, though not at a high level, often transmitted in groups.

Literature Ascribed to Justin

Of works ascribed to Justin, the *Exhortation* and *Sole Rule of God,* for example, are preserved in Codex Parisinus graecus 450. A thirteenth-century manuscript once at Strasbourg contained *Sole Rule of God, Exhortation, Exposition of Orthodoxy, Oration,* and *Epistle to Diognetus,* all ascribed to Justin; in addition there were excerpts from Sibylline and Greek oracles and the two works ascribed to Athenagoras. The Arethas manuscript from the year 914 (Codex Paris. gr. 451) contained only the *Exhortation.*

The *Exhortation* is the longest of the works supposedly by Justin, but like the others it is almost entirely based on anthologized information. The author explicitly says that this is a *logos parainetikos* or "exhortation." Such a type of address was already known to the Stoic Aristo, who refused to engage in such elementary teaching.[1] Posidonius, on the other hand, thought it was "necessary,"[2] and Clement praises the genre at the beginning of his *Tutor.* Methodius refers to the *parainesis* of Paul (in 1 Cor. 7:35),[3] and Epiphanius speaks of the *paraineseis* of the Gnostic Isidore, son of Basilides.[4] Since Epiphanius knows Isidore and his *Ethics* entirely through quotations in Clement of Alexandria, he must regard paraenesis as a proper term for ethical teaching.

In the *Exhortation* the topic is divided into two parts: first, a criticism of Greek poets as religious authorities, especially Homer (with a mention of Hesiod); second, an encomium of the Hebrew prophets, especially Moses, with praise of their reliability. Justin will show "clearly and openly that we follow the religion of our ancestors in God." This allusion may look ahead to the end of the work, where he speaks of Christianity.

The first part begins with an attack on the ignorance of the ancient poets, especially Homer, in regard to the gods (1–2), and then turns to the contradictions of the philosophers (3–6), even with themselves (7). The teachers of the Greeks taught them nothing true about religion (8). One must therefore turn to the "prophet and legislator" Moses, earliest of all as even Greek historians admit (9–10; cf. 25).

The "proof" of this point is supposedly based on the *Antiquities* of Josephus but really on his apologetic *Against Apion,* and on a quotation from Diodorus Siculus 1.94 about Moses' ancient legislation. Unfortunately Diodorus was writing about an Egyptian named Mneves (the first king, Menas); Pseudo-Justin deletes Diodorus' statement that Mneves claimed to have received his laws from Hermes, then continues with his statement that "among the Jews Moyses referred his laws to the god invoked as Iao" and his discussion of later Egyptian legislators. Diodorus was not including "Moyses" in a chronological list, but the apologetic author first identifies Mneves with Moses and then treats the statements as if they were chronological. With Moses now prior to all other wise men (and with the Jews originally from Chaldea), he can explain that all Greek wisdom was derived from the Jewish teacher, whose prophetic books in Hebrew were written before the Greeks could write (11–12). Later when a Ptolemy built the library at Alexandria he had identical Greek versions made by seventy scholars in seventy cells, whose ruins the author has seen (13). The true theology of Greek poets such as Orpheus, the Sibyl, Homer, and Sophocles (14–18), and the philosophers Pythagoras and Plato (19–27), along with Homer (28–35), comes from the Hebrew scriptures. The Sibyl, whose grotto the author has seen at Cumae, also agreed with them; and so did Hermes (Trismegistus) (36–37).

The *Exhortation* certainly contains direct quotations from Homer[5] and Plato. Much of the rest, however, is secondhand and comes from anthologies of poetry[6] and collections of philosophical opinions.[7]

The originality of the work lies in the author's appeal to archaeological evidence as well as in details of his argument. His praise of "the most wise" Philo and Josephus (9–10) suggests a Hellenistic Jewish origin, as do the doctrines discussed along the way. Only in his last chapter does he mention "the advent of our Savior Jesus Christ," who was the Logos of God but "recovered the man formed after the image and likeness of God" and "recalled us to the memory of our first parents." He also refers to Christ's future coming. The bulk of the book is not related to this Christological doctrine, however, and he is probably modifying a Hellenistic Jewish source.[8]

The *Exhortation* was used by Cyril of Alexandria in his *Against Julian,* probably because he found it in a manuscript with the *Preparation for the Gospel* by Eusebius.[9]

The brief oration *To the Greeks* begins as a "farewell address" in the manner of Tatian's *Oration* (see chapter 13). "Do not suppose, O Greeks, that my separation from your customs is irrational or uncritical: I found nothing in them that was either holy or pleasing to God." From this point the author turns directly to analysis of Greek poets from Homer through Hesiod, then to criticism of myths about various gods, especially Heracles, to prove that they were all promiscuous. His epic sources go beyond *Iliad* and *Odyssey* to the Homeric cycle.[10] After a short discussion of tragedy, festivals (with an echo of Amos 5:21), and poets in general, he exhorts Greeks to be taught by the divine Logos and probably alludes to Galatians when he calls his readers to "become as I am, for I was as you are" and avoid various passions.[11]

There is also a Syriac version in which the work is called *Hypomnēmata* and ascribed to "Ambrose, a chief man of Greece."[12] Since the word can mean "notes" or "memoranda," as well as "treatises" or even "commentaries," it is well chosen for the title of a work more valuable for its sources than for its analysis.

A little treatise called *Sole Rule of God* consists of almost nothing but excerpts from anthologies of lines from the poets, arranged to show how inconsistent they were except when they anticipated Christianity.[13]

Theological Use of the Apologists in the Third Century

Melito as Theologian

Melito is cited by an anonymous author of the late second century as opposed to adoptionism. He asks, "Who is ignorant of the books of Irenaeus and Melito and the others who proclaimed Christ as God and man?"[14] A generation later Origen criticized him, however, because he merely stated that Absalom, son of David, was "a model of the devil who rebelled against the kingdom of Christ," and did not investigate the passage further.[15]

Clement in Arnobius

The end of the third century saw the publication of Arnobius' seven books against the pagans, in which we find many Greek sources, with fourteen citations from Plato and two apiece from Aristotle, Sophocles, Mnaseas of Patara (interpreter of unusual myths), Myrtillus, and Posidippus. Festugière showed that in his second book Arnobius relied on Plotinus and other Neoplatonic authors as well as the "mystical" literature of the *Orphica,* the *Hermetica,* the *Chaldaean Oracles,* and the Chaldean sages Zoroaster and Ostanes. An especially important source of information about mythology was Clement's *Exhortation,* cited at either first or second hand (G. E. McCracken analyzes the question fully).[16] Arnobius was naturally much better acquainted with Latin sources, which include Varro, Cicero, Lucretius, Tertullian's *Apology* and *To the Nations,* and the *Octavius* of Minucius Felix.[17]

Theophilus in Lactantius

Early in the fourth century the Latin apologist Lactantius admires and follows both Tertullian and Minucius Felix, and in addition names and uses the work of one Greek apologist. This is what he calls the "book on chronology addressed to Autolycus" (book 3) by Theophilus. Lactantius quotes a few passages directly, including Theophilus' own unique quotations from the *Sibylline Oracles.*[18] As O. P. Nicholson has shown, he carefully follows Theophilus' whole chronological scheme but gives it an apocalyptic orientation by arranging it into a "cosmic week."[19]

Theological Details in Methodius

A bit of Athenagoras' *Embassy,* with a reference to the author, appears in Methodius' treatise *On the Resurrection* in the early fourth century.[20] It is striking that Methodius carefully avoids what Athenagoras says about the Trinity. He probably gives another echo of the work in his *Freedom of Choice* 12.1, where the phrase *haplē kai monoeidēs* is more likely to come from Athenagoras than from the pre-Socratics Anaximenes or Anaxagoras.[21]

Methodius also used Theophilus' work, though without naming him. Perhaps the best evidence occurs in his treatise *On the Resurrection,* where he claims that paradise was on earth because Genesis mentions the Tigris and the Euphrates.[22]

Eusebius as Preserver of the Apologists

Since Eusebius himself was an able and famous apologist, his *Chronicle* and *Church History* contain notices of almost all the second-century apologists. He relates Quadratus and Aristides to Hadrian's visit to Athens and discusses the apologetic works of Justin, Apollinaris, Melito, Miltiades, Tatian, Theophilus, and Clement, and even quotes from a Greek version of the *Apology* by Tertullian. Evidently the church libraries at Caesarea and/ or Jerusalem contained their writings.

The earliest apology, by Quadratus, apparently disappeared except from the library at Caesarea or Jerusalem. Eusebius supplies the one fragment of his work. Presumably he did not consider the rest of it very important. The most important apologist was evidently Justin, whose writings

Eusebius discussed at considerable length.[23] He accepted as genuine Justin's *Refutation* (of the Greeks), *On the Sovereignty of God* = *On the Sole Rule of God* (not the one handed down among his writings), *Psaltēs,* and discussion *On the Soul.*

Eusebius was aware that Melito was a leading member of the Asian Quartodecimans. Polycrates bishop of Ephesus named him as such in a list that began with Philip "of the twelve apostles" and ended with "the eunuch Melito, who lived entirely in the Holy Spirit and lies at Sardis awaiting the visitation from heaven when he will rise from the dead."[24]

On the other hand, Eusebius knew nothing about Athenagoras. If he found him mentioned by Methodius he was unlikely to use his work.[25]

As for Tatian, he knew that this author had composed many works, but he mentioned only two of them, the *Diatessaron* or *Harmony of the Four Gospels* and the *Oration Against the Greeks,*[26] using the latter for the biography of Justin. Like Clement, Eusebius lay emphasis on chapters 36–41 on the antiquity of Moses, and in his *Preparation for the Gospel* cites these chapters along with 31 and 42,[27] quoting them not from Clement but directly from Tatian. From Irenaeus he learned of Tatian's fall from orthodoxy.

Eusebius refers to Theophilus' "three elementary treatises" *To Autolycus,* works against the heresies of Hermogenes and Marcion, and some catechetical books.[28] He may have looked at the attack on Hermogenes, but nothing shows that he opened the other books.

A Special Case: Transmission and Recovery of Aristides

Two papyri found in modern times prove that the apology of Aristides was read in fourth-century Egypt.[29] One is an Oxyrhynchus papyrus (xv.1778) containing Aristides 5.5–6.1, the other a British Museum papyrus (inventory no. 2486) with Aristides 15.6–16.1.[30]

The apology survives as a whole only in Armenian and Syriac versions. In 1878 Mechitarist monks on the island of S. Lazzaro, Venice, published a Latin version of the beginning of the apology from an Armenian manuscript in their library. F. C. Conybeare later found an eleventh-century copy of the same text at Etchmiadzin near Mount Ararat, where the church had been established in the late third century.[31] Presumably the Mechitarists possessed a copy of the Etchmiadzin text.

Rendel Harris found the Syriac version, almost complete, in a seventh-century manuscript on Mount Sinai in 1889, and Armitage Robinson, who was working on a text of the eighth- or tenth-century Greek novel *Barlaam and Josaphat,* noticed that an apologetic speech ascribed to a Christian missionary in India was a slightly revised version of the same work.[32]

Apologetic Learning in the Late Fourth Century

Toward the end of the fourth century Gregory of Nazianzus used Tatian's materials on barbarian originality against the Hellene Julian.[33] Similarly a scholion on another oration by Gregory (*Oration* 31.16) is clearly based on Athenagoras 18, since it omits the same words, required by the sense, from an Orphic fragment.[34]

A reference to Athenagoras by Philip of Side in the fifth century is entirely worthless, for it places Athenagoras in the first half of the second century and makes him the first head of the Christian school at Alexandria, with Clement as his disciple and Pantaenus, known to be Clement's teacher, as the disciple of Clement. Philip knew that Athenagoras addressed the *Embassy* to two emperors but wrongly identified them as Hadrian and Antoninus Pius. Concern for school tradition has eradicated the historical circumstances of Athenagoras' political writing.

The notorious heresy-hunter Epiphanius clearly admired Theophilus and imitated his first sentence at the beginning of his *Panarion*.[35] In addition, some of the information about mythology that he used in his *Ancoratus* 104–106 came from Theophilus.[36]

In his edition of the homilies on the Hexaemeron,[37] S. Giet argued that Basil of Caesarea frequently used Theophilus on Genesis and indeed referred to him. If Basil read Theophilus he may not have admired his work, though he was willing to take some ideas, as opposed to expressions, from the bishop of Antioch. The most significant passage occurs in *Homily* 2.6, where Basil asks how the Spirit was "borne" above the waters and comments thus: "I shall not give you my own explanation, but that of a Syrian who was as far removed from worldly wisdom as he was close to the understanding of what is true. He used to say that in Syriac the word *(epephereto)* was more expressive and because of its close relation to Hebrew came closer to the meaning of the scriptures. . . . It means 'warmed' and 'made alive' *(ezōogonei)* the substance of the waters like a setting bird; by warming them it communicated a certain vital force to them." Some aspects of this explanation are paralleled in Theophilus' exegesis,[38] but there is not a trace of Syriac in the apology. There seems to have been little communication between Greeks and Syrians, in the second century as in the time of John Chrysostom.

23
The Apologists
in the Middle Ages
and Later

In the sixth century Theophilus was sometimes read in the school of Gaza, and in Procopius' commentaries on the Hexateuch there are two anonymous citations of his exegesis (2.19, 24; 2.25).[1] In addition, Procopius knows the treatise *On the Resurrection* ascribed to Justin.[2]

From the eighth century come theological excerpts in the *Sacra Parallela* of John of Damascus, who relied on the library of St. Saba near Jerusalem. The only apologists included are Justin and Theophilus.[3] Justin is represented by eight quotations from the apologies, one from the *Dialogue with Trypho*, and four from works he did not write (one from the *Epistle to Zenas and Serenus*, three from the *Cohortatio*.[4] Most of the "quotations" come from the treatise *On the Resurrection* and unidentified works or are incorrectly ascribed to Justin.[5] Of the six citations from Theophilus four are authentic while one belongs to Eusebius of Caesarea and one to Eusebius of Alexandria.[6] The manuscripts do not give much credit to Theophilus, however. The first fragment is assigned to Theophilus or Theotimus of Scythia or Theophanes, the second to Amphilochius of Iconium, and the fourth to Eleutherius of Tyana. In addition, one sentence comes from Clement's *Exhortation*.[7]

Theophilus is also echoed in a Christian version of a late Antiochene work on geography, the *Expositio totius mundi*, but its date is most uncertain.[8]

Probably before Photius became patriarch of Constantinople around 855, he prepared an analysis of his readings in classical and theological literature for his brother. This "library" contains 280 notices of authors from Herodotus to Nicephorus, patriarch in 806. Not surprisingly, he gives little space to the apologists of the second century, and mentions Quadratus only in passing as a source of Eusebius of Thessalonica; it is not obvious that he knows who he was.[9] He refers to Athenagoras, perhaps our apologist, as recipient of a treatise *On the Difficult Terms in Plato*, and reproduces

Methodius' reference to his *Embassy,* [10] but mentions Tatian only because he was denounced by Irenaeus. [11] On the other hand, he has read Apollinaris' *To the Greeks, On Religion,* and *On Truth* and knows he was bishop of Hierapolis in Asia under Marcus Aurelius. He has heard of other works by this author but has not been able to find them. [12] The list overlaps that of Eusebius but does not coincide with it. [13]

The only apologist Photius treats adequately is Justin. He refers to the (authentic) *Apology for the Christians, Against the Greeks,* and *Against the Jews* (presumably the *Dialogue with Trypho*), and adds some inauthentic treatises against Aristotle: *Against the First and Second Books of Physics* (or "Against Form, Matter, and Privation"; Photius praises the rigorous argumentation), as well as *Against the Fifth Body, Against Eternal Motion,* and *Summary Solutions of Difficulties Raised Against the Religion.* Some of the anti-Aristotelian treatises later appear in Codex Parisinus graecus 450. [14]

Photius also discusses, but does not claim to have read, the books already listed by Eusebius, i.e., his two apologies addressed to Antoninus Pius and his successors, a book on demons, and a *Refutation.* There is also a treatise *On the Monarchy of God* and a *Psaltēs.* [15] Two other titles, *Against Marcion* and *Against All Heresies,* also come from Eusebius, as do biographical details and the account of Justin's martyrdom. [16]

Photius' enthusiastic description of Justin's philosophical skill, erudition, and scientific language is based on the nonauthentic works. It is not clear why he did not coordinate his two lists of works. [17] A discussion by Stephanus Gobarus (a sixth-century tritheist quoted by Photius) is based on the nonauthentic *Exhortation,* but Photius does not seem to know the author of the work in question. [18]

We have already seen how important the libraries of the early church were for preserving such works as those of the apologists, and after the destruction of those at Caesarea and Jerusalem when the Arabs invaded, the others gained importance. N. G. Wilson lays emphasis on the four at Constantinople. For us the most important was the patriarchal, unfortunately burned in 726 though Photius still used it. There were also monastic and provincial libraries like that of St. Saba, used by John of Damascus. Later the monk Antiochus put together his *Pandectes* with its citations of patristic works otherwise lost. [19] Wilson suggests that "so many copies of the leading fathers exist that their number is more an embarrassment than a source of pleasure to the modern scholar who has to edit the text." This is true of "the leading fathers" but not of the apologists, of whom few manuscripts survive.

Arethas, archbishop of Caesarea in Cappadocia after about 902, was an avid collector of classical manuscripts. He rediscovered the *Meditations* of Marcus Aurelius, [20] arranged for copies of classical authors like Plato (Bodleian, Clark. 39) and Euclid (Bodleian, D'Orville MS. XI inf. 2.30), and wrote scholia on Aelius Aristides and Dio Chrysostom.[21] He certainly studied the satirist Lucian[22] and the emperor Julian.[23]

In addition, Arethas wrote dogmatic works and many orations, including one "on the translation of St. Euthymius, archbishop of Constantinople," in which he mentioned Gregory Thaumaturgus. Recently published letters and orations do not refer to early Christian literature.[24]

Because he made use of a commentary on the Apocalypse by Andreas of Caesarea, he encountered the names of "the more ancient" fathers such as Papias, Irenaeus, Hippolytus, and Methodius.[25] In the year 914 he had the scribe Baanes make a collection of early Christian apologies for him, along with some works of the same kind by Eusebius. This is now the Codex Parisinus graecus 451, which contains the *Exhortation* and *Tutor* by Clement of Alexandria, the *Epistle to Zenas and Serenus* and *Exhortation* supposedly by Justin, the *Oration* of Tatian (now lost from the manuscript), books 1–4 of Eusebius' *Preparation for the Gospel,* the *Embassy* and treatise *On the Resurrection* ascribed to Athenagoras, and Eusebius' treatise *Against Hierocles.* [26] Baanes joined Arethas in writing on Clement, while Arethas alone composed scholia on Tatian.[27] In the longest of Arethas' comments he claims that Tatian was not far from Arianism.

The manuscript almost certainly belonged to Cardinal Bessarion, who acquired it after he gave his library to the Senate of Venice in 1467–1468. No manuscript with these contents appears in the first inventory of 1468, but one is listed in 1474 and again in 1524, only to disappear by 1543.[28] Somehow it was transferred to Paris.

Five quaternions (40 leaves) have been lost from the beginning of the manuscript with the first 95 sections of Clement's *Exhortation,* as well as four quaternions between leaves 187 and 188, with the end of the *Exhortation* of "Justin," Tatian's *Oration,* and the beginning of Eusebius' *Preparation for the Gospel.* Three later manuscripts preserve the *Oration:* the mid-eleventh-century Codex Marcianus Venetus 343, from Bessarion's collection; the twelfth-century Codex Mutinensis III D 7, with Athenagoras' apology and treatise on the resurrection; and the twelfth-century Codex Parisinus graecus 174, which belonged to the church of Paphos in the fourteenth century and contains Athenagoras as well.[29] Fifteen later copies have no independent value.

An important "Justin" manuscript of the thirteenth century was once preserved at Strasbourg. This contained the treatise *On the Sole Rule of God,* the *Exhortation,* the *Exposition of Orthodoxy,* and the *Oration,* as well as "by the same author" the *Epistle to Diognetus,* some oracles, and the works of Athenagoras. Justin's authentic works, along with many not his, survive in one manuscript of the year 1364, Codex Parisinus graecus 450. It is a "corpus Iustinianum" with genuine as well as nongenuine works, and was based on research, since it begins with excerpts from Photius and

Eusebius to show what is being compiled. It contains the only extant texts of the *Apologies* and *Dialogue;* the *Epistle to Zenas and Serenus* and the *Exhortation,* which is not mentioned in Eusebius or Photius but in the *Sacred Parallels;* and the *Refutation of Some Aristotelian Doctrines, Questions and Answers for the Orthodox,* and *Christian and Greek Questions and Answers.* The occasion for writing the manuscript remains unknown. One might imagine that the pro-Platonist Petrarch owned it and left it to Venice in 1374, but it has nothing to do with him. Petrarch could not read Greek and there is no reliable evidence that he actually gave his books to the city.[30]

The transmission of Theophilus' works differed from that of other apologies. The oldest extant manuscript is the eleventh-century Codex Venetus Marcianus 496, which belonged to Cardinal Bessarion, as a note in his handwriting shows. He gave it to the Senate of Venice in 1468 and it appears in all the inventories thereafter. It contains the *Reply Against Apollinarius* by Gregory of Nyssa, Eusebius' *Against Marcellus* and *Church Theology,* Adamantius' *Dialogue on Orthodoxy,* Zacharias Scholasticus' *On the Creation of the World,* Aeneas of Gaza's *Theophrastus,* and finally Theophilus. A note by Bessarion states that it ended with Epiphanius' *Twelve Gems,* but there is no trace of it; the manuscript really ended with Theophilus. From this manuscript were copied the sixteenth-century Codex Bodleianus graecus MS. Auct. E. 1.11, without independent value, and in 1540 the Codex Parisinus graecus 887, which contains only the third book. Since most of the other treatises in the latter manuscript deal with the Trinity, the scribe probably copied book 3 by mistake for book 2, where in chapter 15 there is a reference to a divine Triad.

Obviously Bessarion was a prime mover in the transmission of the Greek apologists, and it is important to note with Mioni that while he could and did obtain manuscripts from Sicily and Calabria, "the most important nucleus" of his collection, both patristic and classical, "was certainly Constantinopolitan." In other words, he inherited the tradition of Photius.[31]

In 1543 the celebrated Swiss physician and naturalist Conrad Gesner visited Venice to collect materials for his *Universal Library,* which was to appear at Zurich in September 1545. In Venice he encountered Diego Hurtado de Mendoza, whose library he inspected, and Arnoldus Arlenius, who showed him a catalog of the library.[32] In the library he found a manuscript of Stobaeus, which he borrowed in order to correct his own edition, printed at Zurich some time after June 13, 1543.[33] He also found a manuscript containing Tatian (presumably a copy of the eleventh-century Codex Marcianus 343) and another with Theophilus (copied from Marcianus 496). He was too busy to do anything about the apologists for a time, but early in 1545 his friend Johannes Frisius visited Venice and brought back copies of the manuscripts with Tatian and Theophilus, given him by Arnoldus Arlenius.[34]

Another famous collector was the French king François I, who joined the humanists in collecting early Christian books and was responsible for the fairly large library at Fontainebleau. By 1550 the manuscript of Justin was in his library. Indeed, it was probably there in 1541, when Codex Claromontanus (= Phillips MS. 3081 in the British Library) was copied from it.

Publication of the Apologies 1541–1557

The first early Christian apologetic work to appear in print was the treatise *On the Resurrection* of Athenagoras, published by Peter Nannius at Louvain in 1541; the *Embassy* did not appear until edited by Conrad Gesner at Paris in 1557.

The first edition of Theophilus was published at Zurich in 1546 by Joannes Frisius, who used a manuscript (copied from that at Venice) supplied by Conrad Gesner and a Latin version made by Conrad Clauser. The volume was entitled *Hoc volumine continentur: Sententiarum vel capitum . . . Tomi tres, per Antonium et Maximum monachos olim collecti . . . Theophili sexti Antiochensis episcopi de Deo et fide Christianorum contra Gentes Institutionum libri tres ad Autolycum. . . .* It also contained the first edition of Tatian.

Five years later Robertus Stephanus (Étienne) published the first edition of Justin's works (genuine and other) at Paris, relying on Codex Parisinus graecus 450 from the royal library. In 1592, probably also at Paris, his son Henri published as Justin's the *Epistle to Diognetus* and the *Oration.* Some of the editors supposed that these works would be of value to the Reformers and the Counter-Reformers as well as to humanists. Indeed, the Latin translator of Theophilus claimed that the apologist's arguments against the pagans could be used against the papists too. But Philip Melanchthon, most learned of the Continental Reformers, knew nothing of the apologists. Indeed, he first encountered a manuscript with Pseudo-Justin's *Exposition of Orthodoxy* in 1549 and expressed doubts about the authenticity of the work.[35] Repeated editions of Justin and other apologists, notably that by Prudentius Maranus, published by Charles Osmont at Paris in 1742, reflect considerable interest, as does the great nineteenth-century edition by J. C. T. Otto, *Corpus Apologetarum Christianorum Saeculi Secundi* (Jena: Dufft, 1842–1861). The place of these authors in early Christianity could not really be assessed, however, before the era of Adolf Harnack. By that time they were overshadowed by Christian authors both earlier and later.

Late Latin Use of the Greek Apologists

After the fourth century, Latin writers made less and less use of authors preserved only in Greek, for changing political and theological circumstances made translations pointless. Latin Christian authors found that the apologists were obsolete. It is significant that in Siegmund's study of transmission in Latin manuscripts only Melito and Tatian are represented, neither of them by apologetic works.[36] Only at the Renaissance did new Latin translations of the apologists come into existence, with Latin versions of Tatian and Theophilus in 1546, Justin and Clement in 1551, and Athenagoras in 1557.[37]

Modern Discoveries Related to the Apologists

Here we largely summarize what we have already discussed but lay emphasis on a few significant points. The manuscripts of Justin, Tatian, and Theophilus were well utilized in the sixteenth century, though it should be noted that no editor before Otto in the mid-nineteenth century made use of the manuscript at Venice. We have seen how Armenian and Syriac versions contributed to the recovery of Aristides at the end of the century. In our century discoveries related to the apologies have not been very significant. Two Greek papyri of Aristides' apology; many papyri and several versions of Melito's *Paschal Homily* but not the *Apology;* a parchment fragment of Tatian's *Diatessaron,* not his *Oration*—that is all. Indeed, these authors were so little read that it is surprising that we have anything. Future work on them will probably be concentrated on the relation between their theologies and the cultural settings in which they wrote.

Conclusion

Christian apologetic in the second century accompanied war and conspiracy and was sometimes occasioned by imperial tours of the provinces. It began with Quadratus and Aristides and their appeals to Hadrian at Athens, continued with Justin (after the martyrdom of Polycarp, perhaps during troubles under Antoninus Pius), and reached a climax with Apollinaris, Melito, and Athenagoras. All these apologists addressed emperors. Tatian and Theophilus, more negative, wrote to a group and an individual; Theophilus mitigated Tatian's hostile attitude toward the empire. An anonymous apology addressed the individual Diognetus, while Clement simply used a conventional literary form, apparently writing after the death of Commodus. After one civil war and on the verge of another, the Latin apologist Tertullian would use the works of his Greek predecessors for making the apologetic case once more.

In the long run the pioneering theological work of the apologists was to mean more than their political achievements. The creativity they showed, as they tried to make sense of mysterious or conflicting biblical passages, pointed toward what greater thinkers might produce. They gave much to the history of Christian thought, not in abiding doctrines but in approaches to doctrinal problems.

Appendixes

1. Parallels Between Pliny on Christians and Livy on Bacchants

Pliny *Epistles* 10.96	Livy 39.8.3ff. (quaestio de clandestinis coniurationibus)	
2 flagitia cohaerentia nomini		
3 pertinacia et inflexibilis obstinatio		
4 amentia . . . cives Romani	velut mente capta	13.12
5 multorum nomina	multorum nomina	17.5
7 stato die	statos dies	13.8
ante lucem convenire	nocturna sacra	8.4
carmen Christo quasi deo	ex carmine sacro	18.3
sacramentum	sacramentum	15.13
non in scelus	ad omne scelus	15.3
ne adulteria	stupra promiscua	8.7
ne fidem fallerent	falsa testimonia, signa adulterina, subjectio	
ne depositum adpellati abnegarent	testamentorum, fraudes aliae	18.4
cibum promiscuum et innoxium	vinum et epulae	8.5
8 ex ancillis per tormenta	ancilla 10.5;	12.6
superstitio	superstitio	16.10
prava	prava religio	16.6
et immodica		
9 periclitantium numerus	supra septem milia	17.6
omnis aetatis	aetatis tenerae maioribus	8.6
omnis ordinis	nobiles quidam viri feminaeque	13.14
utriusque sexus	mixti feminis mares	8.6
in periculum	quid . . . periculi	14.4
vici atque agri	tota Italia 14.7; 15.6;	16.4
superstitionis contagio	veluti contagione morbi	9.1

(Tacitus *Histories* 5.5 inter   nihil nefas ducere, hanc summam
se nihil illicitum)   inter eos religionem esse   13.11

97.2   conquirendi non sunt   sacerdotes . . . seu viri
                                         seu feminae essent, non Romae
                                         modo sed per omnia fora et
                                         conciliabula conquiri   14.7

These parallels show that Pliny's language and thought about the Christians were influenced by the Bacchanalian precedent. This does not mean that he did not report reliably to the emperor.[1] It means that his report was influenced by what he expected to encounter.

2. Parallels Between Fronto on Christians and Livy on Bacchants

P. Frassinetti has suggested that the consular opponent of Christianity, Cornelius Fronto, also relied on the tradition of Livy.[2] His vehement attack, delivered at an unknown date, is partly preserved by Minucius Felix. Frassinetti gives a short table of parallels, though he suggests that Fronto may have relied on Cato's lost *De coniuratione* or on an annalist summarizing Livy or Cato.

Minucius Felix *Octavius*		Livy 39	
6.1	disciplina maiorum	maiores vestri	15.2
8.4	profana coniuratio	coniuratio	15.10
		coniuratio impia	16.3
8.4	nocturnae congregationes	nocturni coetus	15.12
9.4	nocturnae ritae	(cf. 15.6, 9)	
9.1	serpentibus perditis moribus	serpit malum	16.3
9.1	sacraria taeterrima	ex obsceno sacrario	15.14
		ex illo uno sacrario	16.2

3. Tacitus: Parallels on Christians and Jews

On Christians: *Annals* 15.44   On Jews: *Histories* 5.4–5

poenis adfecit quos per   Novos ritus contrariosque ceteris
flagitia invisos   mortalibus
vulgus Christianos   Profana omnia quae apud nos sacra,
appellabat.   rursum concessa apud illos quae
                                                        nobis incesta

Auctor nominis eius Christus   Moyses dux
Tiberio imperitante
per procuratorem Pontium Pilatum
supplicio adfectus erat;

repressaque in praesens
exitiabilis superstitio
rursum erumpebat, non modo per
Iudaeam, originem eius mali. . . .

instituta sinistra, foeda, pravitate
valuere . . . inter se nihil illicitum

multitudo ingens . . .
odio humani generis
convicti sunt

adversus omnes hostile odium

The only "fact" in Tacitus' account is that Christ suffered under Pontius Pilate in the reign of Tiberius. The rest of it is based on rhetorical amplification.

The point of these three appendixes is that Latin writers (often with Greek sources) thought of Christianity in stereotypes and possessed virtually no reliable information about it. What Christians would have to aim for would not be better information but a change of attitude.

Notes

Chapter 1: The Background of Christian Apologetic

1. Tertullian *Apology* 40.1–2 (tr. J. E. B. Mayor).
2. E. N. Luttwak, *The Grand Strategy of the Roman Empire* (Baltimore: Johns Hopkins, 1977), 55.
3. Josephus *Against Apion* 1.129–30.
4. W. G. Waddell, *Manetho* (Cambridge: Harvard University Press, 1940), 2–3.
5. Eusebius *Church History* 2.17.
6. Cf. A. Terian, *Philonis Alexandrini De Animalibus* (Chico, Calif.: Scholars Press), 1981.
7. For a biblical precedent cf. the accusation in Ps. 106:34: "They did not destroy the peoples as the Lord had commanded them."
8. Eusebius *Preparation for the Gospel* 8.6–7.
9. Ibid., 8.11.1–18; a somewhat different account in *Every Good Man* 75–87.
10. Cf. H. Box, *Philonis Alexandrini In Flaccum* (London: Oxford University Press, 1939).
11. Philo *Immutability* 176; *Agriculture* 45; *Confusion of Tongues* 108.
12. Philo *Embassy* 147, 149.
13. Hystaspes frag. 13 Bidez-Cumont = Lactantius *Divine Institutes* 7.15.11.
14. Justin *Apology* 1.44.12.
15. Suetonius *Galba* 9.2.
16. Cf. Suetonius *Claudius* 25.5; Pliny *Natural History* 29.54; 30.13.
17. Tacitus *Histories* 4.54; cf. H. Last, "Rome and the Druids," *Journal of Roman Studies* 39 (1949), 1–5.
18. Cf. M. P. Nilsson, *Geschichte der griechischen Religion* II.2 (Munich: Beck, 1961), 111.
19. Cf. L. Koenen, "Die Prophezeiungen des 'Töpfers,'" *Zeitschrift für Papyrologie und Epigraphik* 2 (1968), 178–209.
20. Apuleius *Metamorphoses* 11.17.
21. *Asclepius* 24.
22. Suetonius *Augustus* 31.1.
23. Dio Cassius 57.18.5.

24. Papyrus Yale inv. 299 as read by J. Rea in *Zeitschrift für Papyrologie und Epigraphik* 27 (1977) 151–56.

25. Dio Cassius 75.13.2; cf. F. Cumont, *L'Égypte des astrologues* (Brussels: Fondation Égyptologique Reine Elisabeth, 1937), 152 n. 4.

26. Cf. F. H. Cramer, *Astrology in Roman Law and Politics,* Memoirs of the American Philosophical Society 37 (1954), 232–83.

27. Suetonius *Vitellius* 14.4.

28. On all this cf. R. MacMullen, *Enemies of the Roman Order* (Cambridge, Mass.: Harvard University Press, 1966).

29. Cicero *Flaccus* 67, 69.

30. Tacitus *Histories* 5.8, presumably following a Greek source.

31. Josephus *Against Apion* 2.95.

32. Ibid. 2.121.

33. Cf. Josephus *Against Apion* 1.1, 3; Origen *Against Celsus* 1.16; 4.11; Eusebius *Church History* 3.10; *Preparation for the Gospel* 8.8, etc.; T. Reinach and L. Blum, *Flavius Josèphe Contre Apion* (Paris: Belles Lettres, 1930), vii.

34. Suetonius *Domitian* 12.2; cf. *Inscriptiones Latinae Selectae* 1519.

35. Dio Cassius 67.14.2.

36. Josephus *Against Apion* 1.318.

37. Josephus *Antiquities* 4.223; 5.135, 234; 6.84–85.

38. Ibid., 11.112; 20.229; 6.35–44.

39. Ibid., 10.143; 11.111; 13.301.

40. Ibid., 20.234.

41. Ibid., 14.91; it was the year when they themselves came under tyranny, 19.187.

42. Ibid., 20.251.

43. Josephus *Against Apion* 2.165.

44. Cf. Josephus *War* 4.319, 358; for the Roman situation, cf. *Antiquities* 19.187 with 75 and 173.

45. Josephus *Antiquities* 10.209; Irenaeus *Against Heresies* 5.26.1; Clement *Stromata* 5.98.2–4.

46. Hippolytus *Commentary on Daniel* 2.12.7; cf. *Antichrist* 27.

47. Tacitus *Histories* 5.2–5. See chapter 3.

48. Ibid. 5.13; cf. Suetonius *Vespasian* 4.4; Josephus *War* 3.404.

Chapter 2: The Beginnings of Christian Apologetic

1. Tertullian *Against Marcion* 5.6.5.

2. Clement *Stromata* 5.25.2.

3. A. von Harnack, *Marcion, das Evangelium vom fremden Gott* (Texte und Untersuchungen 45, 1924), 108*.

4. *Martyrdom of Polycarp* 10.2.

5. Theophilus *To Autolycus* 3.14.

6. Ibid., 1.11.

7. Irenaeus *Against Heresies* 5.24.1.

8. Origen *Against Celsus* 8.65.

9. Ibid., 1.1.

10. A. Strobel, "Zum Verständnis von Röm. 13," *Zeitschrift für die neutestamentliche Wissenschaft* 47 (1956), 67–93.

11. E. Käsemann, "Grundsätzliches zur Interpretation von Röm. 13," *Exegetische Versuche und Besinnungen* II (Göttingen: Vandenhoeck & Ruprecht, 1965), 204–22.

12. Josephus *War* 2.140.

13. Josephus *Antiquities* 15.374.

14. Ibid., 15.387.

15. Xenophon *Memorabilia of Socrates* 2.3.18–19.

16. Livy 2.32; Dionysius of Halicarnassus 6.86; cf. W. Nestle, "Die Fabel des Menenius Agrippa," *Klio* 21 (1927), 350–60.

17. Cicero *Duties* 3.22.

18. Seneca *On Clemency* 1.5.1; 2.2.1.

19. Justin *Dialogue* 81.5.

20. *1 Clement* 60.4–61.1.

21. Tertullian *Apology* 21.24.

22. *1 Clement* 24–25; cf. *Miracle and Natural Law in Graeco-Roman and Early Christian Thought* (Amsterdam: North Holland, 1952), 236–40.

23. Seneca *Epistle* 36.11.

24. Cf. my *Gods and the One God* (Philadelphia: Westminster, 1986), 25–26.

25. A similar emphasis on seasons and weather is found in Aratus; see below.

26. For this theme cf. Rom. 1:19–20.

27. Justin *Apology* 2.13.4.

28. Eusebius *Church History* 3.16.

29. Cf. N. Zeegers-Vander Vorst, *Les citations des poètes grecs chez les apologistes chrétiens du IIe siècle*, Receuil de travaux d'histoire et de philologie, 4th ser., fasc. 47 (University of Louvain, 1972), 19.

30. S. Jaekel, *Menandri Sententiae* (Leipzig: Teubner, 1964), no. 808.

31. Athenaeus 567C.

32. Clement *Tutor* 2.50.4; *Stromata* 1.59.4.

33. Clement *Stromata* 1.59.2.

34. *Stoicorum Veterum Fragmenta* II.282 = Cicero *Academica* 2.96 *(Lucullus); Stoicorum Veterum Fragmenta* II.281 = Jerome, *Epistle* 69.2; Diogenes Laertius 7.196–97.

35. Diogenes Laertius 2.108; 5.49; Athenaeus 401E.

36. Jerome, loc. cit. (see note 34 above).

37. R. Pfeiffer, *Callimachus* (Oxford: Clarendon, 1949), frag. 202.

38. Tatian *Oration* 27; Theophilus *To Autolycus* 1.10; 2.3; Clement *Exhortation* 37.4.

39. Athenagoras *Embassy* 30.3.

40. Aelius Aristides *Oration* 43.7–8.

41. Origen *Against Celsus* 3.44.

42. Clement notes the source, *Stromata* 1.91.5.

43. Eusebius *Preparation for the Gospel* 13.12.6–7.

44. Clement *Stromata* 5.101.2–4.

45. Origen *Commentary on John* 10.7.

46. Aelius Aristides *Oration* 43.26; 45.30; cf. J. Amann, *Die Zeusrede des Ailios Aristeides,* Tübinger Beiträge zur Altertumswissenschaft 12 (1931), 94.

47. H. J. Cadbury, *The Book of Acts in History* (New York: Harper, 1955), 46–49.

48. Origen *Against Celsus* 4.5.

Chapter 3: The Reign of Trajan

1. Dio Cassius 68.15.1; for earlier lavish games see Pliny *Panegyric* 34.3.
2. Hegesippus in Eusebius *Church History* 3.32.3, 6.
3. Cf. Pliny *Epistles* 10.8–9; *Panegyric* 52.
4. Pliny *Epistles* 10.96.
5. Livy 39.8–9; no crimes lacking, 39.13.10; cf. *Corpus Inscriptionum Latinarum* I.196 = *Inscriptiones Latinae Selectae* 18.
6. See my "Pliny and the Christians," *Harvard Theological Review* 41 (1948), 99–101 = *After the New Testament* (Philadelphia: Fortress, 1967), 55–56; cf. independently F. Fourrier, "La lettre de Pline à Trajan sur les chrétiens," *Recherches de Théologie Ancienne et Médiévale* 31 (1964), 161–74.
7. A. N. Sherwin-White, *The Letters of Pliny* (Oxford: Clarendon, 1966), 692.
8. Pliny *Epistles* 6.20.5.
9. Cicero *Laws* 2.35–37.
10. Livy 39.8–19; cf. also the allusions in Dionysius of Halicarnassus 2.19.2. The main parallels appear in Appendix 1 and Appendix 2.
11. Cf. E. G. Hardy, *C. Plinii Caecilii Secundi Epistulae ad Trajanum Imperatorem cum eiusdem Responsis* (London: Macmillan, 1889), 78; Pliny, *Panegyric* 34–35, 41–42; *Epistles* 10.1.2.
12. "Some Observations on Ruler-Cult Especially in Rome," *Harvard Theological Review* 28 (1935), 34.
13. The basic discussion is still that of K. Scott, "The Elder and Younger Pliny on Emperor Worship," *Transactions of the American Philological Association* 63 (1932), 156–65.
14. Pliny *Panegyric* 2.3; 52.2, 6; 11.1–4; 35.4.
15. Pliny *Epistles* 10.8–9.
16. Ibid., 10.100, 102.
17. Tacitus *Annals* 15.44.
18. *Histories* 5.4–5.
19. Suetonius *Nero* 16.2.
20. Minucius Felix *Octavius* 9.
21. H. Chadwick, *Origen Contra Celsum* (Cambridge: University Press, 1953), 343 n. 1.
22. Dio Cassius 68.32.
23. Eusebius *Church History* 4.2.
24. Cf. A. Fuks, "The Jewish Revolt in Egypt (A.D. 115–117) in the Light of the Papyri," *Aegyptus* 33 (1953), 131–58; "Aspects of the Jewish Revolt in A.D. 115–117," *Journal of Roman Studies* 51 (1961), 93–104.
25. Eusebius *Church History* 4.6.3.
26. Suetonius *Claudius* 25.4.
27. Cf. W. R. Schoedel, *Ignatius of Antioch* (Philadelphia: Fortress, 1985), 11–12.
28. Ignatius *Magnesians* 8.1; 9.1, 3; *Philadelphians* 6.1.
29. Schoedel, *Ignatius,* 14–17.
30. Ibid., 19.

Chapter 4: The Reign of Hadrian

1. Eusebius (revised by Jerome) *Chronicle,* p. 198 Helm; on chronology see W. Weber, *Untersuchungen zur Geschichte des Kaisers Hadrianus* (Leipzig: Teubner, 1907).

2. P. L. Strack, *Untersuchungen zur römischen Reichsprägung des zweiten Jahrhunderts* (Stuttgart: Kohlhammer, 1933), II.100–8.

3. *Inscriptiones Graecae,* ed. 2, II.1099 = *Sylloge Inscriptionum Graecarum,* ed. 3, 834 + *Inscriptiones Latinae Selectae* 7784.

4. Pausanias 1.20.7.

5. *Sylloge Inscriptionum Graecarum,* ed. 3, 833.

6. Justin *Apology* 1.68; Eusebius *Church History* 4.9, and Melito in ibid., 4.26.10.

7. Plutarch *Solon* 17.1; cf. Aristotle *Constitution of Athens* 7.1.

8. *Inscriptiones Graecae,* ed. 2, II.1075.

9. Plutarch *Solon* 24.1; *Inscriptiones Graecae,* ed. 2, II.1100; cf. P. Graindor, *Athènes sous Hadrien* (Cairo: Imprimerie Nationale, 1934), 30–31, 73–79.

10. Cf. G. E. Mylonas, *Eleusis and the Eleusinian Mysteries* (Princeton: University Press, 1961), 239–43.

11. Cf. F. Millar, *The Emperor in the Roman World* (Ithaca: Cornell University Press, 1977), 36–39.

12. Eusebius *Church History* 4.3.2.

13. Irenaeus *Against Heresies* 2.32.4.

14. Cf. Justin *Apology* 1.21–22.

15. Sextus Empiricus *Against Professors* 9.35; skeptical criticism of the Euhemerist view.

16. Irenaeus *Against Heresies* 2.31.2.

17. Theophilus *To Autolycus* 1.13; cf. Luke 16:31.

18. J. R. Harris, *The Apology of Aristides,* Texts and Studies I.1 (1893).

19. *Oxyrhynchus Papyrus* xv.1778; *Papyrus London* (Literary) 223; cf. H. J. M. Milne, "A New Fragment of the Apology of Aristides," *Journal of Theological Studies* 25 (1923–24), 73–77.

20. Cf. W. C. van Unnik, "Die Gotteslehre bei Aristides und in gnostischen Schriften," *Theologische Zeitschrift* 17 (1961), 166–74.

21. Porphyry *On Vegetarianism* 2.56.

22. Cf. Ignatius *Smyrnaeans* 6.2; Justin *Apology* 1.67.6; Tertullian *Apology* 39.5–6.

23. Cf. Hermas *Similitudes* 5.3.7.

24. Justin *Apology* 1.29.4; Tatian *Oration* 10; Clement *Exhortation* 49; cf. Celsus in Origen *Against Celsus* 3.36; 5.63; Athenagoras *Embassy* 30.2 explains away; cf. Aurelius Victor 14.6–9.

25. J. Geffcken, *Zwei griechische Apologeten* (Berlin and Leipzig: Teubner, 1907), 28–31.

26. Theophilus *To Autolycus* 1.14; Clement *Stromata* 6.39–41, 43, 48, 58, 128; *Prophetic Selections* 58.

27. Origen *Commentary on John* 13.17.

28. Cf. A. J. Malherbe, "The Apologetic Theology of the *Preaching of Peter,*" *Restoration Quarterly* 13 (1970), 205–23; my thanks to the author.

29. Hermas *Mandates* 1.1.

30. Clement *Stromata* 6.41.2–3; 128.1; 43.3.

31. On these, Mylonas, *Eleusis,* 243–85.

32. *Sylloge Inscriptionum Graecarum,* ed. 3, 872.

33. *Sylloge Inscriptionum Graecarum,* ed. 3, 842; Weber, *Untersuchungen,* 182–83.

34. Cf. A. S. Benjamin, "The Altars of Hadrian at Athens and Hadrian's Panhellenic Program," *Hesperia* 32 (1963), 57–86.

35. Eusebius-Jerome, *Chronicle,* p. 200 Helm.

36. Suetonius *Augustus* 60.

37. Philostratus *Sophists* 533.

38. *Inscriptiones Graecae* III.401–402.

39. P. Benoit, J. T. Milik, R. de Vaux, *Les grottes de Murabba'at,* Discoveries in the Judaean Desert II (Oxford: University Press, 1961), nos. 29, 30.

40. A. Reifenberg, *Ancient Jewish Coins,* 2nd ed. (Jerusalem: Rubin Mass, 1947), 60–66.

41. *Inscriptiones Latinae Selectae* 1065; cf. Miltner in Pauly-Wissowa, *Real-Encyclopädie der classischen Altertumswissenschaft* 13:1392–93.

42. Dio Cassius 69.13.3.

43. Eusebius-Jerome *Chronicle,* p. 200 Helm; cf. H. Mantel, "The Causes of the Bar Kokba Revolt," *Jewish Quarterly Review* 58 (1967/68), 224–42, 274–96.

44. Justin *Apology* 1.31.6.

45. Tertullian *Against the Jews* 13.4.

46. Eusebius *Church History* 4.6.1–3; cf. H. Strathmann, "Der Kampf um Beth-Ter," *Palästina-Jahrbuch* 23 (1927), 92–123.

47. Occasional phrases may be Eusebius' own, e.g., language about the madness of revolt, from a passage already quoted from Josephus *War* 5.424 in *Church History* 3.6.1.

48. Ibid., 4.6.4.

49. Ibid., 4.7.7.

50. A. von Harnack, *Marcion, das Evangelium vom fremden Gott,* Texte und Untersuchungen 45 (1924), 20*, 29*.

Chapter 5: Antoninus Pius and the Christians

1. P. Petit, *Pax Romana* (Berkeley: University of California, 1976), 79, 101–2, 108–10, 165.

2. E. N. Luttwak, *The Grand Strategy of the Roman Empire* (Baltimore: Johns Hopkins, 1977), 88–89.

3. *Augustan History, Antoninus Pius* 5.4–5; cf. Aelius Aristides *Oration* 26.70.

4. *Epitome,* in F. Pichlmayr, *Sexti Aurelii Victoris Liber De Caesaribus,* rev. by R. Gründel (Berlin: Teubner, 1970), 15.6.

5. Marcus Aurelius *Meditations* 1.16.2.

6. Melito in Eusebius *Church History* 4.26.10.

7. Cf. J. A. O. Larsen, "Cyrene and the Panhellenion," *Classical Philology* 47 (1952), 7–16; A. S. Benjamin, "The Altars of Hadrian in Athens and Hadrian's Panhellenic Program," *Hesperia* 32 (1963), 57–86.

8. *Orientis Graeci Inscriptiones* 506 = *Inscriptiones Graecae ad res Romanas*

pertinentes IV.575; cf. J. H. Oliver, *Marcus Aurelius: Aspects of Civic and Cultural Policy in the East, Hesperia,* suppl. 13 (Princeton, 1970), 114–15.

9. A. S. Benjamin, "Two Dedications in Athens to Archons of the Panhellenion," *Hesperia* 37 (1968), 340–41.

10. Cf. Origen *Against Celsus* 1.29: "Our Jesus . . . is reproached for having come from a village, and that not a Greek one"; also John 1:46.

11. E. Nash, *Pictorial Dictionary of Ancient Rome,* 2nd ed. (New York: Praeger, 1968), I.508.

12. *Corpus Inscriptionum Latinarum* VI.567 = *Inscriptiones Latinae Selectae* 3474.

13. *Corpus Inscriptionum Latinarum* VI.568 = *Inscriptiones Latinae Selectae* 3473.

14. *Corpus Inscriptionum Latinarum* VI.30994 = *Inscriptiones Latinae Selectae* 3472; cf. 4375 and 3476.

15. G. Radke, *Der Kleine Pauly* IV.1540, treats this as "the full cult name of the god," but Augustine (*City of God* 18.19), presumably following Varro, regards the terms as alternatives.

16. Irenaeus *Against Heresies* 1.23.4.

17. Justin *Apology* 1.26.3.

18. Ibid., 1.64.5; cf. G. Lüdemann, *Untersuchungen zur simonianischen Gnosis* (Göttingen: Vandenhoeck & Ruprecht, 1975), 56 n. 12.

19. Justin *Apology* 1.64.1; Porphyry *The Cave of the Nymphs* 10; Numenius frag. 30 Des Places.

20. Justin *Apology* 1.26.4.

21. Ibid. 1.26.5; cf. A. von Harnack, *Marcion, das Evangelium vom fremden Gott,* Texte und Untersuchungen 45 (1924), 19*–20*.

22. Justin *Apology* 1.26.5; 29.4; 31.6; 42.4; 63.10.

Chapter 6: Justin's Conversion and Works

1. An inscription reads "Zeus Olympios," as at Athens, but it was found in a well.

2. Cf. Pauly-Wissowa, *Real-Encyclopädie der classischen Altertumswissenschaft* 23 (1957): 3–11.

3. Marcus Aurelius *Meditations* 1.6.

4. His pupil Tatian would call himself an Assyrian.

5. *Stoicorum Veterum Fragmenta* II.42; Plutarch *The Contradictions of Stoics* 1035A.

6. Justin *Dialogue* 2.3–6.

7. Ibid., 3–8; cf. J. M. C. van Winden, *An Early Christian Philosopher: Justin Martyr's Dialogue with Trypho Chapters One to Nine* (Leiden: Brill, 1971).

8. Ibid., 2.1–2.

9. Numenius frag. 24 Des Places = Eusebius *Preparation for the Gospel* 14.5.1; cf. frags. 25–28; for a Peripatetic version cf. Aristocles in Eusebius, ibid., 11.3.

10. Irenaeus *Against Heresies* 1.23.

11. Justin *Dialogue* 1.1; Eusebius *Church History* 4.11.8.

12. Justin *Apology* (cited hereafter without name) 2.12.1.

13. Eusebius *Church History* 4.17; 18.6.

14. Cf. Dio Cassius 69.21.2.

15. Josephus *Antiquities* 14.389; 17.191, 342; also Dio Cassius 55.27.6.

16. L. Mitteis and U. Wilcken, *Grundzüge und Chrestomathie der Papyruskunde* I.2 (Leipzig and Berlin: Teubner, 1912), no. 19.

17. M. I. Rostovtzeff, *Social and Economic History of the Roman Empire* (2nd ed., Oxford: Clarendon, 1957), 677 n. 52.

18. See my "Eternal Fire and the Occasion of Justin's Apology," in *Studies in Honor of Antonio Orbe* (Rome, forthcoming).

19. Irenaeus *Against Heresies* 3.3.4; also a letter in Eusebius *Church History* 5.24.16–17.

20. *Martyrdom of Polycarp* 6–7; 12.2.

21. G. W. Bowersock, *Greek Sophists in the Roman Empire* (Oxford: University Press, 1971), 84–86.

22. *Martyrdom of Polycarp* 11.2.

23. A thousand years in Plato, *Phaedrus* 249A; *Republic* 615A.

24. *Martyrdom of Polycarp* 5.1; 7.3–8.1.

25. Ibid., 14.

26. Ibid., 10.2.

27. Philostratus *Sophists* 576.

28. Justin *Apology* 1.1; 68.3; Eusebius *Church History* 4.18.2.

29. D. A. Russell and N. G. Wilson, *Menander Rhetor* (Oxford: Clarendon, 1981), 164–70.

30. Cf. P. Keresztes, "The Literary Genre of Justin's First Apology," *Vigiliae Christianae* 19 (1965), 99–110.

31. Eusebius *Church History* 4.16.1; 14.9.

32. Ibid., 4.18.2.

33. Justin *Apology* 2.14–15.

34. W. Schmid, "Eine Inversionsphänomen und seine Bedeutung im Text der Apologie des Justin," *Forma Futuri: Studi in onore del cardinale Michele Pellegrino* (Torino: Bottega d'Erasmo, 1975), 253–81.

35. Cf. F. Millar, *The Emperor in the Roman World* (Ithaca: Cornell University Press, 1977), 562–63.

36. P. Keresztes, "The 'So-Called' Second Apology of Justin," *Latomus* 24 (1965), 858–69.

Chapter 7: Justin: Church, Bible, and Theology

1. Justin *Apology* 1.13.2.

2. Justin *Dialogue* 41.1, tr. C. C. Richardson.

3. Ibid., 29.1; cf. D. Gill in *Harvard Theological Review* 59 (1966), 98–100.

4. Justin *Apology* 1.61; cf. Heb. 6:4; Eph. 5:14; 2 Cor. 4:6; John 8:12, etc.

5. Note that Moses is among the prophets, *Apology* 1.32.1.

6. Ibid., 65–67.

7. Justin *Dialogue* 7.

8. Justin *Apology* 1.31.8.

9. Josephus *Antiquities* 1.13; cf. *Against Apion* 1.5, 39.

10. Justin *Apology* 1.32.1.

11. Ibid. 1.31.2–5; Josephus (*Antiquities* 1.10; 12.11) named Ptolemy II Philadelphus, who reigned from 283 to 245 B.C.

12. Justin *Dialogue* 68.7; 71.1–2; 84.3; cf. O. Skarsaune, *The Proof from Prophecy* (Leiden: Brill, 1987), 42.

13. Justin *Dialogue* 18–19.

14. Justin *Apology* 1.66.3; 67.3; notably in exegesis of Psalm 22, *Dialogue* 99–107.

15. A. J. Bellinzoni, *The Sayings of Jesus in the Writings of Justin Martyr,* Supplements to *Novum Testamentum* 17 (1967).

16. Justin *Dialogue* 81.4.

17. Ibid., 105.1.

18. Justin *Apology* 1.61.4–5.

19. Justin *Dialogue* 103.8.

20. Ibid., 106.3.

21. *1 Clement* 47.1; 35.5–6.

22. Justin *Dialogue* 81.4; 80.5.

23. Justin *Apology* 1.59.

24. Ibid., 1.6.1–2; 13.3–4; 61.3; cf. 65.3.

25. L. W. Barnard, *Justin Martyr: His Life and Thought* (Cambridge: University Press, 1967), 79–84.

26. Justin *Dialogue* 56.1.

27. Numenius frag. 11 Des Places = Eusebius *Preparation for the Gospel* 11.18.3; frag. 12 = 11.18.8; frag. 15 = 11.18.21.

28. Diogenes Laertius 7.147, cited by J. Dillon, *The Middle Platonists* (London: Duckworth, 1977), 163.

29. Justin *Apology* 2.6.1–2.

30. Ibid., 1.22.1.

31. Justin *Dialogue* 61.1, 3; 62.4; 100.4; 126.1.

32. Ibid. 61.2; cf. Tatian *Oration* 5.

33. Numenius frag. 14 = Eusebius *Preparation for the Gospel* 11.18.16.

34. Justin *Apology* 1.21.1; cf. 33.6.

35. Philo *Drunkenness* 30–31; *Virtues* 62.

36. Justin *Dialogue* 129.1.

37. Numenius frag. 21 = Proclus *Commentary on the Timaeus* I.303 Diehl; frag. 11 = Eusebius *Preparation for the Gospel* 11.18.3.

38. Justin *Apology* 1.33.6.

39. Ibid., 1.21.1.

40. These constellations are named in the *Phenomena* of Aratus: Gemini (not Dioscuri), 147, etc.; Perseus, 248, etc.; Horse, 205, etc.

41. Aratus *Phenomena* 72; Pseudo-Eratosthenes *Catasterisms* 5.

42. Justin *Apology* 22–23. Perseus, Asclepius, and Dionysus, though not the Logos Hermes, recur in *Dialogue* 67–70.

43. Plato *Timaeus* 36B–C; Justin *Apology* 1.60.1–2.

44. Justin *Apology* 1.55.

45. Plato *Epistle* 2.312E; Justin *Apology* 1.60.7.

46. Athenagoras *Embassy* 23.7; Clement *Stromata* 5.103.1; Origen *Against Celsus* 6.18; Hippolytus *Refutation* 6.37.5–6.

47. Numenius frag. 15 = Eusebius *Preparation for the Gospel* 11.18.20.

48. Numenius frag. 30 = Porphyry *Cave of the Nymphs* 10.

49. On Numenius cf. E. Des Places, *Numénius* (Paris: Belles Lettres, 1973), 10–14; J. Dillon, *The Middle Platonists* (London: Duckworth, 1977), 366–72.

50. *1 Clement* 36; Hermas *Similitudes* 8.3.3.
51. Ignatius *Smyrnaeans* 6.1; *Trallians* 5.2.
52. 1 Tim. 4:1 is not Pauline.
53. Xenocrates frag. 15 in R. Heinze, *Xenokrates, Darstellung der Lehre und Sammlung der Fragmente* (Leipzig: Teubner, 1892).
54. Cf. also Plutarch *The Decline of Oracles* 419A: evil *daimones* in Empedocles, Plato, Xenocrates, Chrysippus.
55. W. Schmid, "Die Textüberlieferung der Apologie des Justin," *Zeitschrift für die neutestamentliche Wissenschaft* 40 (1941), 119.
56. Justin *Apology* 1.28.1; Matt. 25:41.
57. Justin *Dialogue* 103.5.
58. Irenaeus *Against Heresies* 5.26.2.
59. Cf. Jude 6; 2 Peter 2:4.
60. Philo *Giants* 6.
61. Papias frag. 4 Harnack.
62. Justin *Dialogue* 80.5; 81.4.
63. Justin *Apology* 1.11.
64. Eusebius *Church History* 3.20.4.
65. Tertullian *Against Marcion* 4.33.8.

Chapter 8: Justin on Moral Questions

1. Cf. Justin *Dialogue* 10.1–2.
2. For a similar simplification, compare Theophilus as described by J. Bentivegna, "A Christianity Without Christ," Texte und Untersuchungen 116 = *Studia Patristica* 13 (1975), 107–30.
3. Is this quite candid? Cf. Justin *Dialogue* 80.4 for Jerusalem after the resurrection.
4. Justin *Apology* 1.14–15; 26–29 (esp. 26.7); 61–68; 2.2; 12–15.
5. Irenaeus *Against Heresies* 1.25.5–6.
6. *Exhortation* 53.4–6; Origen *Against Celsus* 1.5.
7. Tatian *Oration* 28; Plutarch refers to "herds" of boys at Sparta, *Lycurgus* 16.4.
8. For such taxes cf. Suetonius *Gaius* 40.
9. Examples in Plutarch *Dialogue on Love* 759F; Apuleius *Apology* 75; K. Schneider, "Meretrix," Pauly-Wissowa, *Real-Encyclopädie der classischen Altertumswissenschaft* 15:1021.
10. Musonius frags. 12, 13a, pp. 86,6; 88,10 Lutz.
11. Athenagoras *Embassy* 33.1.
12. *1 Clement* 55.2; Tertullian *Apology* 39; Ignatius *Smyrnaeans* 6.2.
13. A. Henrichs, *Die Phoinikika des Lollianos,* Papyrologische Texte und Abhandlungen 14 (1972), 19–23.
14. He has just used *mystērion* of pagan rites: 25.1; 27.4.
15. Suetonius *Domitian* 7.1.
16. Ulpian in *Digests* 48.8.4.2.
17. Modestinus in *Digests* 68.8.8.11.
18. L. Mitteis and U. Wilcken, *Grundzüge und Chrestomathie der Papyrusurkunde* I.2 (Leipzig and Berlin: Teubner, 1912), nos. 74–77.
19. Eusebius *Church History* 6.8.3.

20. Theophilus *To Autolycus* 2.27.

21. Among many witnesses (including Roman poets), cf. Dio Chrysostom *Oration* 4.36; Galen *The Use of the Parts of the Body* 14.11, p. 321,22 Helmreich; Jerome *Epistle* 107.11; *Against Jovinian* 1.47 (Migne, *Patrologia Latina* 22:289C) = Seneca frag. 51.

22. This discussion is abbreviated from my article in *Church History* 54 (1985), 461–72.

23. Aulus Gellius 10.23.4; cf. Dionysius of Halicarnassus 2.25.6.

24. Cato (?) in Pliny *Natural History* 14.90.

25. Cf. generally R. Saller, "Roman Dowry and the Devolution of Property in the Principate," *Classical Quarterly* 34 (1984), 195–205.

26. Musonius frag. 12, p. 86,36 Lutz; Justin *Apology* 2.8.1.

27. Artemidorus *Dream Interpretation* 1.78, p. 88,5 Pack.

28. *Tutor* 3.32.3; cf. Cicero *For Caelius* 57–58.

29. 1 Tim. 2:9; Titus 2:5, 12; Musonius frag. 3, p. 41,17 Lutz.

30. *Tutor* 2.97.2–3; cf. Musonius (?) in Stobaeus *Florilegium* 3.6.23, p. 286,8 Hense.

31. Text and commentary by H. Chadwick, *The Sentences of Sextus* (Cambridge: University Press, 1959).

32. Chastity: 235; self-castration: 13, 273; right reason and right: 264a, 65; license: 68, 71b; pleasure: 70, 232, 272, 411.

33. Cf. the exegesis in Clement *Tutor* 2.87.3; 88.3.

34. See *1 Clement* 35.5–6.

35. Hermas *Mandates* 4.1.5, 9.

36. Musonius Rufus frag. 13A, p. 88,24 Lutz.

37. Plutarch *Marital precepts* 16–17, 140B–C.

38. For examples cf. K. Schneider, "Meretrix," Pauly-Wissowa, *Real-Encyclopädie der classischen Altertumswissenschaft* 15:1021.

39. Cf. L. Friedländer, *M. Valeri Martialis Epigrammaton Libri* (Leipzig: Hirzel, 1886), II.104, 203.

40. H. L. Strack and P. Billerbeck, *Kommentar zum Neuen Testament aus Talmud und Midrasch* III (Munich: Beck, 1926), 68–69.

41. Cf. Clement *Tutor* 2.87.1–2; 95.3.

42. Musonius frag. 12, pp. 84,31 and 86,3 Lutz; followed by Clement *Tutor* 2.97.2; 98.1; Epictetus 1.6.9, with *Tutor* 2.87.1–3.

43. Quintilian 1.2.7; Dio Cassius 51.17.1; Athenaeus 420E.

44. *Synebiou* occurs at the beginning of the narrative; for *symbiōsis* cf. E. Levy, *Der Hergang der römischen Ehescheidung* (Weimar: Bohlaus Nachfolger, 1925), 111; G. Delling, "Eheleben," *Reallexikon für Antike und Christentum* 4:697.

45. Levy, *Hergang,* 59; cf. 84.

46. See on marriage contracts in Mitteis and Wilcken, *Grundzüge* (n. 18 above), II.2, pp. 313–39 (nos. 280–300); A. S. Hunt and C. C. Edgar, *Select Papyri* I (London: Heinemann, 1932), pp. 2–31 (nos. 1–9).

47. H. J. Wolff, "Das iudicium de moribus und sein Verhältnis zur actio rei uxoriae," *Zeitschrift der Savigny-Stiftung für Rechtsgeschichte (Romanistische Abteilung)* 54 (1934), 315–21.

48. Cf. F. Millar, *The Emperor in the Roman World* (Ithaca: Cornell University Press, 1977), 465–549, esp. 472, 547.

49. Valerius Maximus 8.2.3, cited by Wolff, "Das iudicium," 318–19; Plutarch *Marius* 38.3–4.

50. *Augustan History, Marcus Antoninus* 19.8–9.

51. Among many examples, cf. a Giessen papyrus (41) in Mitteis and Wilcken, *Grundzüge,* no. 18; in which a *stratēgos* requests sixty days' leave "to put his affairs in order"; cf. also sixty days *ad consultandum* for a complaisant husband, Tacitus *Annals* 2.85.4.

52. *Studies in Gnosticism and Hellenistic Religions,* ed. R. van den Broek and M. J. Vermaseren (Leiden: Brill, 1981), 169–70.

53. *Stoicorum Veterum Fragmenta* III, p. 199.

54. See the comments in *Zeitschrift für Papyrologie und Epigraphik* 9 (1972), 284 (Merkelbach); 12 (1973), 183–95 (Tsantsanoglu, with a note by Merkelbach); and 13 (1974), 281–82 (Luppe).

55. For the theme cf. Lucretius 4.1160–70; Ovid *Art of Love* 2.657–62; also Plato *Republic* 5.474D; in general, Horace *Satires* 1.3.38–54.

Chapter 9: Marcus Aurelius and the Christians

1. Cf. A. Birley, *Marcus Aurelius* (New Haven: Yale University Press, 1987), 152–55.

2. Justin *Apology* 2.8, 11; Tatian *Oration* 19.

3. Galen 2.218; 14.612 Kühn.

4. Seneca *Epistle* 56, translation from P. D. Arnott.

5. Hippolytus *Commentary on Daniel* 1.20.3.

6. Marcus Aurelius *Meditations* 1.7; 17.5.

7. Minucius Felix *Octavius* 9.6–7; 31.1–2.

8. Lucian *Alexander* 25, 38.

9. Ibid. 30–35.

10. Ibid. 36, 48.

11. A. Vogliano and F. Cumont, "La grande iscrizione bacchica del Metropolitan Museum," *American Journal of Archaeology* 37 (1933), 215–70 (on the family, 219–24).

12. Marcus Aurelius *Meditations* 11.3.

13. C. Carena compares *Meditations* 8.41, 48; Epictetus 4.7.6; *Marco Aurelio I ricordi* (Torino: Einaudi, 1968), 172. On the text cf. A. S. L. Farquharson, *The Meditations of the Emperor Marcus Antoninus* (Oxford: Clarendon, 1944), 859–60.

14. Origen *Against Celsus* 6.34.

15. "Marcus Aurelius, Emperor and Philosopher," *Historia* 18 (1969), 570–87; cf. Birley, *Marcus Aurelius,* 227.

16. Epiphanius *Heresies* 49.1; Tertullian *Flight in Persecution* 9.4.

17. Cf. A. Henrichs, *Die Phoinikika des Lollianos,* Papyrologische Texte und Abhandlungen 14 (1972), 48–51.

18. Dio Cassius 71.4; on the legate, cf. Maria Laura Astarita, *Avidio Cassio* (Rome: Storia e Letteratura, 1983).

19. Dio Cassius 71.8, 10.

20. Dio Cassius 71.22.3; cf. Astarita, *Avidio Cassio.*

21. Papyri in R. Rémondon, "Les dates de la révolte de C. Avidius Cassius," *Chronique d'Égypte 1951,* 364–77.

22. Cf. E. Ritterling, "Epigraphische Beiträge," *Rheinisches Museum* 59 (1904), 196–99.

23. Dio Cassius 23.3; 27.1a.

24. *Mosaicarum et Romanarum legum collatio* 15.2.5.

25. *Augustan History, Marcus Antoninus* 13.6.

26. Dio Cassius 30.1–2; 27.3.2; 28.2–3.

27. Athenagoras *Embassy* 1.2–3.

28. For various itineraries cf. Astarita, *Avidio Cassio,* 154–62.

29. H. Mattingly, *Coins of the Roman Empire in the British Museum* IV (London: Trustees of the British Museum, 1940; repr. 1968), cxxvii; *Inscriptiones Latinae Selectae* 372.

30. J. Vogt, *Die alexandrinischen Münzen* (Stuttgart: Kohlhammer, 1924) I.144.

31. *Inscriptiones Latinae Selectae* 373.

32. Dio Cassius 71.29.1; cf. W. G. Spencer, *Celsus De Medicina* I (London, 1935), 463–65.

33. P. B. Watson, *Marcus Aurelius Antoninus* (New York: Harper, 1884), 222.

34. *Corpus Inscriptionum Latinarum* III.12213; cf. *Augustan History, Marcus Antoninus* 26.5.

35. Philostratus *Sophists* 562–63.

36. Cf. Cicero *To Atticus* 5.21.14, cited by D. Magie, *Roman Rule in Asia Minor* (Princeton: University Press, 1950), 1154 n.36.

37. A dedication in *Inscriptiones Graecae ad res Romanas pertinentes* IV.878.

38. Ammianus Marcellinus 22.5.5.

39. Astarita, *Avidio Cassio,* 162.

40. *Inscriptiones Graecae ad res Romanas pertinentes* III.833.

41. Ibid., III.449.

42. Dio Cassius 71.23.2.

43. For this cf. Aelius Aristides *Oration* 19.1–2, p. 12 Keil; cf. R. Pack, "Two Sophists and Two Emperors," *Classical Philology* 42 (1947), 17.

44. On the roads cf. S. E. Johnson, "Laodicea and Its Neighbors," *Biblical Archaeologist* 13 (1950), 12–18; Magie, *Roman Rule* II.786–802.

Chapter 10: Apollinaris of Hierapolis

1. Cf. A. H. M. Jones, *Cities of the Eastern Roman Provinces* (Oxford: Clarendon, 1937), 73–75; R. L. Fox, *Pagan and Christian* (New York: Knopf, 1986), 233–36.

2. Philostratus *Sophists* 606.

3. *Inscriptiones Graecae ad res Romanas pertinentes* IV.841.

4. Ibid., 818 = C. Humann et al., *Altertümer von Hierapolis,* Jahrbücher des kaiserlichen Deutschen Archäologischen Instituts, Supplementband 4 (1898), Inschriften (W. Judeich) no. 32,4.

5. *L'année épigraphique* 1924, 69; cf. *Orientis Graeci Inscriptiones* 532,6.

6. *L'année épigraphique* 1982, 894; cf. 895.

7. *Inscriptiones Graeci ad res Romanas pertinentes* IV.1756; note the "priest of Roma" at Sardis, ibid., 1757.

8. Cf. S. R. F. Price, *Rituals and Power: The Roman Imperial Cult in Asia Minor* (Cambridge: University Press, 1984), 264.

9. Eusebius *Church History* 5.5.4.

10. J. Guey, "La date de la pluie miraculeuse (172 après J. C.) et la colonne Aurélienne," *Mélanges d'Archéologie et d'Histoire* 60 (1948), 105–27; 61 (1949), 93–118.

11. Dio Cassius 71.8; Arnuphis a sacred scribe of Egypt, *L'année épigraphique* 1934, no. 245; generally, G. Barta, "Legende und Wirklichkeit—das Regenwunder des Marcus Aurelius," *Marc Aurel,* ed. R. Klein (Darmstadt: Wissenschaftliche Buchgesellschaft, 1979), 347–58.

12. "Le monete di Marco Aurelio con Mercurio," *Annali dell' Istituto Italiano di Numismatica* 5–6 (1958–1959), 41–55.

13. *Suda,* nos. 433 and 434, II 641–42 Adler; Claudian, *Panegyric on the 6th Consulship of Honorius* 348–50.

14. Marcus Aurelius *Meditations* 1.6; cf. 9.40 on true prayer.

15. Suetonius *Vespasian* 4.5; Josephus *War* 2.540–55; 5.41; 7.18.

16. Dio 55.23.5; inscriptions from the Flavian period include *Inscriptiones Latinae Selectae* 1032, 1379, 2647.

17. Cf. "Forms and Occasions of the Greek Apologists," *Studi e Materiali di Storia delle Religioni* 52 (1987), 213–26.

18. Origen *Against Celsus* 8.68–69.

19. Tertullian *Apology* 5.6; 35.9.

20. Eusebius *Church History* 4.27.

21. Humann, *Altertümer von Hierapolis,* inscriptions nos. 69, 4, 7; 212,4.

22. Inscription no. 342.

23. Inscriptions nos. 80,3; 222,1; 225,4.

24. *Sibylline Oracles* 5.318; 12.280 (in a context emphasizing Rome).

25. Eusebius *Church History* 3.39.4.

26. Ibid., 5.16.3–4; Acts 21:9.

27. Irenaeus *Against Heresies* 5.33.3–4.

28. 2 Esdr. 10:25–27, 53–54; 9:26. Cf. Montanus' native "Ardabau" in Eusebius *Church History* 5.16.7.

29. Ibid., 5.16.6–9.

30. Ibid., 5.24.2.

31. Inscription no. 319.

32. *Apology* 1.22.5; 54.10; *Dialogue* 69.3; E. J. and L. Edelstein, *Asclepius* I (Baltimore: Johns Hopkins, 1945), T 94–95, 332; statements recalling Xenophon *Hunting* 1.6 = T 243.

33. Eusebius *Church History* 4.27.

34. Ibid., 5.19; cf. 16.17; 16.10.

35. Ibid., 5.19.

36. The "acute suggestion" by G. Salmon, *Dictionary of Christian Biography* III.937; Fox, *Pagan and Christian,* 408 n. 18.

37. Ibid., 5.3.4.

38. Ibid., 5.1.3.

39. Ibid., 5.1.10, 34; 3.3.

40. Ibid., 5.2.2–4.

41. Ibid., 5.3.4.

42. Tertullian *Against Praxeas* 1.5.

43. *Martyrdom of Polycarp* 4.

44. Eusebius *Church History* 5.23.

45. Ibid., 5.25.
46. Ibid., 6.9–10; 11.3.
47. Irenaeus, Syriac frag. 27, II 456 Harvey.
48. Socrates *Church History* 3.7.
49. Cf. A. Houssiau, *La christologie de saint Irénée* (Louvain: Publications Universitaries, 1955), 246–47.
50. Eusebius *Church History* 5.17.1, 5.
51. Ibid. 5.28.4; cf. Tertullian *Against the Valentinians* 5.1.
52. Eusebius *Church History* 5.16.3; 17.1.
53. Jerome *Famous Men* 39.
54. G. Salmon in *Dictionary of Christian Biography* III.916.
55. T. D. Barnes, *Tertullian* (Oxford: Clarendon, 1971), 104.
56. Tatian *Oration* 4; Theophilus *To Autolycus* 1.11; 3.14.
57. Irenaeus *Heresies* 5.24.1.
58. Cf. Tertullian *Against Marcion* 5.6.8.

Chapter 11: Melito of Sardis

1. J. T. Wood, *Discoveries at Ephesus* (London: Longmans, Green, 1877), App. 3, Inscr. 16, p. 18.
2. *Inscriptiones Graecae ad res Romanas pertinentes* IV.1507; cf. 361, 460.
3. W. H. Buckler and D. M. Robinson, *Sardis* VII (Leiden: Brill, 1932), no. 62.
4. Ibid., no. 63.
5. Ibid., no. 15.
6. Cf. G. M. A. Hanfmann, *Letters from Sardis* (Cambridge, Mass.: Harvard University Press, 1972), 38–39, Figs. 17–18.
7. Buckler and Robinson, *Sardis,* no. 79 C; *Inscriptiones Graecae ad res Romanas pertinentes* IV.1519.
8. Eusebius *Church History* 4.26; S. G. Hall, *Melito of Sardis* On Pascha *and Fragments* (Oxford: Clarendon, 1979), frag. 1.
9. Luke 2:1, from which he takes the word *dogma:* ibid., 4.26.5.
10. Ibid., 5.1.4, 7, 9, 14, 27, 57.
11. Irenaeus *Heresies* 1, pr. 3; though this seems unlikely for Lyons.
12. Eusebius *Church History* 5.1.7, 17.
13. Ibid., 4.26.5–6, 10.
14. Ibid., 5.1.7–8, 17; 13–14.
15. Origen *Against Celsus* 8.69.
16. *Acts of Apollonius* 23.
17. Eusebius *Church History* 5.1.47.
18. D. A. Russell and N. G. Wilson, *Menander Rhetor* (Oxford: Clarendon, 1981), 94.
19. Aelius Aristides *Oration* 26.109.
20. J. H. Oliver, *The Ruling Power,* Transactions of the American Philological Association 43.4 (1953), 887.
21. *Inscriptiones Graecae ad res Romanas pertinentes* IV.1756,10.
22. Ibid., 145,21 (A.D. 37); 1398; *Supplementum Epigraphicum Graecum* XI.923 (A.D. 15); *Bulletin de Correspondance Hellénique* 11 (1887), 306.
23. Eusebius *Church History* 4.26.7.

24. Russell and Wilson, *Menander,* 80–81.
25. Theophilus *To Autolycus* 3.27.
26. References in A. S. Pease, *M. Tulli Ciceronis De Natura Deorum Libri III,* II (Cambridge, Mass.: Harvard University Press, 1958), 566–67.
27. Jerome *Famous Men* 24.
28. Nero in Marcus Aurelius *Meditations* 3.16.1; cf. Epictetus 3.22.30.
29. F. W. Norris, "Melito's Motivation," *Anglican Theological Review* 68 (1986), 16–24.
30. Cf. S. E. Johnson, "Christianity in Sardis," *Early Christian Origins: For H. R. Willoughby,* ed. A. P. Wikgren (Chicago: Quadrangle, 1961), 81–90.
31. Jerome *Famous Men* 24, cf. 11.
32. Eusebius *Church History* 5.24.5.
33. Ibid., 4.26.3; on Sagaris a Quartodeciman, 5.24.5.
34. See Hall, *Melito,* xxi–xxii.
35. Eusebius *Church History* 6.13.9.
36. Ibid., 4.26.13–14.
37. "The Old Testament Canon in Palestine and Alexandria," *Zeitschrift für die neutestamentliche Wissenschaft* 47 (1956), 196–97.
38. Eusebius *Church History* 6.25.2.
39. Origen *Selections on Genesis* 1:26; Migne, *Patrologia Graeca* 12:93A; Eusebius *Church History* 4.26.2.
40. Hall, *Melito,* xv.
41. Text in A. von Harnack, *Marcion, das Evangelium vom fremden Gott,* Texte und Untersuchungen 45 (1924), 422*–23*; for a few philosophical and poetic parallels to the text, see *Vigiliae Christianae* 4 (1950), 33–36.
42. Hall, *Melito,* xxxii nn. 3 and 4.
43. Theophilus *To Autolycus* 1.12–13.
44. Tertullian *Baptism* 3.6: "I am afraid of seeming to collect praises of water rather than reasons for baptism."
45. Theophilus *To Autolycus* 1.3; cf. 1 Cor. 15:28 (God); Col. 3:11 (Christ).
46. Clement *Tutor* 1.24.2–3; cf. Irenaeus *Heresies* 3.19.2–3.
47. Eusebius *Church History* 5.28.5.

Chapter 12: Athenagoras of Athens

1. *Inscriptiones Graecae,* ed. 2, II.3620 = *Sylloge Inscriptionum Graecarum,* ed. 3, 872; cf. 869.
2. Ibid., 872.
3. Philostratus *Sophists* 563, 566.
4. T. D. Barnes, "The Embassy of Athenagoras," *Journal of Theological Studies* 26 (1975), 111–14.
5. Note that in *Sylloge Inscriptionum Graecarum,* ed. 3, 872, only the last two epithets, "German and Sarmatian," are mentioned.
6. *Augustan History, Commodus* 12.4.
7. Themistius *Orations* 6, p. 121,4 Downey; *Augustan History, Avidius Cassius* 3.6. Ursula Treu informs me that Clement of Alexandria did not know them.
8. Aelius Aristides *Orations* 19, pp. 12,4; 13,29 Keil; F. Millar, *The Emperor in the Roman World* (Ithaca: Cornell University Press, 1977), 423–24.

9. D. A. Russell and N. G. Wilson, *Menander Rhetor* (Oxford: Clarendon, 1981), 180–81.

10. Millar, *Emperor,* 562–63.

11. See chapter 4.

12. See M. Goedecke, *Geschichte als Mythos. Eusebs "Kirchengeschichte"* (Frankfurt: Peter Lang, 1987), 100–108.

13. For such charges around this time cf. the Gallican martyrs in Eusebius *Church History* 5.1.14, 60.

14. Cf. E. Champlin, *Fronto and Antonine Rome* (Cambridge, Mass.: Harvard University Press, 1980), 64–66.

15. A. J. Malherbe, "The Structure of Athenagoras, 'Supplicatio pro Christianis,' " *Vigiliae Christianae* 23 (1969), 1–20.

16. Homer *Odyssey* 8.296–98, 308–9, both cited in *Embassy* 21.3.

17. Marcus Aurelius *Meditations* 6.42.

18. P. Corssen, *Athenische Mitteilungen* 38 (1913), 1–22; cf. *Inscriptiones Graecae ad res Romanas pertinentes* IV.1532, 1540.

19. O. Kern, *Orphicorum Fragmenta* (Berlin: Weidmann, 1922), frags. 57–58; cf. M. L. West, *The Orphic Poems* (Oxford: Clarendon, 1983), 176–226.

20. J. Geffcken, *Zwei griechische Apologeten* (Berlin and Leipzig: Teubner, 1907), 223 n. 4.

21. Ibid., 161, 188, 223.

22. Ibid., 195.

23. Pliny *Natural History* 35.15, 151.

24. Cf. K. Jex-Blake and E. Sellers, *The Elder Pliny's Chapters on the History of Art* (London, 1896; repr. Chicago: Argonaut, 1982), 225–27.

25. N. Sciveletto, "Cultura e scoliastica in Atenagore," *Giornale Italiano di Filologia* 13 (1960), 236–48.

26. H. Diels, *Doxographi Graeci* (Berlin: De Gruyter, 1879), 287,10; Sextus Empiricus *Against Professors* 10.315; R. M. Grant, "Some Errors in the Legatio of Athenagoras," *Vigiliae Christianae* 12 (1958), 145–46.

27. H. Diels, *Die Fragmente der Vorsokratiker* 44 B 15, 46 A 4.

28. On these martyrs for philosophy see Geffcken, *Apologeten,* 229–30.

29. Justin *Apology* 1.46.3; 2.8.1.

30. Eusebius *Church History* 4.23.3; cf. P. Nautin, *Lettres et écrivains chrétiens des IIe et IIIe siècles* (Paris: Du Cerf, 1961), 18–19.

31. Justin *Apology* 2.12.4; Eusebius *Church History* 5.1.14.

32. Tatian *Oration* 23; Theophilus *To Autolycus* 3.15; Irenaeus *Heresies* 1.6.3.

33. Eusebius *Church History* 5.19.3.

34. Philo *The Creation* 8; *Migration of Abraham* 192–93.

35. Aristides *Apology* 1.5.

36. Clement *Stromata* 4.155.2; cf. G. C. Stead, "The Concept of Mind and the Concept of God in the Christian Fathers," *Substance and Illusion in the Christian Fathers* (London, 1985), essay XIV.

37. Diels, *Die Fragmente der Vorsokratiker* 21 A 28.

38. Cf. W. Jaeger, *The Theology of the Early Greek Philosophers* (Oxford: Clarendon, 1947), 51–54.

39. Irenaeus *Heresies* 2.2.1–2; Tertullian *Against Marcion* 1.3–11.

40. As Philo (*Drunkenness* 31) too understood it.

41. Justin *Dialogue* 61.3–5.

42. Philo *Giants* 25; Justin *Dialogue* 61.2; 128.3.

43. Tertullian *Against Praxeas* 8.5.

44. R. M. Grant, "Athenagoras or Pseudo-Athenagoras," *Harvard Theological Review* 47 (1954), 121–29.

45. Cf. J. L. Rauch, *Greek Logic and Philosophy and the Problem of Authorship in Athenagoras* (Diss. Chicago, 1968); B. Pouderon, "L'authenticité du traité sur la résurrection attribué à l'apologiste Athénagore," *Vigiliae Christianae* 40 (1986), 226–44.

46. Galen 7.663, 12.254 Kühn; other references by W. R. Schoedel in his edition of Athenagoras, pp. 99, 101, 103.

47. Cf. R. Walzer, *Galen on Jews and Christians* (London: Oxford University Press, 1949), 13–16.

48. Walzer, *Galen,* 43–44, 68–69.

49. See further my note on "Paul, Galen, and Origen," *Journal of Theological Studies* 34 (1983), 533–36.

Chapter 13: The Gallican Martyrs and Tatian

1. Eusebius *Church History* 5.1.2–3.

2. Dio Cassius 71.31.3; Philostratus *Sophists* 566.

3. Cf. J. H. Oliver, *Marcus Aurelius: Aspects of Civic and Cultural Policy in the East, Hesperia,* suppl. 13 (1970), 80–82.

4. J. H. Oliver, *The Civic Tradition and Roman Athens* (Baltimore: Johns Hopkins, 1983), 86–87.

5. R. M. Grant, "The Date of Tatian's Oration," *Harvard Theological Review* 46 (1953), 99–101; G. W. Clarke, "The Date of the Oration of Tatian," ibid., 60 (1967), 122–26, rejecting extraneous arguments.

6. *Inscriptiones Latinae Selectae* 5163; Oliver and R. E. A. Palmer, "Minutes of an Act of the Roman Senate," *Hesperia* 24 (1955), 320.

7. *Inscriptiones Latinae Selectae* 9340.

8. Lines 1–4.

9. Eusebius *Church History* 5.1.62–63; 37.

10. Marcus Aurelius *Meditations* 8.18.

11. Origen *Against Celsus* 3.55–57.

12. Ibid., 8.73, 75.

13. Marcus Aurelius *Meditations* 11.3.

14. R. C. Kukula, *Tatians sogenannte Apologie* (Leipzig: Teubner, 1900).

15. L. Alfonsi, "Appunti sul Logos di Taziano," *Convivium* 14 (1942), 273–81; my thanks to U. Bianchi for a copy.

16. Herodotus 7.63; cf. the Syrian Elagabalus' nickname "the Assyrian," Dio Cassius 79.11.2.

17. D. A. Russell and N. G. Wilson, *Menander Rhetor* (Oxford: Clarendon, 1981), 194–95.

18. Ibid., 124–25.

19. Cf. J. H. Oliver, *The Civilizing Power,* Transactions of the American Philological Association 58.1 (1968), sec. 13.

20. J. H. Oliver, *Marcus Aurelius,* 7 (plaque I, line 57); for the date, see p. 34.

21. Cf. C. D. Buck, *Introduction to the Study of the Greek Dialects* (Boston: Ginn, 1928), 12–14.
22. Compare Lucian's use of Ionic in *On the Syrian Goddess.*
23. Sextus Empiricus *Against Professors* 1.87–89.
24. Aristotle, *Politics* 2.3.3 *(to kainotomon).*
25. Lucian *Zeuxis* 1.
26. Aulus Gellius 1.2.
27. Cf. Sextus Empiricus *Against Professors* 1.99–119 (esp. 103); 142–58.
28. Plutarch *Common Conceptions* 1081F = *Stoicorum Veterum Fragmenta* II.517.
29. Cf. Apollonius Dyscolus frag., pp. 78–79 Schneider.
30. C. L. Heiler, *De Tatiani Apologetae Dicendi Genere* (Marburg, 1909), esp. 86–101.
31. On this cf. A. D. Nock, *Essays on Religion and the Ancient World,* ed. Z. Stewart (Oxford: Clarendon, 1972), 642–52.
32. Ignatius *Polycarp* 1–2; cf. W. R. Schoedel, *Ignatius of Antioch* (Philadelphia: Fortress, 1985), 261–65.
33. Cf. T. W. Rein, *Sprichwörter und sprichwörterliche Redensarten bei Lucian* (Tübingen: Laupp, 1894), I, with *Ignorant Collector* 23 and *Hermotimus* 79.
34. Lucian *False Critic* 5; *Apology* 4.
35. Lucian *Double Jeopardy* 21.
36. Lucian *Hermotimus* 61; other references in Rein, *Sprichwörter,* 18.
37. Aesop 40 Hausrath; cf. Plato *Theaetetus* 174A.
38. Cf. G. O. Rowe, "The Adynaton as a Stylistic Device," *American Journal of Philology* 86 (1965), 387–96.
39. Athenaeus 164E.
40. Rein, *Sprichwörter,* 26; Diogenes Laertius 9.28.
41. Cf. K. Thraede, "Erfinder II," *Reallexikon für Antike und Christentum* V.1251–53, on Tatian.
42. Clement *Stromata* 1.74.1–77.2.
43. Cf. 9.4–6 and Marcus Aurelius *Meditations* 3.3.
44. Cf. *Stoicorum Veterum Fragmenta* I.109, III.658, I.159.
45. Empedocles: see Diogenes Laertius 8.69–70; Pherecydes: ibid., 8.1–2; 3.6.
46. Diogenes Laertius 6.97; Demetrius *Symposium,* in Clement *Stromata* 4.121.6; Apuleius *Florida* 14; Sextus Empiricus *Pyrrhonian Outlines* 1.153; 3.200.
47. Cf. J. Bidez and F. Cumont, *Les mages hellénisés* (Paris: Belles Lettres, 1938), II.293–96.
48. Map in W. A. Heidel, *The Frame of the Ancient Greek Maps* (New York: American Geographical Society, 1937), 6.
49. Pseudo-Eratosthenes *Catasterisms* 9, p. 12,6 Olivieri.
50. Justin *Apology* 1.21.3, just after a mention of Ariadne among the stars; A. Puech, *Recherches sur le Discours aux Grecs de Tatien* (Paris: Alcan, 1903), 121.
51. Ptolemy *Syntaxis* 7.5, p. 74,10 Heiberg; Dio Cassius 69.11.4.
52. Cf. Pindar *Nemean Odes* 10.55–90.
53. Cf. Apollodorus *Library* 3.11 = 134–37.
54. Cf. Apollodorus *Epitome* 6.30.
55. Plutarch *On the Face in the Moon* 942F, 944C.

56. Euripides *Orestes* 1635–37; 1673–74; 1683–90; Helen a star in Pliny *Natural History* 2.101.

57. Cf. A. Kalkmann, "Tatians Nachrichten über Kunstwerke," *Rheinisches Museum*, n.f. 42 (1887), 489–524.

58. Plutarch *The Fortune of Alexander* 336CD; cf. *The Pythian Oracle* 401A; Athenaeus 591B; cf. Diogenes Laertius 6.60.

59. Plutarch *Children's Education* 18AB.

60. Cicero *Against Verres* 4.57.126–27; Pausanias 2.20.8; 9.22.3.

61. Demetrius in Seneca *Epistles* 88.37; Aelian *Various Stories* 12.19; cf. Athenaeus 596E.

62. Strabo 617; Plato *Phaedrus* 235C; *On the Sublime* 10.2.

63. Athenaeus 600E.

64. Clement *Stromata* 1.10.3–4; 4.20.3; 4.122.4.

65. Clement *Tutor* 2.72.3 = Stobaeus *Florilegium* 3.4.12, so from an anthology.

66. Cf. Pliny *Natural History* 34.71.

67. According to Aelian, *Animals* 1.38.i, elephants love beautiful women.

68. Pliny *Natural History* 7.34 mentions both statues and names the elephant's mother (Alcippe).

69. Ibid., 7.51.

70. In spite of Pliny *Natural History* 34.70; see Kalkmann, "Tatians Nachrichten," 492.

71. Tertullian *To the Nations* 2.10; Lactantius *Divine Institutes* 1.17, 20; A. Reifferscheid, *C. Suetonii Tranquilli reliquiae* (Leipzig: Teubner, 1860), 349–52.

72. Cf. W. Krenkel, "Pornographie," *Der Kleine Pauly* IV.1061.

73. Clement *Exhortation* 61.2; *Tutor* 2.97.2; cf. Stobaeus *Florilegium* 3.6.22.

Chapter 14: Tatian on the Bible and Theology

1. T. W. Allen, *Homeri Opera* V (Oxford: Clarendon, 1912), 250–53.

2. Clement *Stromata* 1.117.1–7.

3. See also the second and fifth *Lives* as printed by Allen, *Homeri Opera*, 244–48.

4. Josephus *Antiquities* 1.107; *Against Apion* 1.8, 70–71.

5. F. Jacoby, *Die Fragmente der griechischen Historiker* 680.

6. Clement *Prophetic Selections* 38.1; Origen *Prayer* 24.5; *Against Celsus* 6.51.

7. Apollonius Dyscolus frag., p. 91,31 Schneider; cf. *Syntax*, p. 366 Uhlig (a second person latent in the third-person imperative).

8. Cf. B. Neuschäfer, *Origenes als Philologe*, Schweizerische Beiträge zur Altertumswissenschaft 18 (1987) I.208–10; my thanks to the author.

9. Irenaeus *Heresies* 3.7.1; Neuschäfer, *Origenes*, 230–32.

10. For "twisting" cf. 2 Peter 3:16; Polycarp *Philippians* 7.1.

11. Eusebius *Church History* 4.29.6.

12. Clement *Stromata* 3.80.3–81.3.

13. Cf. *1 Clement* 24.5.

14. Irenaeus *Heresies* 4.26.1.

15. Clement *The Rich Man* 17.2–4.

16. Irenaeus *Heresies* 1.28.1; Eusebius *Church History* 4.29.

17. Cf. Irenaeus *Heresies* 1.2.2: "the perfect Father."

18. Ibid. 2.28.5; 13.8.

19. Apollonius Dyscolus *Construction,* p. 519 Uhlig (index).
20. Apollonius *Pronouns* 12.15; *Syntax* 24.18.
21. Apollonius *Syntax* 6.11.
22. Herodes Grammaticus *Forms* (L. Spengel, *Rhetores Graeci* III, 94,22).
23. M. Elze, *Tatian und seine Theologie* (Göttingen: Vandenhoeck & Ruprecht, 1960), 76–79.
24. Ignatius *Romans* 6.3.
25. Elze, *Tatian,* 105.
26. Cf. Clement *Stromata* 2.36.1.
27. Cf. Sextus Empiricus *Pyrrhonian Outlines* 2.26; *Against Professors* 8.270–71.
28. Aelian *Animals* 2.9; 5.39, 46; Sextus Empiricus *Pyrrhonian Outlines* 1.57, 71.
29. Plutarch *Brute Animals* 991E, with hogs and river crabs.
30. Origen *Against Celsus* 4.85–87.

Chapter 15: Celsus Against the Christians

1. Cf. K. Pichler, *Streit um das Christentum. Der Angriff des Kelsos und die Antwort des Origenes,* Regensburger Studien zur Theologie 23 (1980).
2. Cf. J. R. Harris, "Celsus and Aristides," *Bulletin of the John Rylands Library* 6 (1921), 163–75.
3. C. Andresen, *Logos und Nomos. Die Polemik des Kelsos wider das Christentum* (Berlin: De Gruyter, 1955), 345–72.
4. J. Schwartz, "L'épitre à Diognète," *Revue d'Histoire et de Philosophie Religieuses* 48 (1968), 46–53.
5. J.-M. Vermander, "De quelques répliques à Celse dans l'Apologeticum de Tertullien," *Revue des Études Augustiniennes* 16 (1970), 205–25; "Celse, source et adversaire de Minucius Felix," ibid., 17 (1971), 13–25.
6. J.-M. Vermander, "De quelques répliques à Celse dans le Protreptique de Clément d'Alexandrie," ibid., 23 (1977), 3–17.
7. J.-M. Vermander, "La parution de l'ouvrage de Celse et la datation de quelques apologies," ibid., 18 (1972), 27–42.
8. J.-M. Vermander, "Théophile d'Antioche contre Celse: A Autolycos III," ibid., 17 (1971), 203–25.
9. Origen *Against Celsus* 4.36.
10. Origen *Against Celsus* 4.31–51; Theophilus *To Autolycus* 3.18–24.
11. Theophilus *To Autolycus* 2.5–6, 9, 18, 28, 35.
12. Origen *Against Celsus* 4.21, 41.
13. Philo, *Prizes* 23; Justin *Apology* 2.7.2; Gen. 5:29.
14. Cf. F. Bolgiani, "L'ascesi di Noe. A proposito di Teophilo ad Autolyco, III, 19," *Forma Futuri: Studi in onore del cardinale Michele Pellegrino* (Torino: Bottega d'Erasmo, 1975), 295–333.
15. Origen *Against Celsus* 5.61; 8.53.
16. Tacitus *Annals* 15.44: *flagitia;* Pliny *Epistles* 10.96.7; Fronto in Minucius Felix *Octavius* 9.6–7.
17. Origen *Against Celsus* 4.45.
18. Philo *Posterity of Cain* 175–77; *Drunkenness* 164–205.
19. Origen *Against Celsus* 1.4; 2.5.
20. Ibid. 1.9.

21. Justin *Apology* 1.29.4; Tatian *Oration* 10; Origen *Against Celsus* 3.36; 5.63.

22. J.-M. Vermander, "Celse et l'attribution à Athénagore d'un ouvrage sur la résurrection des morts," *Mélanges de Science Religieuse* 35 (1978), 125–34.

23. Origen *Against Celsus* 8.68, 73 (singular); 71 (plural).

24. Justin *Apology* 1.14.17; H. Chadwick, *Origen Contra Celsum* (Cambridge: University Press, 1953), xxvii.

25. Origen *Against Celsus* 8.69.

26. Ibid., 1.3.

27. T. D. Barnes, "Eusebius and the Date of the Martyrdoms," *Les Martyrs de Lyon (177)* (Paris: Centre Nationale de la Recherche Scientifique, 1978), 137–41.

28. Andresen, *Logos und Nomos,* 32–33.

29. Cf. A. Momigliano, "The Disadvantages of Monotheism for a Universal State," *Classical Philology* 81 (1986), 285–97; Dio Cassius 52.36.2–3.

30. Origen *Against Celsus* 3.5.

31. Ibid. 3.10, 12, 14.

32. Ibid. 5.59.

33. Ibid. 8.68–69.

34. Ibid. 8.65; cf. *Martyrdom of Polycarp* 4, perhaps as early as 156.

35. Ibid. 8.67; Epictetus 1.14.14; 4.1.14.

36. Justin *Apology* 1.16.5; cf. *Martyrdom of Apollonius* 3, 6; also Justin *Apology* 1.21.3: you produce a [false] witness who will swear he saw the cremated Caesar ascending into the sky.

37. *Martyrdom of Polycarp* 9; cf. Tertullian *Apology* 32, 35.10; Minucius Felix *Octavius* 29.

38. *Passion of the Scillitan Martyrs* 5–6.

39. Origen *Against Celsus* 8.67.

40. Ibid. 8.67–75.

41. Cf. Andresen, *Logos und Nomos,* 108–238; R. M. Grant, *The Letter and the Spirit* (London: SPCK, 1957), 1–30.

42. Origen *Against Celsus* 2.31.

43. Philo, *Farming* 51; *Confusion of Tongues* 146; Chadwick, *Origen Contra Celsum* 93 n. 3.

44. E.g., Justin *Apology* 1.21.1; 22.1–2; 23.2; 32.10; 63.4.

45. Andresen, *Logos und Nomos,* 345–72.

Chapter 16: Theophilus of Antioch

1. Eusebius *Church History* 5.21; Perennius himself was executed by Commodus in 185.

2. He thus refers to the nature of the vision of God, discussed in the first book of Theophilus, *To Autolycus.*

3. Text in H. Musurillo, *The Acts of the Christian Martyrs* (Oxford: Clarendon, 1972), 90–105.

4. Cf. J. Geffcken, *Zwei griechische Apologeten* (Leipzig and Berlin: Teubner, 1907), 246–48; H. Paulsen, "Erwägungen zu Acta Apollonii 14–22," *Zeitschrift für die neutestamentliche Wissenschaft* 66 (1975), 117–26.

5. J. Schwartz, "Autour des Acta Apollonii," *Revue d'Histoire et de Philosophie Religieuses* 50 (1970), 257–61.

6. *Acts of Apollonius* 16–22; Philo, *Immutability* 35; Paulsen, "Erwägungen," 119–24.

7. Cf. R. Freudenberger, "Die Überlieferung vom Martyrium des römischen Christen Apollonius," *Zeitschrift für die neutestamentliche Wissenschaft* 60 (1969), 111–30 (esp. 128–30).

8. S. Laeuchli, *The Language of Faith* (New York: Abingdon, 1962), 163–66.

9. The language comes from Justin *Apology* 1.4.9.

10. Tertullian *To Scapula* 5.1.

11. Irenaeus *Heresies* 4.30.3.

12. Ibid. 5.24.2–3; A. A. T. Ehrhardt, *Politische Metaphysik von Solon bis Augustin* II (Tübingen: Mohr, 1969), 113–14.

13. Ibid. 5.30.3.

14. Cf. Eusebius *Chronicle,* pp. 205, 207 Helm; *Church History* 4.24.

15. Eusebius *Church History* 4.24.

16. Anonymus *Art of Rhetoric* (L. Spengel, *Rhetores Graeci* I; Leipzig: Teubner, 1853), 428,4; on *prooemia;* Hermogenes *On Method* 12, p. 427,11 Rabe.

17. Justin *Dialogue* 68.8.

18. Cf. Diogenes Laertius 8.80.

19. Demetrius *Elocution* 191.

20. Eusebius *Church History* 3.3.6; 6.15.

21. Quintilian 4.1.9.

22. Herodian 1.1.1; further in C. R. Whittaker, *Herodian* I (London: Heinemann, 1969), 3 n. 2.

23. *Supplementum Epigraphicum Graecum* 11.922.

24. Polycarp *Philippians* 12.3; 1 Tim. 2:1–2.

25. *Augustan History, Marcus Antoninus* 25.9–10; *Avidius Cassius* 9.1.

26. Malalas, *Corpus Scriptorum Historiae Byzantinae* 15:283–86.

27. Full discussion by G. Downey, *A History of Antioch in Syria* (Princeton: University Press, 1961), 229–35.

28. Cf. Malalas, *Corpus Scriptorum Historiae Byzantinae* 15:199.

29. H. J. Schoeps, *Theologie und Geschichte des Judenchristentums* (Tübingen: Mohr, 1949), 101.

30. Ibid., 121–22.

31. Hippolytus, *Commentary on Daniel* 4.30.8.

32. *Augustan History, Commodus* 11.9; Hippolytus *Refutation of All Heresies* 9.12.10–11.

33. Dio Cassius 72.22; 74.16.5.

34. *Apology* 35.9; cf. Dio 72.13.4–5; 22.4–5; Herodian 1.12.2; 17.11.

Chapter 17: Theophilus and Literature

1. Melito in Eusebius *Church History* 4.26.13; Tatian *Oration* 41; Athenagoras *Embassy* 2.1, 6; 9.1.

2. Theophilus *To Autolycus* 2.29, 30, 32, 38 (the text would make better sense if we read, "The lover of learning must also love the truth"); 3.15, 17.

3. Isocrates *To Demonicus* 18.

4. Musaeus frag. 7, p. 225 Kinkel; Lactantius *Divine Institutes* 1.21.39; R. M. Ogilvie, *The Library of Lactantius* (Oxford: Clarendon, 1978), 13–14.

5. Cf. Musaeus frag. 12 Kinkel.

6. E. Maass, *Arati Phaenomena* (Berlin: Weidmann, 1893), xix.

7. *Stoicorum Veterum Fragmenta* II.1077–78.

8. Ibid., 1073.

9. Ibid., 1074 = Origen *Against Celsus* 4.48.

10. Ibid., 1072 = *Clementine Homilies* 15.18.5–6.

11. Diogenes Laertius 10.3.

12. Athenaeus 611B.

13. *Stoicorum Veterum Fragmenta* II.1071; Diogenes Laertius 7.187–88.

14. J. Bidez and F. Cumont, *Les mages hellénisés* (Paris: Belles Lettres, 1938), I.96.

15. Plutarch *Stoic Contradictions* 1052B; Sextus Empiricus *Pyrrhonian Outlines* 3.218.

16. Diogenes Laertius 10.26.

17. Ibid., 10.131.

18. Cicero *Academica* 2; *Lucullus* 109; cf. Sextus Empiricus *Pyrrhonian Outlines* 2.244.

19. Xenophon *Memorabilia of Socrates* 3.3.9; cf. *Education of Cyrus* 1.6.21.

20. Origen *Against Celsus* 1.11.

21. Cf. B. Wisniewski, *Karneades, Fragmente* (Wroclaw: Naradowy, 1970), "fragments" 93–94 = Sextus Empiricus *Against Professors* 9.139–90; Cicero *Nature of the Gods* 3.29–34, 43–52; 38.

22. Sextus Empiricus *Pyrrhonian Outlines* 1.145–63; 3.197–234; the fifth mode in Diogenes Laertius 9.83–84.

23. Ibid., 148.

24. Theophilus *To Autolycus* 3.3, myth versus custom and law; 3.5, dogma versus custom; 3.6, dogma versus law; 3.7, dogma versus dogma.

25. H. Diels, *Doxographi Graeci* (Berlin: De Gruyter, 1879), 593,6.

26. Hippolytus *Refutation* 1.22.3 (p. 572 Diels; cf. p. 589,9).

27. S. Jaekel, *Menandri Sententiae* (Leipzig: Teubner, 1964), no. 81 = no. 107.

28. Herodotus 1.119; 3.99.

29. Thucydides 1.134; 8.81.

30. *Die Fragmente der griechischen Historiker* 661.

31. R. Merkelbach in *Zeitschrift für Papyrologie und Epigraphik* 2 (1968), 11–12.

32. *Die Fragmente der griechischen Historiker* 661.

33. Censorinus *Birthdays* 21.10.

34. Johannes Lydus, *Months* 3.16; other calculations given by A. S. Pease, *M. Tulli Ciceronis De Natura Deorum* II (Cambridge: Harvard University Press, 1958), 669–70.

35. See my edition, *Theophilus of Antioch: Ad Autolycum* (Oxford: Clarendon, 1970), 32–35.

36. Epictetus 2.19.14; cf. Aulus Gellius 1.2.10.

37. *Die Fragmente der griechischen Historiker* 256; Tertullian *Apology* 19.2, Fuldensian version, took this from Theophilus.

38. Homer *Iliad* 14.201; 21.196.

39. Hesiod *Theogony* 27; A. Davids, "Hésiode et les prophètes chez Théophile d'Antioche," *Fides Sacramenti Sacramentum Fidei* (Assen: Van Gorcum, 1981), 206–7.

40. A similar critical question is raised in Sextus Empiricus *Against Professors* 10.18–19.

41. Homer *Iliad* 2.489; A. Hoefler, *Der Sarapishymnus des Aelios Aristides* (Stuttgart: Kohlhammer, 1935), 45.

42. Clement *Stromata* 3.73.3; cf. A. Otto, *Die Sprichwörter und sprichwörterlichen Redensarten der Römer* (Leipzig, 1890; repr. Hildesheim: Olms, 1971), 119.

43. J. Daniélou, *Théologie du judéo-christianisme* (Tournai: Desclée, 1958), 364.

44. Eusebius *Church History* 4.24.

Chapter 18: Theophilus and the Bible

1. Aelius Aristides *Orations* 45.6–7.

2. R. P. C. Hanson, *Allegory and Event* (London: SCM, 1959), 109.

3. Cf. M. J. Shroyer, "Alexandrian Jewish Literalists," *Journal of Biblical Literature* 55 (1936), 261–84.

4. *Midrash Rabbah,* ed. H. Freedman and M. Simon, 1 (London: Soncino, 1939).

5. *Philo, Supplement* I, *Questions and Answers on Genesis,* tr. R. Marcus (London: Heinemann, 1953).

6. A. Marmorstein, "Jews and Judaism in the Earliest Christian Apologies," *Expositor* VIII 17 (1919), 104–9.

7. R. M. Grant, "Theophilus of Antioch to Autolycus," *Harvard Theological Review* 40 (1947), 237–41.

8. L. Ginzberg, *Die Haggada bei den Kirchenvätern* (Berlin: Calvary, 1900); above all, his *The Legends of the Jews* (6 vols., Philadelphia: Jewish Publication Society, 1909–1939).

9. Emendation by Marcovitch: *pērōsōsin* for *plērōsōsin.*

10. M. Marcovich, "Theophilus of Antioch: Fifty-five Emendations," *Illinois Classical Studies* 4 (1979), 80.

11. Irenaeus *Heresies* 1.18.1; 1.8.4.

12. Eusebius *Church History* 4.24.

13. A. von Harnack, *Marcion, das Evangelium vom fremden Gott,* Texte und Untersuchungen 45 (1924), 414*.

14. Irenaeus *Heresies* 4.38.1.

15. Clement *Stromata* 3.103.1.

16. Irenaeus *Heresies* 1.24.1.

17. von Harnack, *Marcion,* 413*, 415*.

18. Ibid., 414*.

19. Ibid., 414*–415*.

20. Ibid., 269*–270*; Theophilus *To Autolycus* 2.26, 29.

21. Ibid., 270*.

22. *Sayings of Sextus* 109; Clement *Stromata* 7.32.8; Origen *Against Celsus* 8.30.

23. Irenaeus *Heresies* 1.24.2; 28.1.

24. Eusebius *Church History* 5.1.26.

25. Contrast the remarks of D. A. Dombrowski, *The Philosophy of Vegetarianism* (Amherst: University of Massachusetts Press, 1984), 5–10.

26. Cf. Philo *Special Laws* 4.62.

27. *Didascalia* 6.16, p. 218 Connolly.

28. Irenaeus *Heresies* 4.15.1; 16.3–5.

29. Cf. *Apostolic Constitutions* 2.9.2; 2.41.1–2; 6.20 (reworks the *Didascalia* but does not mention the "judgments").

30. *Clementine Homilies* 3.49.2.

31. Quotations from the poets have fallen out of 2.37.

32. The Gospel passages have fallen out of *To Autolycus* 3.12.

33. O. Stählin, *Clemens Alexandrinus* III (Leipzig: Hinrichs, 1909), 199: *Outlines,* frag. 12.

34. Cf. *Stoicorum Veterum Fragmenta* III.314.

35. Epiphanius *Heresies* 33.3.4; 5.3; 7.4.

36. Theophilus *To Autolycus* 2.10, 38; 3.13.

37. Ibid. 3.11; 2.29; R. M. Grant, "The Bible of Theophilus of Antioch," *Journal of Biblical Literature* 66 (1947), 173–86; "Patristica," *Vigiliae Christianae* 3 (1949), 228–29.

38. Ibid. 2.9, 30, 36, 38.

39. Accepting the emendation of M. Marcovich, "Theophilus of Antioch: Fifty-five Emendations," *Illinois Classical Studies* 4 (1979), 87.

40. Cf. Codex Bezae and Irenaeus *Heresies* 3.12.14.

41. Theophilus *To Autolycus* 1.14; 2.34; 3.19.

42. Cf. Origen *First Principles* 2.8.3.

43. F. Bolgiani, "Sullo scritto perduto di Teofilo d'Antiochia 'Contro Ermogene,'" *Paradoxos Politeia: In onore di G. Lazzati* (Milan: Vita e Pensiero, 1979), 77–118, esp. 94.

44. Justin *Dialogue* 81.4.

45. Eusebius *Church History* 4.24.

46. For this see P. Nautin, "Irénée et la canonicité des épîtres pauliniennes," *Revue de l'Histoire des Religions* 182 (1972), 113–36.

47. Cf. N. Zeegers-Vander Vorst, "Les citations du Nouveau Testament dans les Livres à Autolycus de Théophile d'Antioche," *Texte und Untersuchungen* 115 = *Studia Patristica* 12 (1975), 371–82.

Chapter 19: The Theology of Theophilus

1. S. Laeuchli, *The Language of Faith* (New York: Abingdon, 1962), 165.

2. Cf. G. W. Clarke, *The Octavius of Marcus Minucius Felix* (New York: Newman, 1974), 30.

3. More correctly in Justin *Apology* 2.6.3.

4. Most recently and reliably, D. A. Fiensy, *Prayers Alleged to Be Jewish,* Brown Judaic Studies 65 (Chico, Calif.: Scholars Press, 1985).

5. R. M. Grant, "The Early Antiochene Anaphora," *Anglican Theological Review* 30 (1948), 91–94.

6. Fiensy, *Prayers,* 138–40. Note that liturgical parallels extend to Theophilus' comments on Genesis in book 2.

7. B. Bischoff, *Anecdota novissima* (Stuttgart: Hiersemann, 1984), 1–9; my gratitude to the late Arnaldo Momigliano.

8. Cf. my "The Book of Wisdom at Alexandria," *Texte und Untersuchungen* 92 (1966), 462–72.

9. Cf. G. T. Armstrong, *Die Genesis in der alten Kirche* (Tübingen: Mohr, 1962).

10. E. R. Goodenough, *Introduction to Philo Judaeus* (New Haven: Yale University Press, 1940), 43–44.

11. Cf. *Corpus Hermeticum* 2:14; Justin *Apology* 2.6.1.

12. Cf. Ex. 20:5–6; 34:6–7; Deut. 5:9–10; 7:9–10.

13. Plutarch *Stoic Contradictions* 1050E.

14. Origen *Against Celsus* 4.71–73.

15. *Corpus Hermeticum* 2:12.

16. E. R. Dodds, *Proclus: The Elements of Theology* (Oxford: Clarendon, 1933), Prop. 80 and pp. 242–43.

17. See E. J. Goodspeed, *Index Apologeticus* (Leipzig: Hinrichs, 1912), 27, 210.

18. Aulus Gellius 19.12.

19. Dionysius of Alexandria (in Eusebius *Preparation for the Gospel* 14.27.8), on the other hand, correctly relates *theein* to sun, moon, and stars while also mentioning *tithēmi.*

20. Cf. Irenaeus' cucumber-aeon in his parody of Gnostic thought, *Heresies* 1.11.4.

21. Philo, *Allegory of the Laws* 1.65.

22. Irenaeus *Heresies* 3.8.3; Clement *Exhortation* 7.3; 110.1, *Tutor* 1.62.4.

23. Tertullian *Against Praxeas* 21.2; Paulinists in Epiphanius *Heresies* 65.1.5.

24. Marcellus frag. 52 Klostermann.

25. Justin *Dialogue* 76.7.

26. Irenaeus *Heresies* 2.13.6; 28.6.

27. Origen *Commentary on John* 1.24, p. 29,23 Preuschen; cf. R. Cadiou, *Commentaires inédits des Psaumes* (Paris: Belles Lettres, 1936), 77.

28. Tertullian *Against Hermogenes* 18.6; *Against Praxeas* 7.1; *Against Marcion* 2.4.1.

29. Hesiod *Theogony* 890, 899, 929h = 7; cf. S. Kauer, *Die Geburt der Athena im altgriechischen Epos* (Würzburg: Triltsch, 1959), 11, 14.

30. *Splanchna,* Hesiod *Theogony* 929n = 13; *Stoicorum Veterum Fragmenta* II.908.

31. Cf. A. B. Cook, *Zeus* III.1 (Cambridge: University Press, 1940), 656, 726.

32. *Stoicorum Veterum Fragmenta* III (Diogenes of Babylon), 33.

33. O. Kern, *Orphicorum Fragmenta* (Berlin: Weidmann, 1922), frag. 56, p. 135,8 = *Clementine Homilies* 6.7.5.

34. Ibid., frags. 65, 168, 169.

35. Cf. M. Muehl, "Der Logos endiathetos und prophorikos in der älteren Stoa bis zur Synode von Sirmium," *Archiv für Begriffsgeschichte* 7 (1962), 7–56.

36. Irenaeus *Heresies* 2.12.5; 13.8; Origen *Against Celsus* 6.65.

37. Philo *Posterity of Cain* 7.

38. Eusebius *Church History* 4.22.3.

39. This is Jewish-Christian; cf. H. J. Schoeps, *Theologie und Geschichte des Judenchristentums* (Tübingen: Mohr, 1949), 100–106.

40. H. J. de Jonge, "Sonship, Wisdom, Infancy: Luke, II, 41–51a," *New Testament Studies* 24 (1977/78), 317–54.

41. Theophilus *To Autolycus* 1.3, 11, 14 (Rom. 2:7); cf. 2.34.

42. Ibid. 2.8, 37; 3.9, 12.

43. Contrast Irenaeus *Heresies* 3.21.10.

44. Theophilus *To Autolycus* 2.10, 28, 30, 35, 38; 3.13.

45. Cf. my *Gods and the One God* (Philadelphia: Westminster, 1986), 133–34.
46. Cf. T. Bohlin, *Die Theologie des Pelagius und ihre Genesis,* Uppsala: Universitets Ärsskrift, 1957, no. 9.
47. *1 Clement* 25.

Chapter 20: Early Alexandrian Christianity

1. *Acts of Appian* in H. A. Musurillo, *Acts of the Pagan Martyrs* (Oxford: Clarendon, 1954), 65–70, 205–20.
2. Herodian 1.17.12; Dio Cassius 71.36.4.
3. M. J. Routh, *Reliquiae sacrae,* ed. 2 (Oxford: Typographeum Academicum, 1846), II.307.
4. Clement *Stromata* 1.144; Eusebius *Church History* 6.6.
5. Cf. W. E. G. Floyd, *Clement of Alexandria's Treatment of the Problem of Evil* (Oxford: University Press, 1971), xxii n. 4.
6. Clement *Exhortation* 20–22.
7. Eusebius *Church History* 2.17.
8. Clement *Stromata* 1.11.2–3.
9. Eusebius *Church History* 5.11.2; cf. M. P. Roncaglia, "Pantène et la Didascalée d'Alexandrie," *A Tribute to Arthur Vööbus* (Chicago: Lutheran Theological Seminary, 1977), 211–33.
10. Eusebius *Church History* 5.10.
11. Clement *Prophetic Selections* 27.1–4.
12. Ibid., 56.2.
13. Justin *Apology* 1.42.1–2; similarly Tertullian, *Against Marcion* 3.5.
14. O. Stählin, *Clemens Alexandrinus* III (Leipzig: Hinrichs, 1909), 219–20.
15. Text in ibid., 224.
16. Clement *Stromata* 6.137.1; cf. 5.93.4.
17. Clement *Tutor* 1.71.1; *Stromata* 5.38.6.
18. Clement *Exhortation* 63.3; *Tutor* 1.26.3; 27.2; *Stromata* 5.92.
19. See also S. R. C. Lilla, *Clement of Alexandria* (Oxford: University Press, 1971), 224–26.
20. A. Méhat, *Étude sur les 'Stromates' de Clément d'Alexandrie* (Paris: Du Seuil, 1966), 427–52, 521.
21. Cf. the edition by H.-I. Marrou, *Diognète* (Paris: Du Cerf, 1951).
22. Theophilus *To Autolycus* 3.15.
23. Origen *Against Celsus* 4.7; 6.78; cf. J. Schwartz, "L'Épître à Diognète," *Revue d'Histoire et de Philosophie Religieuses* 48 (1968), 49–51.
24. *To Diognetus* 5.17; 7.7.
25. *1 Clement* 6.2, "Dircae"; Ignatius *Romans* 4–5; Eusebius *Church History* 5.1.37; cf. *Martyrdom of Polycarp* 11–12.
26. Melito frag. 2 Hall.
27. Marcus Aurelius *Meditations* 1.6.
28. Cf. A. S. L. Farquharson, *The Meditations of the Emperor Marcus Antoninus* (Oxford: Clarendon, 1944), 440.
29. H. G. Meecham, *The Epistle to Diognetus* (Manchester: University Press, 1949), 93.
30. Marrou, *Diognète,* 244–47; 259–68.

31. L. Mitteis and U. Wilcken, *Grundzüge und Chrestomathie der Papyruskunde* I.2 (Leipzig and Berlin: Teubner, 1912), no. 81.

32. Ibid., no. 171; cf. H. G. Pflaum, *Les carrières procuratoriennes sous l'Haut-Empire romain* II (Paris: Geuthner, 1960), 659–62, no. 246.

33. Clement *Tutor* 1.1.1–2.

34. Seneca *Epistles* 95.65; cf. P. Hartlich, "De Exhortationum a Graecis Romanisque scriptarum historia et indole," *Leipziger Studien* 11 (1889), 283, 332–33.

35. Hartlich, "De Exhortationum," 333; Aristotle frag. 10b Walzer and Ross.

36. Cf. C. Mondésert, *Clément d'Alexandrie: Le Protreptique* (Paris: Montaigne, 1942), 26–36.

37. G. E. Mylonas, *Eleusis and the Eleusinian Mysteries* (Princeton: University Press, 1961), 288–305.

38. H. Diels, *Doxographi Graeci* (Berlin: De Gruyter, 1879), 129–32.

39. *Sibylline Oracles* frag. 1.10–13 Geffcken = Theophilus *To Autolycus* 2.36.

40. *Stoicorum Veterum Fragmenta* I.557, 560; Pythagoras *Sentences* 35; cf. Pseudo-Justin *Exhortation* 19.

41. G. Butterworth, "Clement of Alexandria's Protrepticus and the Phaedrus of Plato," *Classical Quarterly* 10 (1916), 198–205.

42. Clement *Exhortation* 122.3–123.1; Plato *Phaedrus* 279C, 252C.

43. Clement *Exhortation* 117.2.

44. Aratus *Phenomena* 13–15.

45. Hesiod frag. 195 Rzach.

46. Euripides frag. 941; Sophocles frag. 1025, also cited by Athenagoras *Embassy* 5.3 and in the *Sole Rule of God* and *Exhortation* of Pseudo-Justin.

47. O. Kern, *Orphicorum Fragmenta* (Berlin: Weidmann, 1922), frags. 246–247.

48. *Sibylline Oracles* 3.624–25.

49. Cf. N. Zeegers-Vander Vorst, *Les citations des poètes grecs chez les apologistes chrétiens du IIe siècle* (Louvain: Publications Universitaires, 1972).

50. Eusebius *Church History* 4.26.4; 6.13.9.

51. Clement *Stromata* 1.101.2.

52. Ibid. 3.81.1–3; *Prophetic Selections* 38(–39).

53. Ibid. 3.92.1.

54. *Tutor* 3.21.5 is not very close to Justin *Apology* 1.27.1, 3.

55. Justin *Apology* 2.8.1.

56. Philo *Noah's Planting* 3, 8; Mondésert, *Clement,* 47 n. 1.

57. Philo *Noah's Planting* 9; J. Daniélou, *Message évangélique et culture hellénistique* (Tournai: Desclée, 1961), 335.

58. Philo, *Dreams* 2.193–94 in Clement *Exhortation* 69.1–3.

59. Clement *Stromata* 1.72.4.

Chapter 21: Early Use of the Apologists

1. Epiphanius *Weights* 17; Irenaeus *Heresies* 3.21.1.

2. Irenaeus *Heresies* 3.3.3.

3. Ibid., 3.11.8.

4. Theophilus *To Autolycus* 1.1; 2.16; 3.14.

5. Irenaeus *Heresies* 5.15.3; cf. 5.14.1; 1.16. 3; 3.3.3–4.

6. Cf. Photius *Library* 232.

7. Irenaeus *Heresies* 5.30.3.

8. Ibid., 2.31.2; 32.3.

9. Ibid., 4.6.2; cf. 5.26.2.

10. Ibid., 3.3.4; 5.33.3; cf. M. Widmann, "Irenaeus und seine theologischen Väter," *Zeitschrift für Theologie und Kirche* 54 (1957), 166.

11. Ibid., 1.28.1.

12. Ibid., 3.23.8.

13. Tatian *Oration* 35.

14. Irenaeus *Heresies* 4.30.3.

15. Cf. F. Loofs, *Theophilus von Antiochien Adversus Marcionem und die anderen theologischen Quellen bei Irenaeus,* Texte und Untersuchungen 46.2 (1930), 10–44 and 67–70; a few more examples added below.

16. Irenaeus *Heresies* 4.20.1; *To Autolycus* 1.4–5 (cf. 2.3); W. R. Schoedel, "Enclosing, Not Enclosed," *Early Christian Literature and the Classical Intellectual Tradition,* ed. W. R. Schoedel and R. L. Wilken (Paris: Beauchesne, 1979), 75–86.

17. Irenaeus *Heresies* 4.20.1; Theophilus *To Autolycus* 1.7; 2.10.

18. Irenaeus *Heresies* 1.22.1; 3.8.3; *Demonstration* 5.

19. Ibid., preface 4; 7.4; 39.2–3; 5.1.3; 5.1; 6.1; 28.4; *Demonstration* 11.

20. Cf. J. Mambrino, " 'Les deux mains de Dieu' dans l'oeuvre de saint Irénée," *Nouvelle Revue Théologique* 79 (1957), 355–70.

21. Theophilus *To Autolycus* 2.25–27.

22. Irenaeus *Heresies* 3.23.6; Theophilus *To Autolycus* 2.25–26.

23. Irenaeus *Heresies* 5.26.2.

24. Theophilus *To Autolycus* 2.25.

25. Irenaeus *Demonstration* 96; *Heresies* 4.26.3.

26. *Sibylline Oracles* 8.132–33, 145–50.

27. S. N. Miller in *Cambridge Ancient History* XII (1939), 12–13; *Inscriptiones Latinae Selectae* 418: DIVO NERVAE ATAVO.

28. Tertullian *To the Nations* 1.17.4; cf. Dio Cassius 76.7.2; T. D. Barnes, *Tertullian* (Oxford: Clarendon, 1971), 33.

29. R. Agahd, *M. Terentii Varronis Antiquitatum Rerum Divinarum libri I, XIV, XV, XVI,* Neue Jahrbücher 24 (1898), 1–220.

30. Tertullian *To the Nations* 1.7.8–9.

31. Ibid., 1.17.3.

32. Jerome *Famous Men* 24.

33. See chapter 10.

34. Barnes, *Tertullian,* 106.

35. Tertullian *Apology* 35.9, 11; 37.4; Barnes, *Tertullian,* 33.

36. See, however, the *Sibylline Oracle* noted above.

37. Herodian 1.12.1; Dio Cassius 72.13.4.

38. Herodian 1.17.11; cf. Aurelius Victor *Caesars* 17.8–9.

39. Dio Cassius 67.15.1.

40. Cf. Dio Cassius 75.8.4.

41. Tertullian *Apology* 1.1; 9.6; 30.7; 50.12.

42. Ibid., 13.9.

43. Barnes, *Tertullian,* 106.

44. Tertullian *Against the Valentinians* 5.1.

45. Tertullian *Apology* 30.4.

46. Ibid., 35.8.
47. Ibid. 19.3; 46.15–16; cf. Barnes, *Tertullian,* 108.
48. Theophilus *To Autolycus* 3.21, 29, 23; 2.36.
49. C. Becker, *Tertullians Apologeticum: Werden und Leistung* (Munich: Kösel, 1954); cf. M. Pellegrino, "Ancora sulla duplice redazione dell'Apologeticum," *Historisches Jahrbuch* 77 (1958), 370–82.
50. R. M. Grant, "Patristica," *Vigiliae Christianae* 3 (1949), 228.
51. F. Bolgiani, "Sullo scritto perduto di Teofilo d'Antiochia 'Contro Ermogene,'" *Paradoxos Politeia in onore di G. Lazzati* (Milan: Vita e Pensiero, 1979), 77–118.
52. Barnes, *Tertullian,* 239.
53. R. Heinze, *Tertullians Apologeticum,* Berichte über die Verhandlungen der königlich sächsischen Gesellschaft der Wissenschaften zu Leipzig, Philologisch-historische Klasse, 62 (1910), 279–490; cf. R. Sider, *Ancient Rhetoric and the Art of Tertullian* (Oxford: University Press, 1971), 5–7, 141.
54. Eusebius *Church History* 5.28.5.
55. Hippolytus *Refutation* 8.16; 10.18.
56. Eusebius *Church History* 5.28; cf. "the God who suffered," Tatian *Oration* 13.
57. Clement *Stromata* 1.11.2.
58. Ibid., 1.74–75, 79–80, 87, 101–22.
59. Ibid., 1.135.3.
60. Photius *Library* 109; O. Stählin, *Clemens Alexandrinus* III (Leipzig: Hinrichs, 1909), 202, frag. 23.
61. Origen *Selections on the Psalms,* Migne, *Patrologia Graeca* 12:1120A; Melito frag. 5 Hall.
62. Novatian *On the Trinity* 3.15.29; *To Autolycus* 1.3; 2.27.

Chapter 22: The Apologists in the Third Century and After

1. *Stoicorum Veterum Fragmenta* I.356, p. 80,23.
2. Seneca *Epistle* 95.65.
3. Methodius *Symposium* 3.13.
4. Epiphanius *Heresies* 32.4.1.
5. Cf. the judicious discussion by N. Zeegers-Vander Vorst, *Les citations des poètes grecs chez les apologistes chrétiens du IIe siècle* (Louvain: Publications Universitaires, 1972), 229–54.
6. Cf. A. Elter, *De Gnomologiorum Graecorum historia atque origine* (Bonn: University, 1893–1896), 157–78.
7. Cf. H. Diels, *Doxographi Graeci* (Berlin: De Gruyter, 1879), 17.
8. On the work cf. my "Studies in the Apologists," *Harvard Theological Review* 51 (1958), 128–34.
9. Cf. my "Greek Literature in the Treatise *De Trinitate* and Cyril *Contra Julianum,*" *Journal of Theological Studies* 15 (1964), 265–79.
10. Cf. "Homer, Hesiod, and Heracles in Pseudo-Justin," *Vigiliae Christianae* 37 (1983), 105–9.
11. Gal. 4:12; 5:20–21.

12. British Museum, Additional MS. 14658, first printed by W. Cureton, *Spicilegium Syriacum* (London: Rivingtons, 1855).

13. Cf. Elter, *De Gnomologiorum,* 123–29, 149–56, etc.

14. Eusebius *Church History* 5.28.5.

15. Origen *Selections on the Psalms,* Migne, *Patrologia Graeca* 12:1120A; Melito frag. 5 Hall.

16. G. E. McCracken, *Arnobius: The Case Against the Pagans* I (Westminster, Md.: Newman, 1949), 34–51.

17. J. Quasten, *Patrology* II (Utrecht: Spectrum, 1953), 386–87.

18. Cf. R. M. Ogilvie, *The Library of Lactantius* (Oxford: Clarendon, 1978), 28–31, 88–95.

19. O. P. Nicholson, "The Source of the Dates in Lactantius' *Divine Institutes,*" *Journal of Theological Studies* 36 (1985), 291–310.

20. Athenagoras *Embassy* 24.2 (p. 58, lines 10–11, 12–14, 19–25 Schoedel; Methodius *On the Resurrection* 1.36.6–37.2, pp. 277,9–278,8 Bonwetsch.

21. *Embassy* 19.4; H. Diels, *Die Fragmente der Vorsokratiker* 13 B 2; 59 B 46.

22. Methodius *On the Resurrection* 1.55.1; Theophilus *To Autolycus* 2.24.

23. Eusebius *Church History* 4.8.3–9.3; 11.8–12.1; 16–18.

24. Ibid., 5.24.5.

25. Cf. my *Eusebius as Church Historian* (Oxford: Clarendon, 1980), 138–40.

26. Eusebius *Church History* 4.29.

27. Eusebius *Preparation for the Gospel* 10.11.

28. Eusebius *Church History* 4.24.

29. J. van Haelst, *Catalogue des papyrus littéraires juifs et chrétiens* (Paris: Sorbonne, 1976), nos. 623 and 624.

30. Published by H. J. M. Milne in *Journal of Theological Studies* 25 (1923/24), 73–77.

31. J. R. Harris, *The Apology of Aristides,* Texts and Studies 1.1 (1893), 29–30.

32. G. R. Woodward and H. Mattingly, *St. John Damascene, Barlaam and Ioasaph* (London, 1914), v–xvi; 396–424; cf. R. L. Wolff in *Harvard Theological Review* 30 (1937), 233–47.

33. *Oration* 4.109 (Migne, *Patrologia Graeca* 35:645A).

34. O. Kern, *Orphicorum Fragmenta* (Berlin: Weidmann, 1922), 137–38 (frag. 57); M. L. West, *The Orphic Poems* (Oxford: Clarendon, 1983), 179–80.

35. Epiphanius *Heresies* 2.2.6, p. 171,3 Holl; cf. p. 169,14.

36. U. von Wilamowitz-Möllendorff, "Ein Stück aus dem Ancoratus des Epiphanios," Sitzungsberichte der königlichen preussischen Akademie der Wissenschaften, Philosophisch-historische Klasse, 38 (1911), 759–72.

37. *Sources Chrétiennes,* Paris 1949; summary pp. 48–56.

38. Theophilus *To Autolycus* 2.13.

Chapter 23: The Apologists in the Middle Ages and Later

1. Migne, *Patrologia Graeca* 87:1, 157B and 164B; M. Richard in *Revue Biblique* 47 (1938), 387–97.

2. *Patrologia Graeca* 87.1.222B; cf. P. Prigent, *Justin et l'Ancien Testament* (Paris: Gabalda, 1964), 42–43.

3. There are also several citations of 1-2 Clement and the genuine letters of Ignatius.

4. K. Holl, *Fragmente vornicänischer Kirchenväter aus den Sacra Parallela,* Texte und Untersuchungen 20.2 (1899), 32–36 (nos. 94–106).

5. Ibid., 36–55 (nos. 107–30).

6. Ibid., 56–57 (nos. 131–34), from 1.1, 4, 5; 2.27.

7. Ibid., 85 (no. 184).

8. Cf. my "The Textual Tradition of Theophilus of Antioch," *Vigiliae Christianae* 6 (1952), 147–48.

9. Photius *Library* 162.

10. Ibid., 155, 234.

11. Ibid., 120.

12. Ibid., 14.

13. Eusebius *Church History* 4.27.

14. On minor fragments, mostly not genuine, cf. A. von Harnack, *Geschichte der altchristlichen Literatur* I.1 (Leipzig: Hinrichs, 1893), 108–13.

15. Eusebius *Church History* 4.18.4; he leaves out *On the Soul.*

16. Ibid. 4.12; 18.9; 11.10; 16.

17. Photius *Library* 125.

18. Ibid., 232.

19. N. G. Wilson, "The Libraries of the Byzantine World," *Greek, Roman and Byzantine Studies* 8 (1967/68), 53–80.

20. A. Sonny, "Zur Überlieferungsgeschichte von M. Aurelius *Eis heauton,*" *Philologus* 54 (1895), 181–83.

21. Cf. A. von Harnack in Texte und Untersuchungen 1.1 (1883), 36–46.

22. H. Rabe, "Die Lukianstudien des Arethas," Nachrichten der Akademie der Wissenschaften zu Göttingen, 1903, 643–56.

23. J. Bidez and F. Cumont, *Recherches sur la tradition manuscrite des lettres de l'empereur Julien,* Mémoires de l'Académie royale de Belgique 57, 4 (1898), 130.

24. Migne, *Patrologia Graeca* 106:799B; F. X. Murphy, "Arethas, Archbishop of Caesarea," *New Catholic Encyclopedia* 1 (1967): 777–78.

25. Migne, *Patrologia Graeca* 106:220B.

26. Cf. O. von Gebhardt, *Der Arethas-Kodex,* Texte und Untersuchungen 1.3 (1883).

27. Cf. O. Stählin, *Clemens Alexandrinus* I (Leipzig: Hinrichs, 1905), xvi–xxiii, 293–340; E. Schwartz, *Tatiani Oratio ad Graecos,* Texte und Untersuchungen 4.1 (1888), 44–47.

28. L. Labowsky, *Bessarion's Library and the Biblioteca Marciana: Six Early Inventories,* Sussidi eruditi 31 (1979), 511.

29. Schwartz, *Tatiani Oratio,* iii–iv.

30. Cf. Labowsky, *Bessarion's Library,* 25–26.

31. E. Mioni, "Bessarione bibliofilo e filologo," *Rivista di Studi Bizantini e Neohellenici,* n.s. 5 (XV) (1968), 61–83.

32. *Bibliotheca Universalis,* folios 205v, 92v; cf. C. Graux, *Essai sur les origines du fonds grec de l'Escurial* (Paris: Vieweg, 1880), 387–400.

33. *Bibliotheca Universalis,* folio 456r.

34. Cf. my "The Textual Tradition of Theophilus of Antioch," *Vigiliae Christianae* 6 (1952), 146–59, esp. 152–53.

35. E. P. Meijering, *Melanchthon and Patristic Thought* (Leiden: Brill, 1983), 73–74.

36. *Die Überlieferung der griechischen christlichen Literatur in der lateinischen Kirche bis zum zwölften Jahrhundert* (Munich: Filser, 1949), 48 n. 1; 131–32.

37. Cf. "Theophilus Antiochenus," *Catalogus translationum et commentarium: Mediaeval and Renaissance Latin Translations and Commentaries: Annotated Lists and Guides,* ed. P. Kristeller and F. E. Cranz (Washington: Catholic University, 1971), II.235–37.

Appendixes

1. R. Merkelbach, "Der Eid der bithynischen Christen," *Zeitschrift für Papyrologie und Epigraphik* 21 (1976), 73–74, compares a priest's oath from Egypt.

2. "L'orazione di Frontone contro i cristiani," *Giornale Italiano di Filologia* 2 (1949), 238–54, esp. 248–49.

Bibliography

The Apologists in General

1883   Harnack, A. von. *Die Überlieferung der griechischen Apologeten des zweiten Jahrhunderts in der alten Kirche und im Mittelalter.* Texte und Untersuchungen 1.1.

1883   Gebhardt, O. von. *Der Arethas-codex, Paris. Gr. 451.* Texte und Untersuchungen 1.3:154–96.

1900   Ginzberg, L. *Die Haggada bei den Kirchenvätern und in der apokryphischen Litteratur.* Berlin: Calvary.

1907   Geffcken, J. *Zwei griechische Apologeten.* Leipzig and Berlin: Teubner.

1912   Puech, A. *Les apologistes grecs du IIe siècle de notre ère.* Paris: Hachette.

1912   Goodspeed, E. J. *Index Apologeticus.* Leipzig: Hinrichs.

1914   ———. *Die ältesten Apologeten.* Göttingen: Vandenhoeck & Ruprecht. Reprinted 1984.

1919   Marmorstein, A. "Jews and Judaism in the Earliest Christian Apologies." *Expositor* VIII 17:73–80, 100–116.

1943/44   Casamassa, A. *Gli apologisti greci.* Lateranum, n.s. 9–10.

1947   Pellegrino, M. *Gli apologeti greci nel II secolo.* Rome: Anonima Veritas.

1947   ———. *Studi su l'antica apologetica.* Rome: Storia e Letteratura.

1947   Grant, R. M. "The Decalogue in Early Christianity." *Harvard Theological Review* 40:1–17.

1948   ———. "Pliny and the Christians." *Harvard Theological Review* 41:273–74.

1949   Frassinetti, P. "L'orazione di Frontone contro i cristiani." *Giornale Italiano di Filologia* 2:238–54.

1950/51   Benz, E. "Christus und Sokrates in der alten Kirche." *Zeitschrift für die neutestamentliche Wissenschaft* 43:195–224.

1954   Ruiz Bueno, D. *Padres apologistas griegos [s. II].* Madrid: Editorial Catolica.

1955   Grant, R. M. "The Chronology of the Greek Apologists." *Vigiliae Christianae* 8:25–33.

1957   Spanneut, M. *Le stoïcisme des pères de l'église de Clément de Rome à Clément d'Alexandrie.* Paris: Du Seuil (rev. ed. 1969).

1960   Schwartz, J. "Du *Testament de Lévi* au *Discours Véritable* de Celse." *Revue d'Histoire et de Philosophie Religieuses* 40:126–37.

1961   Daniélou, J. *Message évangélique et culture hellénistique.* Tournai: Desclée (E.T., *Gospel Message and Hellenistic Culture;* Philadelphia: Westminster, 1973).

1962   Laeuchli, S. *The Language of Faith: An Introduction to the Semantic Dilemma of the Early Church.* New York: Abingdon.

1963   Carpenter, H. J. "Popular Christianity and the Theologians in the Early Centuries." *Journal of Theological Studies* 14:294–308.

1965   Grant, R. M. "Early Christianity and Pre-Socratic Philosophy." *Harry Austryn Wolfson Jubilee,* I, 357–84. Jerusalem: American Academy for Jewish Research.

1965   ———. "Early Christianity and Greek Comic Poetry." *Classical Philology* 60:157–63.

1966   Chadwick, H. *Early Christian Thought and the Classical Tradition.* Oxford: Clarendon.

1966   Grant, R. M. *The Early Christian Doctrine of God.* Charlottesville: University Press of Virginia.

1972   Zeegers-Vander Vorst, N. *Les citations des poètes grecs chez les apologistes chrétiens du IIe siècle.* Louvain: Publications Universitaires.

1973   Joly, R. *Christianisme et philosophie: Études sur Justin et les apologistes grecs du deuxième siècle.* Brussels: Éditions de l'Université de Bruxelles.

1973   Beaujeu, J. "Les apologètes et le culte du souverain." *Le culte des souverains dans l'Empire romain.* Fondation Hardt, Entretiens XIX. 101–42.

1979   Schoedel, W. R. "Enclosing, Not Enclosed: The Early Christian Doctrine of God." *Early Christian Literature and the Classical Intellectual Tradition in honorem Robert M. Grant,* ed. W. R. Schoedel and R. L. Wilken, 75–86. Paris: Beauchesne.

        Barnard, L. W. "Apologetik I (Alte Kirche)." *Theologische Realenzyklopädie* 3:371–411.

1986   Grant, R. M. "Forms and Occasions of the Greek Apologists." *Studi e Materiali di Storia delle Religioni* 52:213–26.

1986   Timpe, D. "Apologeti cristiani e storia sociale della chiesa antica." *Annuario della Facoltà lettere e filosofia, Università di Siena,* 7:99–127.

Background

1904   Decharme, P. *La critique des traditions religieuses chez les grecs.* Paris: Picard.

1915   Clerq, C. *Les théories relatives au culte des images chez les auteurs grecs du IIme siècle après J.-C.* Diss. Paris.

1918   Borries, B. von. *Quid veteres philosophi de idololatria senserint.* Göttingen: Dieterich.

1945   Amand [de Mendieta], D. *Fatalisme et liberté dans l'antiquité grecque.* Louvain: Bibliothèque de l'Université.

1945–54   Nock, A. D., and A. J. Festugière. *Corpus Hermeticum.* 4 vols. Paris: Belles Lettres.
1973   Places, E. des. *Numénius Fragments.* Paris: Belles Lettres.
1977   ———. *Atticus Fragments.* Paris: Belles Lettres.
1977   Dillon, J. *The Middle Platonists.* London: Duckworth.
1981   Russell, D. A., and N. G. Wilson. *Menander Rhetor.* Oxford: Clarendon.
1983   West, M. L. *The Orphic Poems.* Oxford: Clarendon.

Beginnings

Hellenistic Judaism

1942   Lieberman, S. *Greek in Jewish Palestine.* New York: Jewish Theological Seminary of America.
1947   Wolfson, H. A. *Philo.* 2 vols. Cambridge, Mass.: Harvard University Press.
1951   Lieberman, S. *Hellenism in Jewish Palestine.* New York: Jewish Theological Seminary of America.
1956   Tcherikower, V. "Jewish Apologetic Literature Reconsidered." *Eos* 48: 169–93.
1984   Bischoff, B. "Der Brief des Hohenpriesters Annas an den Philosophen Seneca—eine jüdisch-apologetische Missionsschrift (Viertes Jahrhundert?)." *Anecdota novissima: Texte des vierten bis sechzehnten Jahrhunderts.* Stuttgart: Hiersemann, 1–9.

Acts of the Apostles

1955   Gaertner, B. *The Areopagus Speech and Natural Revelation.* Uppsala: Gleerup.
1961   Dibelius, M. "Paulus auf dem Areopag." *Sitzungsberichte der Heidelberger Akademie der Wissenschaften* 1938–1939 = *Aufsätze zur Apostelgeschichte,* ed. H. Greeven. Göttingen: Vandenhoeck & Ruprecht.
1963   Conzelmann, H. *Die Apostelgeschichte.* Tübingen: Mohr.

Individual Apologists

Justin Martyr

1923   Goodenough, E. R. *The Theology of Justin Martyr.* Jena: Frommann.
1941   Schmid, W. "Die Textüberlieferung der Apologie des Justin." *Zeitschrift für die neutestamentliche Wissenschaft* 40:87–138.
1944   Weis, P. R. "Some Samaritanisms of Justin Martyr." *Journal of Theological Studies* 45:199–205.
1952   Schmid, W. "Frühe Apologetik und Platonismus." *Hermeneia Regenbogen* (Heidelberg: Winter), 163–82.
1952/53   Andresen, C. "Justin und der mittlere Platonismus." *Zeitschrift für die neutestamentliche Wissenschaft* 44:157–95.
1953   Ehrhardt, A. "Justin Martyr's Two Apologies." *Journal of Ecclesiastical History* 4:1–12.

1953   Barthélemy, D. "Redécouverte d'un chaînon manquant de l'histoire de la Septante." *Revue Biblique* 60:18–29.

1953   Milik, J. T. "Une lettre de Simon bar Kokheba." *Revue Biblique* 60:276–94.

1955   Andresen, C. *Logos und Nomos.* Berlin: De Gruyter.

1956   Grant, R. M. "Aristotle and the Conversion of Justin." *Journal of Theological Studies* 7:246–48.

1958   Schmid, W. "Ein rätselhaften Anachronismus bei Justinus Martyr." *Historisches Jahrbuch* 77:358–61.

1964   Prigent, P. *Justin et l'Ancien Testament.* Paris: Gabalda.

1965   Keresztes, P. "The Literary Genre of Justin's First Apology." *Vigiliae Christianae* 19:99–110.

1965   Chadwick, H. "Justin Martyr's Defence of Christianity." *Bulletin of the John Rylands Library* 47:275–97.

1965   Keresztes, P. "The 'So-Called' Second Apology of Justin." *Latomus* 24:858–69.

1966   Hyldahl, N. *Philosophie und Christentum. Eine Interpretation der Einleitung zum Dialog Justins.* Acta theologica Danica 9.

1967   Barnard, L. W. *Justin Martyr: His Life and Thought.* Cambridge: University Press.

1967   Bellinzoni, A. J. *The Sayings of Jesus in the Writings of Justin Martyr.* Supplements to *Novum Testamentum* 17.

1968   Glockmann, G. *Homer in der frühchristlichen Literatur bis Justinus.* Texte und Untersuchungen 105:99–195.

1971   Winden, J. C. M. van. *An Early Christian Philosopher: Justin Martyr's Dialogue with Trypho Chapters One to Nine.* Leiden: Brill.

1973   Osborn, E. F. *Justin Martyr.* Tübingen: Mohr.

1975   Schmid, W. "Eine Inversionsphänomen und seine Bedeutung im Text der Apologie des Justin." *Forma Futuri: Studi in onore de cardinale Michele Pellegrino,* 253–81. Torino: Bottega d'Erasmo.

1976   Skarsaune, O. "The Conversion of Justin Martyr." *Studia Theologica* 30:53–73.

1977/78 Strecker, G. "Eine Evangelienharmonie bei Justin und Pseudoklemens?" *New Testament Studies* 24:297–316.

1978   Vogel, C. J. de. "Problems Concerning Justin Martyr." *Mnemosyne* 31:360–88.

1979   Lüdemann, G. "Zur Geschichte des ältesten Christentums in Rom." *Zeitschrift für die neutestamentliche Wissenschaft* 70:86–114, esp. 97–114: Ptolemäus und Justin.

1981   Grant, R. M. "Charges of 'Immorality' Against Various Religious Groups in Antiquity." *Studies in Honor of Gilles Quispel,* ed. R. van den Broek and M. J. Vermaseren, 161–70. Leiden: Brill.

1983   Bisbee, G. A. "The Acts of Justin: A Form-Critical Study." *Second Century* 3:129–57.

1984   Saller, R. "Roman Dowry and the Devolution of Property in the Principate." *Classical Quarterly* 34:195–205.

1985   Grant, R. M. "A Woman of Rome: Justin, Apol. 2, 2." *Church History* 54:461–72.

1987　Skarsaune, O. *The Proof from Prophecy: A Study in Justin Martyr's Proof-Text Tradition: Text-Type, Provenance, Theological Profile.* Supplements to *Novum Testamentum* 66.

1987　Droge, A. J. "Justin Martyr and the Restoration of Philosophy." *Church History* 56:303–19.

Marcus Aurelius

1944　Farquharson, A. S. L. *The Meditations of the Emperor Marcus Antoninus.* 2 vols. Oxford: Clarendon.

1983　Astarita, M. L. *Avidio Cassio.* Rome: Storia e Letteratura.

1987　Birley, A. *Marcus Aurelius.* New Haven: Yale University Press.

Apollinaris of Hierapolis

1943　Roos, A. G. *Het regenwonder op de zuil van Marcus Aurelius.* Mededeelingen der Nederlandsche Akademie van Wetenschappen, n.r. 6:1–32.

1948–49　Guey, J. "La date de la pluie miraculeuse (172 après J. C.) et la colonne Aurélienne." *Mélanges d'Archéologie et d'Histoire* 60:105–27; 61:93–118.

Melito of Sardis

1951　Rémondon, R. "Les dates de la révolte de C. Avidius Cassius." *Chronique d'Égypte* 26:364–77.

1958　Daniélou, J. "La symbolisme baptismale du véhicule." *Sciences Ecclésiastiques* 10:127–38 (Melito).

1974　Schneemelcher, W. "Histoire du salut et Empire romain: Meliton de Sardes et l'État." *Bulletin de Littérature Ecclésiastique* 2:81–98.

1979　Hall, S. G. *Melito of Sardis:* On Pascha *and Fragments.* Oxford Early Christian Texts. Oxford: Clarendon.

Athenagoras

1947　Ubaldi, P., and M. Pellegrino. *Atenagora: La Supplica per i cristiani, Della risurrezione dei morti.* Torino.

1954　Grant, R. M. "Athenagoras or Pseudo-Athenagoras." *Harvard Theological Review* 47:121–29.

1958　―――. "Some Errors in the Legatio of Athenagoras." *Vigiliae Christianae* 12:145–46.

1960　Sciveletto, N. "Cultura e scoliastica in Atenagora." *Giornale Italiano di Filologia* 13:236–48.

1968　Rauch, J. L. *Greek Logic and Philosophy and the Problem of Authorship in Athenagoras.* Diss. Chicago.

1969　Malherbe, A. J. "The Structure of Athenagoras, 'Supplicatio pro Christianis.'" *Vigiliae Christianae* 23:1–20.

1972　Barnard, L. W. *Athenagoras.* Paris: Beauchesne.

1972　Schoedel, W. R. *Athenagoras:* Legatio *and* De Resurrectione. Oxford Early Christian Texts. Oxford: Clarendon.

1975   Barnes, T. D. "The Embassy of Athenagoras." *Journal of Theological Studies* 26:111–14.
1979   Schoedel, W. R. "In Praise of the King: A Rhetorical Pattern in Athenagoras." *Disciplina Nostra: In Memory of Robert F. Evans,* ed. D. F. Winslow 69–90. Cambridge, Mass.: Philadelphia Patristic Foundation.
1985   Jones, C. P. "Neryllinus." *Classical Philology* 80:40–45.

Tatian

1887   Kalkmann, A. "Tatians Nachrichten über Kunstwerke." *Rheinisches Museum,* n.f. 42:489–524.
1888   Schwartz, E. *Tatiani Oratio ad Graecos.* Texte und Untersuchungen 4.1.
1900   Kukula, R. C. *"Altersbeweis" und "Künstlerkatalog" in Tatians Rede an die Griechen.* Vienna: Author.
1900   ———. *Tatians sogenannte Apologie.* Leipzig: Teubner.
1903   Puech, A. *Recherches sur le Discours aux Grecs de Tatien.* Paris: Alcan.
1909   Heiler, C. L. *De Tatiani Apologetae Dicendi Genere.* Marburg.
1942   Alfonsi, L. "Appunti sul *logos* di Taziano." *Convivium* 14:273–81.
1953   Grant, R. M. "The Date of Tatian's Oration." *Harvard Theological Review* 46:99–101.
1954   ———. "The Heresy of Tatian." *Journal of Theological Studies* 5:62–68.
1957   ———. "Tatian and the Bible." *Texte und Untersuchungen* 63:297–306.
1958   ———. "Studies in the Apologists." *Harvard Theological Review* 51:123–34.
1960   Elze, M. *Tatian und seine Theologie.* Göttingen: Vandenhoeck & Ruprecht.
1964   Grant, R. M. "Tatian *(Or. 30)* and the Gnostics." *Journal of Theological Studies* 15:65–69.
1964   Hawthorne, G. F. "Tatian and His Discourse to the Greeks." *Harvard Theological Review* 57:161–88.
1967   Clarke, G. W. "The Date of the Oration of Tatian." *Harvard Theological Review* 60:122–26.
1968   Barnard, L. W. "The Heresy of Tatian—Once Again." *Journal of Ecclesiastical History* 19:1–10.
1969   Osborne, A. E. *Tatian's Discourse to the Greeks.* Diss. Cincinnati.
1982   Whittaker, M. *Tatian:* Oratio ad Graecos *and Fragments.* Oxford Early Christian Texts. Oxford: Clarendon.

Celsus

1924   Glöckner, O. *Celsi Alethes Logos.* Bonn: Marcus & Weber.
1940   Bader, R. *Der* Alethes Logos *des Kelsos.* Stuttgart and Berlin: Kohlhammer.
1941/42 Wifstrand, A. *Die Wahre Lehre des Kelsos.* Bulletin de la Société Royale des Lettres de Lund V.
1953   Chadwick, H. *Origen Contra Celsum.* Cambridge: University Press. Reprinted 1965.

1955   Andresen, C. *Logos und Nomos.* Berlin: De Gruyter. (Comments by W. den Boer in *Mnemosyne* 9 [1956]:361–62; J. H. Waszink in *Vigiliae Christianae* 12 [1958]:166–77.)

1960   Schwartz, J. "Du Testament de Lévi au Discours véritable de Celse." *Revue d'Histoire et de Philosophie Religieuses* 40:126–45.

1964   ———. "La 'conversion' de Lucien de Samosate." *L'Antiquité Classique* 33:384–400.

1968   ———. "L'Épître à Diognète." *Revue d'Histoire et de Philosophie Religieuses* 48:46–53.

1970   Vermander, J.-M. "De quelques répliques à Celse dans l'Apologeticum de Tertullien." *Revue des Études Augustiniennes* 16:205–25.

1971   ●———. "Celse, source et adversaire de Minucius Felix." *Revue des Études Augustiniennes* 17:13–25.

1971   ———. "Théophile d'Antioche contre Celse: A Autolycos III." *Revue des Études Augustiniennes* 17:203–25.

1971   Lilla, S. R. C. *Clement of Alexandria,* 34–41. Oxford: University Press.

1972   Vermander, J.-M. "La parution de l'ouvrage de Celse et la datation de quelques apologies." *Revue des Études Augustiniennes* 18:27–42.

1973   Schwartz, J. "Celsus Redivivus." *Revue d'Histoire et de Philosophie Religieuses* 53:399–405.

1977   Vermander, J.-M. "De quelques répliques à Celse dans le *Protreptique* de Clément d'Alexandrie." *Revue des Études Augustiniennes* 23:3–17.

1978   ———. "Celse et l'attribution à Athénagore d'un ouvrage sur la résurrection des morts." *Mélanges de Science Religieuse* 35:125–34.

1980   Pichler, K. *Streit um das Christentum. Der Angriff des Kelsos und die Antwort des Origenes.* Regensburger Studien zur Theologie 23.

Theophilus of Antioch

1911   Wilamowitz-Möllendorff, U. von. "Ein Stück aus dem Ancoratus des Epiphanios." *Sitzungsberichte der königlich preussischen Akademie der Wissenschaften* 38:759–72.

1936   Shroyer, M. J. "Alexandrian Jewish Literalists." *Journal of Biblical Literature* 55:261–84.

1947   Grant, R. M. "The Bible of Theophilus of Antioch." *Journal of Biblical Literature* 66:173–96.

1947   ———. "Theophilus of Antioch to Autolycus." *Harvard Theological Review* 40:227–56.

1948   Bardy, G. (Tr. J. Sender, from Maran.) *Théophile d'Antioche: Trois livres à Autolycus.* Paris: Du Cerf.

1948   Grant, R. M. "The Early Antiochene Anaphora." *Anglican Theological Review* 30:91–94.

1950   ———. "The Problem of Theophilus." *Harvard Theological Review* 43:179–96.

1951   ———. "Note on the Petrine Apocrypha" (with G. Quispel). *Vigiliae Christianae* 5:31–32.

1952   ———. "The Textual Tradition of Theophilus of Antioch." *Vigiliae Christianae* 6:146–59.

1957   Nautin, P. "Notes critiques sur Théophile d'Antioche, Ad Autolycum Lib. II." *Vigiliae Christianae* 11:212–25.

1958   Grant, R. M. "Notes on the Text of Theophilus, *Ad Autolycum* III." *Vigiliae Christianae* 12:136–44.

1959   ———. "Scripture, Rhetoric and Theology in Theophilus." *Vigiliae Christianae* 13:33–45.

1961   Downey, G. *A History of Antioch in Syria.* Princeton: University Press.

1965   Malley, W. J. "Four Unedited Fragments of the *De universo* of the Pseudo-Josephus Found in the *Chronicon* of George Hamartolus (Coislin 305)." *Journal of Theological Studies* 16:13–25.

1970   Grant, R. M. *Theophilus of Antioch: Ad Autolycum.* Oxford Early Christian Texts. Oxford: Clarendon.

1970   Zeegers-Vander Vorst, N. "Les versions juives et chrétiennes du fr. 245–7 d'Orphée." *L'Antiquité Classique* 39:475–506.

1971   Vermander, J.-M. "Théophile d'Antioche contre Celse: *A Autolycos* III." *Revue des Études Augustiniennes* 17:203–25.

1971   Grant, R. M. "Theophilus Antiochenus." *Catalogus translationum et commentarium: Mediaeval and Renaissance Latin Translations and Commentaries. Annotated Lists and Guides,* ed. P. Kristeller and F. E. Cranz, II, 235–37. Washington, D.C.: Catholic University Press.

1972   ———. "Jewish Christianity at Antioch in the Second Century." *Recherches de Science Religieuse* 60:97–108.

1972   Simonetti, M. "La sacra scrittura in Teofilo d'Antiochia." *Epektasis: Mélanges Jean Daniélou,* 197–207. Paris.

1973   Nautin, P. "Ciel, pneuma et lumière chez Théophile d'Antioche (notes critiques sur *Ad Autol.* 2, 13)." *Vigiliae Christianae* 27:165–71.

1975   Bolgiani, F. "L'ascesi di Noe: A proposito di Theophilo ad Autolyco, III, 19." *Forma futuri: Studi in onore del cardinale Michele Pellegrino,* 295–333. Torino: Bottega d'Erasmo.

1975   Zeegers-Vander Vorst, N. "Notes sur quelques aspects judaïsants du Logos chez Théophile d'Antioche." *Actes de la XIIe Conférence Internationale d'Études Classiques,* 69–87. Amsterdam.

1975   ———. "Les Citations du Nouveau Testament dans les livres à Autolycus de Théophile d'Antioche." *Texte und Untersuchungen* 115:371–82.

1975   Bentivegna, J., S.J. "A Christianity Without Christ by Theophilus of Antioch." *Texte und Untersuchungen* 116:107–30.

1976   Keary, M. B. "Un fils cannibale de Poseidon (Théophile d'Antioche, *Ad Autolycum,* II, 7)." *Revue des Études Grecques* 89:101–2.

1976   Zeegers-Vander Vorst, N. "La création de l'homme (Gn 1, 26) chez Théophile d'Antioche." *Vigiliae Christianae* 30:258–67.

1979   Marcovich, M. "Theophilus of Antioch: Fifty-five Emendations." *Illinois Classical Studies* 4:76–93.

1979   Dörrie, H. "Der Prolog zur Evangelium nach Johannes im Verständnis der älteren Apologeten." *Kerygma und Logos: Festschrift für Carl Andresen,* ed. A. M. Ritter, 136–52. Göttingen: Vandenhoeck & Ruprecht.

1979   Bergamelli, F. "Il languaggio simbolico delle immagini nella catechesi missionari di Teofilo di Antiochia." *Salesianum* 41:273–97.

1980   Bolgiani, F. "Sullo scritto perduto di Teofilo d'Antiochia Contro Ermogene." *Paradoxos Politeia. Studi patristici in onore di Giuseppe Lazzati,* ed. R. Cantalamessa and L. F. Pizzolato, 77–118. Milan: Vita e Pensiero.

1980   Bunt, A. van de, and A. van den Hoek. "Aristobulus, Acts, Theophilus, Clement Making Use of Aratus' Phainomena: A Peregrination." *Bijdragen* 41:290–99.

1980   Sijpestein, P. J. "The Historian Apollonides alias Horapios." *Mnemosyne* 33:364–66.

1981   Zeegers-Vander Vorst, N. "Satan, Eve et le serpent chez Théophile d'Antioche." *Vigiliae Christianae* 35:152–69.

1981   Davids, A. "Hésiode et les prophètes chez Théophile d'Antioche (Ad Autol. II, 8–9)." *Fides Sacramenti Sacramentum Fidei: Studies in Honour of Pieter Smulders,* ed. H. J. Auf den Maur et al. Assen: Van Gorcum.

Use of Theophilus

1930   Loofs, F. *Theophilus von Antiochien Adversus Marcionem und die anderen theologischen Quellen bei Irenäus.* Texte und Untersuchungen 46.2.

The Acts of Apollonius

1965   Krüger, G., and G. Ruhbach. *Ausgewählte Märtyrerakten,* ed. 4, 30–35. Tübingen: Mohr.

1969   Freudenberger, R. "Die Überlieferung vom Martyrium des römischen Christen Apollonius." *Zeitschrift für die neutestamentliche Wissenschaft* 60:111–30.

1970   Schwartz, J. "Autour des Acta Apollonii." *Revue d'Histoire et de Philosophie Religieuses* 50:257–61.

1972   Musurillo, H. *The Acts of the Christian Martyrs,* 90–105. Oxford: Clarendon.

1975   Paulsen, H. "Erwägungen zu Acta Apollonii 14–22." *Zeitschrift für die neutestamentliche Wissenschaft* 66:117–26.

The Early School of Alexandria

1889   Hartlich, P. "De Exhortationum a Graecis Romanisque scriptarum historia et indole." *Leipziger Studien zur classischen Philologie* 11:207–336.

1915   Bousset, W. *Jüdisch-christlicher Schulbetrieb in Alexandria und Rom.* Göttingen: Vandenhoeck & Ruprecht.

1966   Grant, R. M. "The Book of Wisdom at Alexandria." *Texte und Untersuchungen* 92:462–72.

1971   ———. "Early Alexandrian Christianity." *Church History* 40:133–44.

1977   Roncaglia, M. P. "Pantène et la Didascalée d'Alexandrie." *A Tribute to Arthur Vööbus,* 211–33. Chicago: Lutheran Theological Seminary.

1983   Grant, R. M. "Paul, Galen, and Origen." *Journal of Theological Studies* 34:533–36.

The Epistle to Diognetus

1928   Geffcken, J. *Der Brief an Diognetos.* Heidelberg: Winter.
1934   Molland, E. "Die literatur- und dogmengeschichtliche Stellung des Diognetbriefes." *Zeitschrift für die neutestamentliche Wissenschaft* 33:289–312.
1947   Andriessen, P. "The Authorship of the Epistula ad Diognetum." *Vigiliae Christianae* 1:129–36 (summary of articles in *Recherches de Théologie Ancienne et Mediévale* 1946/47).
1949   Meecham, H. G. *The Epistle to Diognetus.* Manchester: University Press.
1957   Billet, B. "Les lacunes de l' 'A Diognète.' " *Recherches de Science Religieuse* 45:409–18.
1965   Marrou, H.-I. *A Diognète,* supplemented. Paris: Du Cerf.
1968   Schwartz, J. "L'Épître à Diognète." *Revue d'Histoire et de Philosophie Religieuses* 48:46–53.

Irenaeus as Continuator and Corrector of the Apologists

1923   Sanday, W., C. H. Turner, and A. Souter. *Novum Testamentum Sancti Irenaei.* Oxford: Clarendon.
1935   Reynders, B. "La polémique de saint Irénée." *Recherches de Théologie Ancienne et Mediévale* 7:5–27.
1949   Grant, R. M. "Irenaeus and Hellenistic Culture." *Harvard Theological Review* 42:41–51.
1957   Widmann, M. "Irenäus und seine theologischen Väter." *Zeitschrift für Theologie und Kirche* 54:156–73.
1959   Schoedel, W. R. "Philosophy and Rhetoric in the *Adversus Haereses* of Irenaeus." *Vigiliae Christianae* 13:22–32.
1964   Hefner, P. "Theological Methodology and St. Irenaeus." *Journal of Religion* 44:294–309.
1972   Nautin, P. "Irénée et la canonicité des épîtres pauliniennes." *Revue de l'Histoire des Religions* 182:113–36.
1977   Unnik, W. C. van. "An Interesting Document of Second Century Theological Discussion (Irenaeus, *Adv. Haer.* 1. 10. 3)." *Vigiliae Christianae* 31:196–228.
1979   ———. "Theological Speculation and Its Limits." *Early Christian Literature and the Classical Intellectual Tradition in honorem Robert M. Grant,* ed. W. R. Schoedel and R. L. Wilken, 33–43. Paris: Beauchesne.
1984   Schoedel, W. R. "Theological Method in Irenaeus (*Adversus Haereses* 2. 25–28)." *Journal of Theological Studies* 35:31–49.

Index